Advanced Praise

"I truly believe that this book will help those who have the desire to make a paradigm shift, that will improve their health and ability to act and think spiritually, to make that shift creating a new life and self."

Bernie Siegel, M.D. author of *365 Prescriptions For The Soul* and *Prescriptions For Living*

"Psychology all too often focuses on the negative and how the individual must spend many years in psychotherapy to undo the negative in his/her life. John Ryder is a positivist, who empowers the individual by providing the tools necessary to change how one thinks and feels. Anyone who reads this book will quickly discover a variety of clever strategies to deal with everyday difficulties in life in a very effective and positive way. This book will help you be more optimistic and positive."

Paul Michael Ramirez, Ph.D. Chairman, Department of Psychology, Long Island University, Professor, Doctoral Program in Clinical Psychology, Brooklyn, New York

"As a brain scientist who studies stress-related disorders, I know John Ryder understands the biology of our nervous system. Integrating this with clinical experience, a humanistic perspective, and his knowledge of Eastern philosophies have produced an uplifting manual for making positive life changes."

Steven Berman, Ph.D.
UCLA Brain Research Institute

"John Ryder's book answered all my questions about what drives us crazy and what we can really do about it to regain balance and harmony. He is very insightful and easy to understand. He delivers simple to follow tools to make you smile and feel strong, while living in today's high pressure jungle. Buy it and read every page of it! You will be glad you did."

A. Brooks, Editor, Talent in Motion Magazine, New York

POSITIVE DIRECTIONS

Shifting Polarities
to Escape Stress
and Increase Happiness

John Ryder, Ph.D.

New York

Published by:

MORGAN · JAMES
THE ENTREPRENEURIAL PUBLISHER™
www.morganjamespublishing.com

Habitat
for Humanity®
Peninsula
Building Partner

Morgan James Publishing, LLC
1225 Franklin Avenue, Suite 325
Garden City, NY 11530-1693
800.485.4943
www.MorganJamesPublishing.com

Design by:
Megan Johnson
www.Johnson2Design.com

Library of Congress Cataloging
Ryder, John G.
Positive Directions
Shifting Polarities to Escape Stress and Increase Happiness

Index:
1. Self Help – Personal Growth.
2. Mind, Body, Spirit – Inspiration and Personal Growth
3. Psychology – Mental Health

ISBN 10: 1-60037-365-8

ISBN 13: 978-1-60037-365-7

Acknowledgments

This book is the result of an enormous effort that was made possible through the help of a great number of people to whom I wish to express my deepest gratitude. Writing this book has been an amazing journey. I am grateful to all those who gave me the inspiration, motivation, direction, and valuable feedback, especially Christina Stroud's diligence to attain excellence. As a result the manuscript went through numerous revisions to make it as clear and straightforward as possible; so thanks to my editors Nina Costanza, Susan Schwartz, and Natalie Reeves.

My deep sense of fulfillment rests on the hearts, minds, souls and shoulders of a vast number of friends, family, colleagues, clients, other authors and visionaries that made my dream a reality. So, thank you Lidia, Peter, Borghild, Marek, Marlena, Rob, Amy, Ben, Yanusz, Jane, John, Stacey, Steve, Susan, Alex, John, Michael, Pete, Matthew, Sammy, Marlenka, Wiesio, Janusz, Barbara, Rafal, Gina, Bendel, Maria, Alex, Ryzard, Keith, Joasia, Brooks, Kasia, Maryam, Agata, Ruth, Ewa, Ula, my parents and all the others.

Many individuals have impressed me with their thinking, theories, passion, and achievements. I have quoted a number of great people throughout the pages of this book. Those who have personally changed my life for the better, I wish to specifically acknowledge and thank here: Mark Victor Hansen for thinking "Mega Big;" Jack Canfield for his insights into achievement; Tony Robbins for his deep understanding of human needs and passion; Martin Seligman for his relentless search for the sources and mechanics of positive psychology; Howard Gardner whose scholarly pursuit of what makes us intelligent helps us all; Daniel Goleman who champions expanding perspectives of emotional intelligence; Gary Zukav whose early insight into the complexity of the world allowed him to simplify it; Deepak Chopra who inspired mind-body medicine by melding Eastern and Western views; Swami Rama whose wisdom and understanding of Eastern philosophy inspired me; and Ken Wilbur who helped me expand and integrate these ideas.

The business of success is another area of great importance, for knowledge alone is not enough. You must have the passion, motivation, and opportunities to excel. I have had the good fortune to encounter many experts in the field of peak performance and excellence. Apart from those mentioned, Brian Tracy has been a leader and innovator who I greatly respect. Others who have helped me in my work and progress are Alex Mandossian, Mitchell Davis, Tom Antion, and Dan Kennedy for their brilliant marketing ideas and insights into business. I am grateful to Rick Frishman and John Kremer for pointing me in the right direction, as their experience in this field is extraordinary. Finally, I wish to thank David Hancock and all the great people at Morgan James Publishing, especially Elise Morrone and Kim Spano who helped put this book together.

I do love what I do. As a strategist, I help people untangle their lives and make life easier. I really appreciate all of my clients who through the years have shared their stories and have given me the opportunity to work with them. They have all participated in paving the road for this book. Of course, all the names in the illustrated examples have been changed to protect everyone's identity.

This small space would have to be multiplied a million times to approach the true depth of my appreciation to all. I thank you for helping me achieve this vision.

CONTENTS

Automatisms, Addictions, Assumptions, Rationalization or
Denial, Responsibility, Sensitivity, Attitudes, Obsessiveness,
Sabotage, Neurotic behaviors

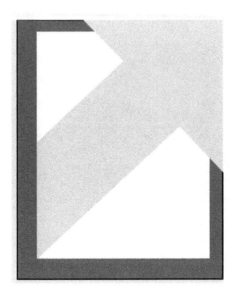

Always Go in Positive Directions

Dedication:

May we all discover what unites us so that we eagerly cooperate to bring peace and prosperity to all.

Preface

Why Read this Book?

Whenever I buy a book, I always check who is the author – what makes this person special, what would make me want to read his or her book. My journey through life has been very challenging and rewarding. I have been forced to learn about dealing with adversity on my own, struggling to achieve goals, enjoying triumphs, coping with despair, resolving complex problems and pushing past all limitations. Just the type of stuff every person has to deal with at least once in a while.

My life has been like a pendulum constantly swinging from highs to lows, from joys to tragedies, from success to failure. Confronted by these extreme polarities, we all try to cope as best as possible. The highs are nice; the lows everyone would like to avoid and yet, that task is extremely difficult. It is normal that difficult events in life can make us angry, anxious, frustrated, or depressed. This has made me wonder why it is faster and easier for us to slip in that negative direction than it is to climb up in the positive or happy direction? It just seems unfair. This inequality has motivated me to figure out what would make life easier?

Just like you, I have always wanted to have a happy and fulfilling life, but in reality it has often been a major ordeal with tremendous challenges at every turn. Through extensive experience with these ordeals, my work as a psychologist, meeting many extraordinary people, traveling and studying around the world, I discovered many fantastic tools to deal with these difficulties or even to turn a crisis in life to my advantage and quickly regain balance. These were important lessons in life that made me curious why we are all often caught on the negative or painful side of life. The reason for this problem has been the inspiration for this book and much of my work; it is about what the mind does wrong.

My life has been obsessed with thinking about one question:

"How does the mind work?"

The answers to this question have helped me resolve three basic problems about life:

♦   **How do you make the best decisions to prevent trouble in your life?**

♦   **What is the best way to deal with unwanted problems or feelings?**

♦   **How do you actualize your talents, potentials, or opportunities?**

These are universal desires that are much simpler to achieve than you think, if you understand 'how the mind works'. In *Positive Directions,* I will introduce you to my system; it contains a unique set of ideas: some are ancient, others contemporary, and many are original, that together offer you a new way to look at the world. My desire is to enlarge your perspective in a good way. So, if you are you searching for a book that is to the point, rich in facts, clear in its theories, and delivers what it promises, here you are!

You have every right to be skeptical - just allow me to prove that *you* are actually holding the keys that will unlock the chains that have been limiting your life. Even if you are a very healthy, strong, and successful individual, what made you assume that life can't be much better? As you read this book you will become convinced that it can be better. If your life is filled with stress, hardships, blockages, fears, anger, and a general lack of progress, it's liberation time! This book is going to turbo charge you. My personal life has been filled with serious challenges and hardships. The tools I have developed have certainly helped me cope and excel in life, and as a psychologist I have used this system to help thousands of my clients, whatever their stories or backgrounds. My mission is to empower as many people as I can with the tools to help them escape stress and maximize their potential.

This book has been written from a very unique point of view merging two opposite perspectives into one. I have dedicated my life to the study of hard-core science as well as training the intuition and the more philosophical perspective of ancient wisdom. I am fortunate to have become fascinated by both camps since my early youth. From the age of 16, I already knew that I was going to pursue a career in psychology; at the same time, I began meditating and studying spirituality. During the following 35 years, my curiosity led me to an in-depth study of the brain and its counter-part, the mind. This book is the first in a series to share the most valuable parts of my journey with you.

What was Special about My Journey?

I earned a doctorate in psychology through the City University of New York. For many years I studied neuropsychology: how the brain's mechanisms can explain all the different behaviors we are capable of. I worked at the Boston VA Hospital, Harvard Medical Center, and the Mount Sinai School of Medicine where I conducted clinical research about brain function. At the latter institution, I served as an assistant professor for several years. Using cutting edge QEEG technology to map the electrical activity of the brain, I continued researching the brain's functions. My work involved the evaluation and treatment of patients who suffered anything from a mild head injury to severe brain diseases. This gave me the unique opportunity to observe the specific changes in behavior associated with discrete parts of the brain. I encountered many tragic cases of debilitating stroke or cancer, although the mild brain injuries revealed much more about the inner workings of the mind.

The effects of a real head injury tend to be permanent, although most people learn to live with the consequences. Actually, everyone has experienced the effects of a mild head injury, at least temporarily. When you have not slept well, have a pounding headache or a fever, your brain cannot operate normally. It is sluggish, easily confused, disoriented, and it becomes difficult to concentrate plus many other problems. Even the common troubles you all experience everyday – stress, pressure to perform, deadlines, noise, and commotion – can easily interfere with the brain's normal function. Fortunately, most of these problems disappear quickly, allowing you to resume your regular activities. With a head injury the problems tend to be permanent. You can appreciate how taxing even normal stress can be. There are many techniques that popular psychology offers to restore balance and improve performance. If you would like to know the best ones, read on.

As a psychologist, I have struggled to understand how the mind works and what you can do to help yourself be more successful in life. This inquiry began with introspection, searching inside my own mind, which is the specialization of Eastern philosophy. Meditation was only one doorway into this arena. My quest for more information took me across five continents around the world meeting with teachers, professors, monks, gurus, swamis, scholars, scientists, doctors, healers, shamans, prophets, psychics, astrologers, and an endless assortment of other interesting people. I have studied the history, ideas, and works of various religions, the mystics, the sciences, and spirituality with the intention to understand their concepts and use of intuition, insight, and the natural intelligence we call wisdom.

In my own search for meaning and purpose in life, my mind has battled with dark forces and has been inspired by light ones. My life has been filled with extraordinary success as well as with tragic and painful events, my work has dealt with both on a continuous basis. Questions about "Why did that happen?" have raged through my mind many times. Yet something powerful has always struck me and given me many reasons to believe in something greater, to have hope, to understand the incomprehensible, to call up the courage to face doubts, pain, and injustice. I believe that our reality does stretch from a very material world all the way to a very spiritual one. This represents the duality of life – the material and spiritual. For those who have the ability to embrace both aspects, as I have learned to do, this brings a soothing comfort to life. I believe that any successful life must include both these opposite polarities. Discovering the best way to balance this duality is one of the ultimate secrets of life.

This double life I have been leading, half immersed in the facts of science and half in the more intuitive work of the mind, has led to the merger of two very opposing fields. This really makes my perspective unique and the information I present you, original. It should not surprise you that one of my major contributions is to highlight this very *duality of life*, the yin and yang, the paradoxes, the extreme polarities that stretch across our reality in every imaginable direction.

My perspective grew out of interviews with all the people I have encountered. Some were exceptionally successful and happy, while others were miserable and barely able to cope. A clear pattern of what works in life and what does not emerged from their stories. Some of this information comes from modern Western thinking, while a lot of it came from the ancient wisdom of other cultures. This division, in general, represents the different styles of thinking between the East and West.

The Western system relies on the rational, logical rules, regulations, facts, and details of a hierarchical organization of society. The Eastern system depends on a more introspective, subjective approach, one that is holistic, intuitive, emotional, flexible, connective, and is driven by a sense of inherent values rather than external controls. At this time, our Western society, despite the wealth and sophistication, is filled with stress where people complain about a lack of happiness and time; while those parts of Eastern cultures that have not yet been Westernized, have, in contrast, been enjoying much more peace of mind. Despite a lack of material wealth among the Eastern people, they report more happiness and less stress. What can possibly explain this strange disparity? Do you remember being told that technology would make our lives easier, give us more free time, help us enjoy a better life? The truth is undeniably the very opposite. Is the lack of "time" in our Western society the reason for many of our troubles, or does it go deeper into our thinking styles?

What is my personal history?

My personal quest for fulfillment has not been easy. I was not born with a silver spoon in my mouth. My parents came from Eastern Europe as immigrants to New York just after WWII. Their lives were more difficult than mine. My mother lost her first husband during the war and spent over four years in a concentration camp despite the fact she was a Christian. My father was in the war, fighting across Europe. They both saw and experienced a great deal of suffering. My father established a small business in Long Island, and I grew up in a rather rural area that slowly transformed into suburbia about 40 miles from New York City. Throughout my childhood, I worked for my father to earn money. Although we were poor compared to all our neighbors, I traveled to Europe nearly every year from the age of fourteen which began to expand my own horizons and curiosity.

I was not the best student in college, but was good enough to get some scholarships in addition to working and paying my own way through to a Ph.D. in psychology. I know what it is like counting the change in your pocket to decide which can of food you can take home to cook. Those financial hardships only motivated me more to work hard and rely on my natural talents. After fifteen years of academic work, I established a private practice in New York City as a psychologist and hypnotherapist. I was able to expand my practice based primarily on word of mouth referrals. During these years I found love, developed a very close wonderful relationship that lasted thirteen years. Then I experienced the hardship and pain of losing it as well. This made me painfully aware of the joys of a healthy partnership and the deep sorrow of its loss. However, I might add that my ex-wife and I remain close friends, so there are ways to cope and adapt to changes in life that are healthy and comforting. The point I wish to make is that my life has been filled with challenges that have forced me to adapt the best way possible, building my resilience and flexibility to go beyond coping effectively. My system is not only based on theories, but rather on experience and the facts of life.

Living a very active life in New York City and traveling around the world (often on my own) has exposed me to a richly stimulating world. My private practice is busy with a colorful variety of clients from every walk of life. This has given me the opportunity to apply my system to a large number of people in different situations to determine how well it actually works. I am proud to report that my system works very well for a vast majority of people. It is easy to learn and apply. It works for most of the common situations you find yourself in and helps rebuild the balance, harmony and peace inside. My system is also a valuable tool to help you identify your potential, talents and achieve more.

What Do I Know That You Want to Know Too?

I have learned a great deal about life. What I want to offer you here are the most precious gems that will increase in their value to you over the years. I can say that because it has been my intention to distill all the brilliant information I have encountered into a brief, focused summary of what I consider the:

♦ **Vital Knowledge** - the most essential information you must have, and

♦ **Required Skills** - to deal with life most effectively and achieve more.

Science has always promised to solve every problem on earth. It hasn't. The mystics have also claimed that they can "see" the future and made many predictions that often have been wrong. There is, however, an approach that bridges these two ways of thinking, uniting the strongest aspects of each together to create the most reliable and effective system to deal with our world and our personal lives.

Part of my system describes the natural evolution of mankind, and I predict this century will give birth to the **Third Renaissance** - a reflection of the growing number of people concerned with improving their personal lives from the <u>inside</u>. That is the surge of interest many of us have to increase the sense of fulfillment by developing our inner strength, our virtues, and our connection to others, rather than only relying on materialistic or external goals.

Integrating the duality of life

It is my firm belief that when you are given the right information and the necessary tools your life will change dramatically. Why? Two reasons; the first is the natural predisposition our mind has to slip into the negative direction. You must learn to counter-act the tendency to get drowned in stress, tension, and frustration. The second reason is that our normal subjective perspective limits what we perceive to only a small part of the whole story. There are many things you can learn to do that will expand your perspective. It is not just a matter of following rules and regulations, as explained by the more scientific approach. Neither is it about listening solely to your intuition and gut feelings as suggested in the Eastern perspective. The question is: when do you rely on one or the other? Neither one is sufficient to make you feel good, resolve conflicts, deal with stress, or help you realize all your potentials. That is why I have written this book, to integrate these two perspectives. *I intend to present you with many simple facts, explanations, and systems that will help you forge your own bigger and better perspective on how to think and live more comfortably.*

The reason I developed the confidence to write this book was years of testing and determining that this system really works well. This book is not about psychological problems some people experience, rather it is a story of what we <u>all</u> experience every day of life. That means what some professionals refer to as psychological problems, I believe is a completely normal part of life, but it is not necessary to spend a long time in anxiety, anger, or pain suffering. Instead, I intend to explain how you can easily change bad feelings or events into good experiences.

The practical tools that I describe here are the same knowledge and skills that I have relied on myself and shared with thousands of my clients for whom these tools have dramatically changed their lives from the inside. Change is a process. It may be instantaneous, quick, or slow. What is usually most noticeable is the difference in energy from the previous state to the new one. Change shifts the energy, preferably in a *positive direction*. And, my system is a completely natural approach to deal with life much more effectively.

So let me end on the following promise. I am certain that the information contained here will give you a great deal of insight into how the mind works, how to make it work better, and what to do to bring you greater prosperity, happiness, and peace of mind. In addition, these tools will make all of your relationships work better; you will be able to deal with "personality issues" very effectively and help others achieve more as well.

It is my most sincere wish that you enjoy and employ this book to make your life easier and more successful!

J.R.

New York

How to Use this Book:

This book has been designed so that you can use it in many different ways; whatever works best for you. This is more than a 'self-help' book. It is an interesting story that you will be glad to hear, and a major reference for you to utilize. I consider this a *personal development* book because if offers a great deal of knowledge that has been integrated from many sources. There are two sections and for those interested in reaching more goals there is a workbook available. The first section contains a lot of information. The second section describes the skills you need to overcome stressful challenges and enjoy life more.

Some of you do not like to read very much or at least may not enjoy the detailed explanations about nature and the mind in the first section. Consequently, I have included at the end of each chapter a *summary of the keys points* that you need to know. So if you do not want to read a whole chapter, please, at least go and read the summary keys. These summary keys are also excellent for reference. I do suggest that you definitely read the *Introduction*, there you will gain an overall perspective about the concepts and tools contained here.

The second section contains the most practical information on how to deal with a variety of common problems we all must work on. First, I explain the tools and then, how to use them. Each chapter contains at least ten examples to illustrate how to resolve difficulties most effectively. You can read through all of the material or just the parts that are particularly relevant to you. You can use the *index* to look-up specific terms or check the table of contents for subject headings.

The *Appendix* contains notes, exercises, and variety of resources. All books and articles mentioned are referenced by numbers in parentheses (#) which are listed in the *bibliography* along with a recommended reading list.

In general, I urge you to mark up this text as much as you like! The idea here is to find subjects with which you really connect with and find stimulating or important. The paragraph headings often pose a question that is subsequently answered in the text.

There are boxes sprinkled through the text with little "Ryderisms" as some people refer to them which contain factoids, exercises, ideas, new words, or just funny ideas to think about. I have also included a good number of quotations by many luminaries from around the world.

> **The Boxes** offer definitions, things to try, or just something to think about.

There is also a separate paperback interactive *Achievement Workbook* available that contains more information with practical skills that is designed to guide you towards greater success and fulfillment. See the Appendix or the website for more information.

Multimedia Resources on the Internet:

I have also constructed a website **www.ShiftingPolarities.com** that contains a vast amount of additional resources for you to use with this book. This information is constantly being expanded and updated. Much of the information is free to anyone who purchases a book. At this website you will find interactive tools to help you best utilize the knowledge in this book. There are many forms, tables and graphs that you can download from the internet site. I also offer a regular newsletter in the form of an Ezine that contains helpful advice and a schedule of events. There are also additional recorded programs, books, videos, and other products available for purchase.

Some of the *Recorded Exercises* described in this book are available from the website to be listened to, or downloaded for free. When you are ready, go to the website and click on the *Resources* button to access these materials and begin exploring the unlimited power of your mind.

Your first task (if you like) is to visit the website and download some of the tools available there. You will find many useful items that you can download and print. There is a bookmark that has a picture of the Triplex Mind and the main ideas from the book for easy reference. I suggest you cut it out and use it.

Come to a Live Event!

There is nothing more powerful than a live event that gives you the opportunity to experience the information presented here and consolidate it into your life. I offer several different formats that include free lectures as well as workshops about the master keys. The workshops are presented in various formats: a single evening (2 - 4 hrs), a whole day (6 - 8 hrs) and multi-day events. You can read about these in the Appendix or look up the most recent developments online. These are educational, experiential, and stimulating workshops that make this information more than just exciting, they make it personal for you!

You can check the website for a schedule of *live events* near you. I would like to personally invite you to join an event to lift up your life to the next level in a positive direction!

If your group, organization, school, corporation or business is interested in requesting a specially prepared keynote address, workshop, or consultation please visit my website **www.JohnRyderPhD.com** and click on Media - Speaking Engagements. I will be glad to develop a program for your group to promote higher levels of performance while maintaining internal balance and harmony. My presentations are content rich and passionately delivered to meet and exceed your specific needs.

I look forward to meeting you soon!

Lean on me when you're not strong

And I'll be your friend

I'll help you carry on

For it won't be long

Till I'm gonna need

Somebody to lean on

Lean on me...

Bill Withers

Introduction

The Keys to Shifting Polarities
Problems You <u>Can</u> Prevent and
Goals You <u>Can</u> Achieve

Create what you can do best that the world needs most.

21ˢᵗ Century Axiom

The keys to our prosperity, health and happiness are not reserved for special people; they are available to all who simply seek them. Do you know where to look? Some keys are fairly obvious, others remain hidden. Unless you discover all the right keys, you cannot enjoy the good life with plenty of success. Instead, your life remains locked in an unpleasant struggle, filled with stress, frustration, and misery. Part of the problem is that our effort is usually focused externally, confronting the difficulties life throws at us with the wrong keys. It does not matter how hard we try to deal with life; we never seem to reach the success we desire. That is because true progress depends on the hidden keys inside our mind and body. Unless you shift your focus to deal with the internal problems we all experience, you will be missing important keys. I am proposing that success requires you to understand how the mind works and, more importantly, how it fails to work correctly. If you learn how and why we make common mistakes, you will be able to avoid many of them and improve your ability to reach your true potential.

Mindmatics: are the automatic parts of your mind that take over your ability to think; it is our tendency to become robotic.

Nobody wants to believe that something is wrong inside of him or her.

Right now, most of your minds are arguing with my basic concept, that your mind does not work right, that you were born more likely to experience problems than pleasure. Your mind does not want to believe that idea for many good reasons. The fact is, we are all locked into a subjective perspective of life and ourselves; consequently your mind must defend its viewpoint at any cost. So your mind will often refuse to believe that it is wrong; after all, it is the only source of experience we have. How could it be wrong? This internal perspective of life will always blame a million outside causes for all our problems. Go ahead; admit it. I dare you; you don't want to be the source of your own difficulties – do you? No one does.

The real reason your mind is struggling with this concept is because there is a natural imbalance in your entire being. You are a victim of our human nature. However, this is not a matter of blame. Your nature is lopsided. The brain and nervous system you were born with are simply unfair to you because the nature of our thinking and feeling becomes the source of many troubles. That means every single person is born with a system that is more likely to spiral downward into the negativity of pain, frustration, or anxiety because that is the way our minds work. This is a matter of balance or the lack of it. We are all prone to easily slide down into the negative direction, and the more skills we develop to reverse our natural tendencies, the faster and farther we can climb up in the *positive direction*. This is the art of what I call *Polarity Shifting*.

Polarities of what?

Just about everything in life is a duality. These dualities exist in two polarities, from good to bad, happy to sad, rich to poor, positive to negative, and so on. The more time you spend in any of the negative, lower directions, the more stress and trouble you will experience. Conversely, if you learn how to shift polarities, to escape the negative side and go up into the *positive direction*, your life will feel much better. Those people who have learned to shift polarities in the positive direction quickly, easily, and more effectively live a happier, healthier, and more prosperous life. The ultimate keys for you to discover are the ones that make you an expert at shifting polarities.

We rarely find balance as life moves across opposite extremes. Usually, it is a matter of counter-balancing any negativity by going as far in the opposite direction as possible. When we shift polarities, we are not seeking the midpoint for balance. The idea is to obtain as much positive, healthy, happy, and good energy as we can. This is not a matter of compromising your life or coping with difficulties, it is about reversing situations for the better.

> **Serious things cannot be understood without laughable things, nor opposites at all without opposites.   Plato**

What do we all agree on?

There are certain universal goals we all share. The *positive direction* of any polarity in life is obvious, as are the rewards it brings or the suffering the opposite direction produces. How we choose and satisfy our goals is unique to every person.

- To live a long, healthy, happy, and prosperous life.

- To leave this world better than we found it for our children.

- To prevent or minimize suffering and troubles.

- To experience as much fulfillment as possible achieving our dreams.

To achieve these basic goals should not be difficult. However most of us experience a constant struggle to reach every small step toward success. The reason for our difficulties is psychological. There are four basic psychological functions that we all use every day. The problem is that these functions rarely work as we need them to; instead they often fail us and drive us crazy. That means they throw us down in the negative polarity. Normally, these four systems are constantly working to deal with circumstances on a wide spectrum from a positive extreme to the opposite negative polarity. Each function plays a significant role in determining what happens in our lives. Just as with everything else in life, each of these psychological functions has a good side and a problem side. I refer to these factors as the **JEEP** system: **J**udgment, **E**motions, **E**nergy, and **P**atterns. See Table 1.

These four simple factors represent the most fundamental and important functions of our brain. If our brains were designed to deal with these four factors perfectly, all of us would live a great life. Unfortunately, the truth is that our brains are inherently flawed with respect to these four factors, causing tons of trouble. We are all born with certain weaknesses. Consequently, sometimes we all end up making bad choices, getting into destructive patterns, fail to get or use the energy we need, or end up feeling miserable, frustrated, angry, anxious or whatever. These are all well accepted facts of life. However, I intend to offer you explanations of how the system works (or fails to) and solutions to improve the way your mind works so that you can prevent these problems from occurring. These represent the keys to shift the polarity of each factor from negative to positive.

Table 1: The JEEP Polarities – The Duality of the Mind with the Four Psychological Sources of Sabotage (Locks) or Success (Keys):

Psychological Factors	**Negative - Locks**	**Positive - Keys**
Judgment: analyzing information you collect to make choices about life	Bad Decisions stress & trouble	Good Decisions growth & reward
Emotions: the intensity and type of feelings we experience and express	Negative Feelings bad, sad, mad...	Positive Feelings happy, confident, accepting, good
Energy: the power we generate, use, keep, exchange, or give away	Negative Losing Draining energy	Positive Charging plenty of energy
Patterns: all our automatic routines, habits, and programs we repeat	Bad Destructive self sabotage	Positive Helpful simplify life

The good news is that the biggest improvements we can make in our lives are free, simple, and relatively easy to accomplish. All you require is knowledge and some specific skills anyone can learn to change the psychology of your mind, making life easier, allowing you to achieve more and suffer less. You simply need the right keys to gain control of the inner system of the brain. By learning to shift polarities, you will spend more time on the more rewarding side of the polarities.

What Keys?

Which came first - the lock or key? A good locksmith will carefully grind each key to perfectly fit and open the lock it is made for. In life, we are confronted by a stream of obstacles, problems, challenges, and moments of pain mixed with the opportunities, rewards, surprises and experiences of pleasure. Are there specific keys to unlock the psychological difficulties life presents? How do we know which keys fit in our locks? I have heard many people claim to be "locksmiths" selling keys to wealth, fame and happiness. At last count, there were many more people still struggling with their keys than those who found the right ones. How do we get the right keys to open the doors we want to? What is the secret? Why is it a secret? Would you like to have a master locksmith customize the right keys for you? I provide answers to all these questions.

The Master Keys

To find the right keys to solve problems and challenges in life is a rather complex task because there are such a tremendous variety of troubles, each requiring a different key to resolve. However, by identifying just four internal factors responsible for our personal sabotage, it is much easier to find the keys to unlock these common problems. That is, the principle goal of this book is to present you the ***nine master keys*** that can always reverse the unwanted direction any of the four JEEP factors may go in. That is how you can conquer most of your psychological challenges. It is not so complex or difficult to deal with these four factors because they are just part of our human nature. When you learn to correct these four psychological factors you will be able to excel more easily, preventing problems, and achieving goals.

What are the locks and keys?

I refer to <u>problems</u> as **"locks"** and to the <u>solutions</u> as **"keys."** Each "lock" limits our freedom to be happy and successful. The four factors of sabotage are the general categories under which we all have our particular problems or locks. Everyone has plenty of specific locks; some cause only minor trouble; others create intense friction, terrible conflicts, and enormous stress. When the conditions become really bad with obstacles, we end up in a metaphorical jail. No one wants to be imprisoned, but that is precisely what life feels like to many people. Are you one of them? If not, I'm sure you know others who are.

Every "lock" has specific "keys" that will open or resolve it. The master keys unlock most of the locks in one category. When you unlock your problems, it is automatically a liberating experience. This is the process of reversing directions so that you start heading for success and happiness. Instead of wasting your time on problems, you will have more time to focus on achieving goals you can reach. I do not promise everyone will become a millionaire. However, I will describe how every individual can access his or her own sense of wealth, health, and joy. These keys also enable you to clearly identify all your potential so that you will be more productive and successful.

> ***Exercise the Subconscious:*** *Think of all your keys; close your eyes and just imagine which key opens which lock and which way the key fits into the lock (teeth up or down) and then which way you turn it to open the lock. Did you use your hands to help remember? These are subconscious programs, or mindmatics;*

Can we make life easier?

Life does not have to be constantly difficult. Certainly, there are all the good and beautiful aspects of life along with all its problems, pressures, and pain. Why do we have a hard time being happy, feeling healthy, and making ends meet? Why is our life dominated by so much anxiety, fear, anger, frustration, sadness, and pain? After all, we have been living in a civilized world, with a great deal of wisdom, sophisticated technology, plus each of us has been accumulating a lifetime of experience. Why haven't we conquered these simple challenges yet? The answer is because the mind, despite its power, is actually a very fragile, easily disturbed system that often fails to provide us with the right response. The mind distorts reality more quickly than it constructs an accurate picture of it. The mind often jumps to conclusions that are wrong. The system was designed to make us more prone to the negative polarity. This is true of our internal experience as well as that of the world around us.

I have simplified this problem by identifying the four basic sources of all of our sabotage (JEEP system). As you learn to use the master keys I provide you, you will begin to limit and ultimately end most of your own sabotage. Develop your skills to reverse unwanted polarities and move in the desired direction. Consequently, it is possible to make life easier by gaining control of what upsets us, drives us crazy, throws us off balance, drains us of energy, or simply stresses us out. Besides these four factors, I will describe two secret locks and two hidden keys that can and do have tremendous effects on your life. This system will help us utilize these four basic factors to achieve more success.

Illustrative example:

> Ted worked on Wall Street. He had an important administrative position supervising a large staff of employees. Ted was a large, stocky fellow who came to my office complaining of terrible stress at the job and feeling he was stuck in a very destructive routine trying to cope with it. He was overeating and drinking heavily after work. As he began to identify why he was reacting with so much frustration and anxiety about the demands his coworkers were putting on him, he was able to change his responses. He also became more aware of the motives for his sabotaging routines, which allowed him to replace those patterns with better ones. Very quickly, Ted reported that he was able to remain calm and comfortable regardless of the demands of the job, and he began exercising much more than overeating. Soon he lost weight, gained more confidence, did not need to drink excessively, and felt much more in control of his life. He discovered just a few keys that liberated him from the stress and enabled him to feel much more productive and healthy. He learned how to relax quickly and to return to his own positive thinking that gave him the strength to change his habits. This was the result of just a few weeks of counseling.

What is the difference between competition and cooperation?

In our Western world everything is based on competition. Is that really necessary? The answer is, unfortunately, yes in our culture. But is there anyone who doubts that we would accomplish more if our system were based on cooperation? The reason for this universal problem is in our very nature. We are all born dominated by the survival instincts - *I must win in order to survive*. Did you ever feel anxious or angry about losing to someone else? Do you remember the pain of failure or sense of disgust with yourself for not winning? We all grow up dominated by these instinctual feelings that have actually caused our society to become increasingly competitive and stressful. If we develop the skills to control these instincts, then we will be able to gain much more from cooperating. The idea of cooperation is a concept rooted in Eastern philosophy. Their culture have advanced the skills of controlling these destructive instincts in us. This book will show you how some insight and a few new skills will allow you to become more successful through cooperating.

What's wrong with the brain?

Our brain is designed to do many amazing things. Despite the brain's power, it can easily do terrible things to our reality. We are born with significant limitations and handicaps, but don't worry, these are all natural and normal problems. We often suffer from poor perceptions, distortions, illusions, false assumptions, and disconnections, which are all problems regarding information processing. The brain's capacity to monitor itself is limited. The brain creates automatic programs very quickly, but they can be very destructive to ourselves or others. The brain is also emotionally prejudiced making us much more vulnerable to stress, fears, anger, and pain. The main commodity of life is energy. Unfortunately, our brain is not well designed to manage these resources automatically. If we do not develop an effective system to control our energy, we will feel weakened, fatigued, drained, confused, frustrated, or disturbed because there is some injustice in our exchange of energy with others. Together, all of these factors make it difficult for us to develop good judgment and make the best decisions. These are only the major problems that the brain does not deal with very well. There are many other problems; however, the factors listed above directly affect the four sources of our success or sabotage: our judgment, emotions, energy, and our patterns.

These limitations reflect our general tendency to slip in the negative direction and get entangled in all the problems. Polarity shifting gives you the knowledge and skills to reverse directions and move towards all the positive and desired goals.

Real Relaxation: Stop for a moment. Are you worried about what is wrong with your mind or body? Don't be. Close your eyes for just 2 minutes and slow down your breathing to about 3 seconds for each breath in and 3 seconds out. Notice your ability to relax deeply, regain balance and harmony inside, or did your brain keep going a hundred miles an hour? One important key is to learn to relax quickly.

I dedicate a separate chapter for each of these four JEEP factors. Every person depends on these factors for either his/her success or problems in life. Each of us has to deal with both aspects, the positive and negative effects of these four systems. Some people have more trouble with one or two of these factors than the others. Most people have trouble with all four of these factors. The main point here is that these factors represent internal problems of how our brain works or fails to work effectively. There is nothing abnormal about these problems. They exist among all people to one degree or another. They interfere with life more for some than others. In my experience, everybody deals with these problems sometimes.

Illustrative examples:

Marcy is an attractive, young lawyer working in New York City. She told me that she has always been very selective with her boyfriends. When she met an attractive businessman who wanted her very much, she was convinced by all his actions that he was the "right" guy. Yet, before getting married she had a very strong intuition that settling with him would be a big mistake. She could not identify what was bothering her exactly. She ignored her doubts and got married. She came to me a few months after the wedding complaining that he was impossible, didn't want to be intimate with her, questioned her constantly, and made her life miserable. None of these behaviors were apparent before her marriage, but she did have a feeling that something was not right.

Her judgment ignored the intuitive sense and led her to a big mistake, a bad choice, and many problems before they separated. After being given the keys to making better choices, Marcy has told me that she feels much more confident making decisions. These keys taught her how to listen to her intuition and still logically prioritize her alternatives with the rules to eliminate bad decisions. Marcy had to recognize the difference between just anxiety and that special feeling she got in her tummy that was telling her something important.

Rochelle described a frightening car accident that fortunately was not very serious, but destroyed her car. She became afraid of driving a car, or riding buses, trains, and planes. She could only drive one specific route to and from work in a roundabout manner. She became eager to overcome her fears after I helped her understand what went wrong in her head. Rochelle had generalized her anxiety from the car accident to anything to do with roads or transportation. The keys I provided her enabled Rochelle to relax, releasing the physical stress, and to shift polarities to transform her anxieties into comfortable feelings. Once she learned how to shift from fear to courage driving, she was able to do the same in other areas of her life. Soon she began to enjoy traveling and has been sending me post cards from foreign cities.

The most common reason we experience a sense of injustice is because of an unfair exchange of energy. You may be working hard on some project at work and your boss takes all the credit when you have finished it. That leaves you with a sense of disrespect, having been taken advantage of. Similarly, you may go to a store to purchase a familiar item and be disturbed by paying twice as much for it as you did not long ago. Consider a housewife who takes care of the home, children, and cooks for her husband who fails to acknowledge her efforts, instead placing more demands on her or just complaining about something else. The wife may be justified in feeling a loss of energy, where a few kind words of gratitude from him would have easily satisfied her needs. Energy constantly changes as it flows from one person to another. We are all very sensitive to the overall balance of energy moving between people. When one gets more than another, it causes discomfort and raises the alarm. There are keys to correct this inequality, and when you learn to use these keys, you will be able to regain balance or not suffer from the lack of it.

The question of patterns can be described on two levels. We are all designed to repeat behaviors to simplify our lives. These appear as our habits and routines. On a deeper, more hidden level, we develop subconscious programs or patterns of thinking that may not be easy to observe, but that do have a significant role in our lives. Joseph is a mother's boy. His thinking includes a compelling command to inform his mother about every event in his life and to get her approval. This has made it nearly impossible for any woman to have a deep relationship with him because there is always a third party involved in everything. This pattern of life has actually been depressing to Joseph, and when he came to me, he was forced to make a choice to shift his thinking and need for his mother's approval or lose his wife. The keys he was given gave Joseph the knowledge of how his patterns do not really satisfy his needs, how to obtain leverage to change his habits and a new better program to replace the old one. Today Joseph gets along with his wife as well as he does with his mother.

> We do what we can, and then make a theory to
> prove our performance the best. R.W. Emerson

Do you doubt the illusions?

If you do not believe that the brain makes mistakes, let me prove it to you. On the next page are a few examples of special figures. Go to them and answer the questions. See if you can find the differences. Perhaps I can convince you that the brain is designed to make mistakes about what it perceives, calculates, interprets, tries to create, and so on. We all have had those embarrassing moments where we made an obvious error that we did not even notice; like trying to open your house door with the office key? Well, let me explain it to you very carefully, but first look at the figures and then continue. (See next page.)

Illusions: What to do you see? Are you sure it is real or not?

Are the horizontal lines straight?

Is this triangle flat or
does it change position?

Straight or not?

How many triangles
do you see below?

Is the distance between A-B smaller or
larger than the distance between B-C ?

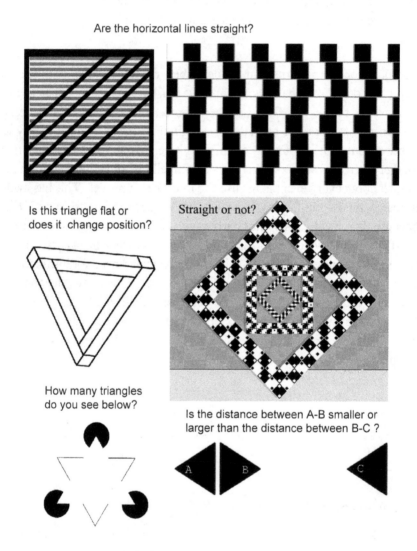

If you had a difficult time with the illusions, do not blame your sensory
perception: it is fine. Your awareness is fine too. In fact, it is the only
thing that can correct the illusions that we observe. Above you were
presented with a few classic illusions to demonstrate how easily your brain
is fooled by the context in which you see something in. The lines are not

crooked; they are straight, the distance between the triangles is the same (A-B = B-C), and so on. They do look different because our brain's perceptual system is prone to making mistakes, just as the other parts of the brain are also vulnerable to making major errors in every area of function. That is a real problem few understand.

My Mission:

As a psychologist, it has been my ambition to constantly learn as much as possible and refine this knowledge for others to utilize. I have always made an effort to develop both my intuition (to "sense" the world) and my rational thinking (to scientifically investigate what is true). With this knowledge, my mission is to enlighten and empower people to make life easier and achieve more. Based on over thirty-five years of my research and experience, I want to offer you the following information, which I have distilled from many other teachers, books, experiences, and insights. The central theme here remains *Polarity Shifting*, becoming aware of going in the wrong or negative direction and reversing polarities to head in a desirable and *positive direction*. I have divided this data into two groups and will present it to you throughout this book in the form of keys.

> *Expander: one who expands awareness, in contrast to the traditional shrink. I intend to expand your perspectives.*

▸ **Vital Knowledge** - The essential group of facts and theories everyone should know and utilize in his or her daily life, those that are necessary for our progress. This includes the rules about reality and the physical laws that govern nature. Without this information you are likely to become the victim of greater hardships, illusions, problems, and a general lack of progress. This knowledge also helps identify your natural talents and abilities to promote progress.

▸ **Required Skills** - These are the most valuable sets of activities that we need to study and exercise to maximize our responsiveness to common challenges. This is a list of easy to learn skills to deal with life and our own inadequacies in the best ways possible. Without these skills, you will be unable to cope effectively. Instead you will experience more stress and fail to actualize your potential. Practicing these skills improves your ability to adapt, cope with stress, and achieve your goals. The master keys represent the special strategies to shift polarities effectively.

What Is the Diamond Master Key?

This book relies on the premise that there is one psychological function that affects all the others: this is our *conscious awareness*, the system that allows us to experience and deal with life. This is the fundamental operating system of our brain, yet, how often do you stop and think about it? The magic of consciousness is that it works invisibly, creating the experience of life without leaving a clue of how it does this amazing feat! Awareness is the ultimate key for us to observe our universe, think about it, and actually find ways to improve the world. The mysterious power of consciousness is not a problem to understand, rather, it is a crucial key for us to utilize and take full advantage of.

> *Cosmic Consciousness: the highest state of awareness, that mystics, sages, prophets and others have described transcending all senses and becoming directly aware of God and the universe.*

The most important point about consciousness is that it is a dynamic factor, constantly changing, shifting, stretching, expanding, or narrowing and focusing. Just as easily as you can redirect your attention, you automatically change your level of awareness. The potential power of your consciousness is nearly unlimited; you can connect memories from your past, make associations in the present or visualize the future. Consciousness is the ultimate bridge to escape limitations set by cosmic or biological laws. With a little training, the mind can conceive almost anything! This is what gives birth to all the creativity in our civilization.(1) The first rule to learn is that we can constantly gain better control of our attention system to direct our awareness where we want to.

What is the difference between focusing and shifting attention?

The brain is designed to move in only two directions. You are either focusing and concentrating on one particular task, or you are shifting attention to the next more important item before you, expanding your awareness. Think about it. Your thinking goes only in these two directions, focusing or shifting attention. These processes reflect a tremendous number of different brain systems that engage our ability to concentrate or become more generally aware of our surroundings. These two functions are responsible for the way we handle everything we do. Either we are able to focus on a given task effectively, or we are able to keep shifting our attention to the next important item.

Normally, we are easily distracted by unimportant stimuli; it is difficult for a person to keep his or her mind focused for long periods of time. Even performing at our best, very few people are able to concentrate or keep shifting their attention for long. Most people are able to do a little of both for short periods of time. Some are better at concentrating, and few are good at shifting and letting go of what they focused on previously. Learning to improve your ability to concentrate or shift and let go of your focus has countless advantages in life.

For example, an individual recognized for his power of concentration is Albert Einstein working on his mathematical formulas. A famous person who has developed the power to shift his focus is James Bond, who constantly is vigilant of every possible source of trouble in his environment.

Why is the CQ most important?

The concept of this book was to highlight the importance of awareness. The series title is *Raising Your CQ* - the *consciousness quotient*. This is my metaphor of *how aware you are*. A

> ***Benius:*** *a person who is a genius at living in the moment, being in the here and now with complete ease and total passion. Are you?*

century ago, the IQ score began to measure what is believed to be intelligence. More recently, the EQ was developed to measure emotional intelligence.(2) Beyond these two measures, I propose a new idea. It is not how smart you are, how emotionally clever, or even how much you know; rather it is a matter of what you are aware of now! This makes our awareness the ultimate measure of our success or failure. The more you are aware of, the higher is your CQ! The secret of raising your CQ is based on the combined process of increasing control of your attention system so you can focus or shift your awareness most effectively. And secondly, you raise your CQ by learning all the keys to unlock your problems and help achieve your goals. This is a matter of becoming a master of your own environment so that you can shift polarities whenever necessary.

Consciousness is a diamond key because it is responsible for operating the brain and mind. The experience of awareness transcends all divisions within the nerves of the brain or functions of the mind. Consciousness is an integral part of every function of the mind. Consequently, it can always help us gain control of the four sources of success and sabotage (judgment, emotions, energy, and patterns). This makes awareness a crucial key to gaining insight, preventing sabotage, or reaping rewards from our internal systems.

Many experts claim that intelligence is mostly inherited.(3) I do not agree. However, everyone agrees that awareness continues to be the spontaneous integration of all the information we process across a lifetime, so it cannot be inborn. Consciousness is different from knowledge, which is stored in memory, or intelligence, which usually refers to a few specific traits and skills. Awareness is a complex psychological system that we naturally develop early in life and should continue improving over a lifetime, but usually don't because no one offers any instructions about it. So I intend to help you increase your awareness by giving you the right tools to do so. This book will explain many ways to expand your awareness. You will learn to better use your consciousness system, to concentrate or shift attention more effectively. This process will help make your life easier too.

Your Past: *Sit comfortably, close your eyes and go back to your childhood to recall your favorite toy or game and how much fun you had playing. Remember as vividly as you can. Consider how this makes you feel. Have you done anything recently that was as much fun? Can you try to?*

How conscious can you be?

There are countless levels of consciousness, from the lowest to the highest. The lower levels reflect a lack of curiosity, knowledge, and a simplified view of reality. The higher levels indicate a person who is not satisfied with a narrow perspective and is constantly expanding everything he or she can be aware of. Success in life is not based on intelligence, knowledge, or just motivation.(4) However, anyone who has excellent control of his or her attention and develops his or her skills of observation and judgment is most likely to enjoy success in life. Anyone can reach the ***superior level of awareness***, which is a heightened state of alertness, clarity of perception, presence of mind, a sense of connectedness, and the preparedness for any event life throws at us. Most people can recall a few moments like that. You can reach this superior awareness relatively easily with practice and clear instructions. This will be described in the chapter 8 on Attention. Developing a superior consciousness means that you are always able to shift your awareness in the direction it needs to go for you to master the situation you are in, while keeping in mind the details as well as the larger picture.

Building bridges

This book attempts to present one of the most balanced perspectives merging the Eastern philosophical system with the Western scientific system. The best way I can support this claim is by asserting that I consider myself both a philosopher and a scientist; and I hold no prejudices against either one. To the contrary, I have invested most of my life trying to find ways that these two apparently separate perspectives can be elegantly integrated and work cohesively. There will be many examples of how these two systems fit together and ultimately are very complementary. To begin building a bridge I wish to focus on two fundamental thinking styles every person uses. Both processes provide us with answers about what we observe and think about, but they are very different from one another.

The Dualities – which path to take?

Wherever you want to go, there is always more than one way to get there. Do you prefer the scenic road or the faster highway? The preference may depend on other factors, like if you are in a hurry or if you are just exploring. The path you pick is an important decision and will change everything that happens. The two most common approaches we all rely on to make decisions are very different; sometimes they are in agreement, but often they are radically apart. Some people use both; others use only one; which one do you favor to help make your decisions?

▸   **The Rational Approach** represents the modern, pragmatic logical system that we must learn to use. It depends on first collecting concrete, objective, detailed information. Secondly, these details must be carefully analyzed and compared to previous experience. The rational approach then leads to a calculated ranking of alternatives. This ultimately becomes the basis for a logical, rational judgment of what appears to be the best choice. This is a conscious, deliberate effort to make a decision.

▸ **The Intuitive Approach** describes the original human radar system we are all born with. It depends on the subjective impression that gives us a "gut" feeling, or some sort of psychic awareness that provides instant knowledge that cannot be explained logically. This intuition creates a strong positive or negative feeling to follow one course of action rather than another. Intuitive knowledge is not learned or intellectual; it is spontaneous awareness that may arise from the subconscious mind or some sort of internal radar we have to evaluate situations.

This is an excellent example of two polarities that are both positive and negative together. Both approaches have strengths and weaknesses, which make it a bit more complex to know

> **Intulytical:** *the ability to combine the power of intuition with being rationally analytical.*

which one to rely on and when. In the West, the rational approach is usually promoted as the superior system because it is supposed to be objective, pragmatic, based on facts, details, and a logical analysis of everything. The resulting decision must be right and have greater value than any other approach.(5) In comparison, the intuitive approach is considered the superior system in the East.(6) The reason using the intuition is considered superior by many people can be attributed to many factors: philosophical, cultural, traditional, but the most powerful reason is that the intuition is often right. Everyone can recall a moment when his or her hunch or intuition turned out to be completely right, in direct contrast to the facts. Intuition can also be wrong, just as the rational path can equally produce faulty results. So which path is the right one? When should we rely more on one system than the other? The short answer is to integrate these two systems and use both. These issues will be addressed in detail in Chapter 22 on Judgment.

At this moment, my concern is that you are aware of these two approaches and begin reflecting on which one you rely on the most and which system others use to make decisions. Is there a time when one approach is really superior? The truth is that even famous scientists who normally rely on the rational approach to make decisions have reported that their most important discoveries were based on a hunch or a feeling to run some experiment. So let's assume that for now both approaches have roles in our decision process. Life is all about decisions. The right choice can catapult you to great success, just as the wrong one can send you spiraling downward. The following stories are meant to demonstrate how choices in real life circumstances can change your destiny.

Heard stories of real success?

Some of the more famous stories are the most revealing. What about the young man who dropped out of college and started his own software company creating the world's leading computer program? This is the story of Bill Gates and Microsoft Corporation. His success was not due to the "right" education or having great wealth to develop his programs and company. He did have a vision and incredible awareness of what computers could offer. Another young man grew up in a rural area of the south. His father died before he was born and his stepfather was a gambler and alcoholic. Despite hardships at home, he applied himself to his studies and excelled. He jumped at the opportunity to visit Washington D.C. and at 16 met President Kennedy. That inspired him to get involved with politics and he worked on a few campaigns. While at college, he won a Rhodes scholarship to study in England for a year. He returned to his home state and eventually became governor. Bill Clinton was elected President at the age of 46. What keys did he have that allowed him to climb so high up the ladder of success from such humble beginnings? He obviously had a plan, great communication skills, and a political awareness that few will ever match.

Consider well respected artists like a poor black boy who grew up in a Brooklyn ghetto and found his calling early on and by the time he was a teenager was appearing in comedy clubs doing stand-up routines. Chris Rock went on to become one of the leading edgy comics in America producing numerous films and television programs. What gave this guy the confidence to stand up in front of crowds to make them laugh? He has an extraordinary awareness of humor and what topics are likely to evoke laughter. This is a talent he has been developing all his life. What keys did he discover early in his life to recognize these abilities? He accessed superior patterns, emotions, energy and judgment.

Another good example is a young girl who moved to New York City from Detroit to become a dancer. She had nothing except her own conviction that she could do it. Despite a lack of resources and financial hardships, she started a band, recorded some songs, ran around the clubs playing her music, and finally got a record deal. Her first single was very successful, which prompted the record company to invest in a full album. Madonna's first album went on to be a multi-platinum record. This began a versatile music career that has made Madonna the "Queen of Pop" by the media. What keys did this young girl have that helped her conquer all the challenges and become a self made star? One obvious answer is recognizing her own talents and investing enormous energy and passion into her work. She has a relentless commitment to her art and always gives her all; this is an example of superior energy, emotion, and pattern awareness.

Other stories you have not heard:

What makes some stories really impressive is that they describe normal people who do extraordinary things. Anthony, one of my clients, riding a train in Brooklyn, saw a crazed man wielding a knife slash a woman in the face. As the doors opened, the man ran out of the train, and Anthony chased him, tackled him to the ground, and waited for the police to arrest the attacker. He suffered a gash to his hand in the incident. He risked his own life to protect others, demonstrating courage and a sense of justice that motivated him. There is the story of Aaron Ralston who was hiking in a remote canyon in Utah when he fell, and a large boulder pinned his arm. After five days without help, he decided to amputate his own arm to escape.

We all can understand his decision to survive at the cost of his own arm, but it forces the question upon us: would you have done the same thing in his place? That is an excellent example of the will to live.

There are many decisions in our lives that can be life changing. Recently, returning from racing my car (an M6 for those who know) at the Pocono Race Track, I was driving leisurely back on an open, nearly empty turnpike. I was in the right lane with nothing straight in front of me for a mile. It was dusk and to be safe, I decided to put on my glasses to see better. They were in my glove box, so I leaned over and began searching for them. Then suddenly, I had a strong intuition to look up. As I peered over the dashboard, to my surprise I saw a giant buck walk into my lane no more than 50 feet ahead of me! My instincts and fast reflexes made my car swerve violently around the beast just in time. Luckily, I knew my car and its handling. More so, I am grateful to that internal signal that commanded me to look up; otherwise I would not be here now.

The external information we obtain from our senses or instruments about our surroundings is equally important. It can be a satellite weather forecast, a thermometer, a traffic light, or a report from some high-tech diagnostic instruments that can help identify medical problems early. I recall one client, a young woman, who had a history of medical problems, whom I insisted get another test to be certain there was nothing wrong. When she complied and went for the examination, she learned that there was something serious that needed immediate treatment. As disturbing as such information can be, the rational, objective approach literally saved her life. The truth is that both approaches are extremely valuable and probably we should not try to ignore either one.

What reality do we count on?

The one we experience is the answer. Whatever we perceive, or think we know, whether it is true or a complete illusion, that is what we assume reality really is. This puts us at a serious disadvantage. If what we assume is wrong, then how do we get to the truth? The only way to find the true reality is with the diamond key, our internal system of conscious awareness. Consciousness allows us to test our thinking, theories, perceptions and conclusions to determine how accurately they reflect reality. The next step is to attempt to integrate all the various elements together. Hence, we should strive to utilize our rational and intuitive approaches together. And in the end, just to be safe, we require a little doubt, questioning our results even if we are very confident of them. Skepticism is a very useful attitude in many situations, until a decision has been made.

The story of reality will begin the first section: *The Nature of the Universe.* In this section, I discuss, in a very simplified form, the various laws that affect our reality, as well as our perceptions of it. This is how I intend to introduce you to the vital knowledge about our universe. With this information, you will be better prepared to deal with reality and your own (faulty) perceptions of it.

> **Cosmush:** *unwanted intervention from the world around you that makes a mess of your plans. You know, like rain, electricity going out, a flat tire, your cell phone dropping out, etc. This is the cosmic chaos making mush.*

How to improve the system?

The skills and knowledge we get early in life are never enough to prevent bad things from happening. The universe is far from perfect; something, somewhere, is constantly going awry in it, disturbing our plans and causing us stress. In addition, the world is getting more crowded and competitive. This is why it is getting progressively more difficult to achieve the goals we want. The reason we have these problems can be blamed, in part, on the way our brains function. The question then is how can we improve the way our brain functions? First, we must recognize how and why our nervous system makes so many mistakes. This information is available, and I will describe it to you in the following chapters on Human Nature. Once you understand the basic function of our mind and body, I will explain the master keys to battle the mistakes we make, so you can expand your awareness and learn to shift polarities, escaping trouble.

Through the process of learning the vital knowledge and required skills, you can keep raising your CQ. Each key allows you to unlock part of the sabotage that limits you and causes stress. With each step, you experience a little more awareness. As you learn how to double-check the impressions your brain gives you for accuracy, you will become more confident and less likely to be fooled by illusions. This will help you prevent many bad things from happening or allow you to resolve them more quickly if they do occur. When you realize the true purpose for all emotions, it becomes easy for you to escape negative feelings and spend more time in positive emotions. You also discover the keys to superior judgment, to improve your skills for making better choices. Finally, increasing your sense of control over the reality you are in, will give you a new sense of mastery, and allow you to adapt more effectively to difficulties and achieve more success whenever possible. Becoming an expert at polarity shifting will help you to escape stress and head in a ***positive direction***. This is how you can progressively make life easier and feel more happy and fulfilled.

> **Riches do not consist in the possession of treasures,**
> **but in the use made of them.** Napoleon

What do you have to realize?

The story comes full circle and returns to the concept of consciousness and the whole system of awareness. Consciousness provides you with the ability to perceive, analyze, focus, concentrate, and exercise either logical judgment or intuition to decide the best course of action to take in life. From the moment you awake until you fall asleep, your conscious awareness processes all the information from the world around you and inside your head to create the experience of being alive. The ability of the brain to be aware is among the greatest mysteries of life. Despite the fact that the brain does a marvelous job at giving us consciousness, there are many shortcomings that limit its reliability. In fact, the brain's main

---

Dreams: *Your dreams are an alternate reality. Can you recall your favorite, most wonderful dream you have had that you would like to have again? Perhaps it was strange or bizarre in some way; have you figured out what it means? This is another example of how our thoughts work under the surface of awareness.*

function is to give us only approximations of what we need to know to deal with life. As you may recall with the graphic illusions presented before; the brain is easily fooled. Consequently, our lives are a constant struggle to overcome a persistent lack of consciousness that limits us in countless ways. And yet consciousness also enables us to constantly expand our awareness, so that anyone can instantly develop a superior awareness with just a little effort of attention.(7)

Increasing your conscious awareness of something is a natural result of focusing your attention on it. The moment you learn to focus on Shifting Polarities in the *positive direction*, you automatically liberate yourself from numerous limitations and expand your mind in the best way possible.

What is next?

This introduction is meant to give you a general overview of what this book is about and to put you into the right "mind set" to take advantage of the material being presented. The book is divided into two sections, separated into small chapters for better digestion.

The first section begins on the most general level and gets progressively more specific about our relationship to the world around us; what limits us and the influences we deal with. Each chapter describes a number of basic concepts that I list for you as keys at the end of each. In Chapter Three, I introduce you to the **Triplex Mind** system that helps you understand how your mind works. Subsequent chapters describe how the locks and keys work. The section ends on what is our quest for fulfillment. All this information prepares you to better understand and appreciate how the nine master keys work.

The second section introduces you to the universal rules about the JEEP polarities. Each of the nine master keys is described in detail. These are the required skills to gain control of your JEEP factors. From Chapter 18, you are presented the JEEP factors and how to deal with the negative influence they have on your life. Each factor is clearly illustrated with examples so that you can easily apply the tools described to your own life. Here you begin to better understand how to make better decisions; why some people drain you of energy while others give you a boost; and how to gain more control over your life in general.

The skills section is summarized in Chapter 23 which offers the ***Gold Keys*** to escape stress and accelerate reaching your goals. It also describes what to do during various crisis and extreme circumstances. Here the worst challenges in life are acknowledged. You are offered further tools to deal with these difficulties most constructively, I refer to these as the ***Fourth*** and ***Fifth ways***. The following chapter addresses spirituality, not as a religion, but rather as a way to redirect energy in a ***positive direction***. It discusses how this is part of a movement I refer to as the Third Renaissance that is leading to a paradigm shift around the world.

The last chapter reviews what I consider the science of success and the art of life. These two approaches to life reflect the Western and Eastern styles of thinking. Integrating these two systems results in the most powerful and successful approach to life. When you finish this book, do not put it away. Leave it within reach to refer to the ideas, suggestions, and tools inside. Let this book remain a major resource to make life easier and it will!

The purpose of this book is to prepare you to achieve more of your true potential. I have also created a companion ***Achievement Workbook*** that continues this journey to help you remove obstacles, clearly define your strengths, and reach more of your goals. This workbook is an interactive system that contains more practical information and a variety of exercises designed to give you the tools to achieve more with less effort and trouble.

It does not matter where you are in life, there is always room to achieve more success and happiness. Are you curious what your <u>true</u> potential is? Is it possible that events in life have lowered your expectations? Do you ever wonder – "what if ___?" There are countless possibilities and opportunities that perhaps you are missing, or may fail to take in the future.

I urge you to get the ***Achievement Workbook*** and go through the exercises inside. You will gain greater self awareness. You will clearly identify your own talents or predispositions. Find every opportunity before you. Learn to develop an excellent strategic plan, organize yourself and set your priorities effectively. Watch yourself excel. This does not mean that every person will become rich and famous. Rather, I believe that you will discover what your true purpose in life is and experience a deep sense of fulfillment learning to master your situation and adapt more successfully to challenges you encounter.

The *Achievement Workbook* will raise your level of performance and help you manage your time more effectively. Refer to the Appendix for more information, visit my website www.ShiftingPolarities.com for details or purchase it at your local (or online) bookstore.

The unexamined life is not worth living.   Socrates

SECTION I THE VITAL KNOWLEDGE

Chapter 1 The Nature of the Universe

The roots of education are bitter, but the fruit is sweet.   Aristotle

This section provides the *vital knowledge* necessary to understand the basic laws that govern our universe and reality. This is an emerging story. No one can claim to know the complete picture because much about the universe remains a deep mystery. What we do know is very fascinating and valuable in many ways. This story is based on the combined wisdom of the ancient and modern thinkers who, in their own brilliance, have recognized the natural laws and described them in many ways. The following is a brief, simplified summary of the most intelligent and aware minds I have studied.(8) You will also notice that I describe both the Eastern and Western perspectives and show you how they relate. Some of what I present may seem obvious to you; some of it will be novel; all of it is important to create a foundation upon which all the other information will be built. Perhaps you will begin to notice how many different dualities exist in our universe and how things continue to move from one end to another. If these details are too much to handle, you can skip down to the end of this chapter to review the keys, although I think you will find it fascinating to read.

The Cosmic Laws

When we think of "our world" we are usually referring to earth and our surrounding environment. The universe includes our world and everything else. There can only be one set of physical laws that determine reality so what we discover here on earth is true everywhere. Cosmic laws refer to the rules or conditions of nature. The principles described below are the necessary rules to understand the nature of life and make it easier to deal with. Without this information, you will experience the locks of ignorance and illusion and limit your progress.

The Law of Cause and Effect

The universe was built from the beginning by the physical laws that state: every event has a cause and a consequence. That means that everything happens because something made it occur. The key factor is to identify the correct and necessary cause for each effect. This can be a complex task, but often an important one. The causes for many events are not obvious, rather, they may even be hidden. This is especially true about human relationships. The concept of **Karma** has been used for thousands of years, in the East, to describe cause and effect in people's lives. It does not refer to rewards or punishment, as many mistakenly think; rather it explains how each action has its consequences. It is said that we accumulate karma. Very simply, our lives are the sum of all of our actions and the consequences they have generated. This follows the saying "As you sow, so shall you reap" reflecting the idea that good things bring on more good things and vice versa.

This law includes the secondary concept that all things have an origin and a destiny. Truly, everything begins and ends somewhere. The notion of destiny may be wrongly interpreted as being without choice or freedom - that your destiny cannot be changed. This is not the case. To the contrary, both the Western and Eastern perspectives largely agree that we are the architects of our future.   Destiny refers to what were the ultimate consequences of some earlier actions. Destiny is not a force causing things to happen; it is a label for the events. The truth is that most of the time we are free to chose among many possible alternatives, and whichever direction we take will determine our consequences.

The origin of each event can in theory be traced backwards through time to find the specific causes responsible. This is how science works. The truth is that, regardless of how many details we consider, we cannot always find the right causes. The reason for this problem is that the true causes can be complicated, or even hidden, making them difficult to identify. The mistake we often make is to attribute causes to the wrong agent. When we blame the wrong cause for some event, we create another injustice and let the true causes escape notice. The key is to understand that every event has causes and consequences. Following that, you must accurately identify what they really are.

Illustrative example:

> Betty came to me because of stress with her parents. She is married and lives far away, but her mother calls to complain about Betty's father, who is abusive. Her mother does not want Betty to confront her father who has a bad temper, screams, and even pushes her mom around. This makes Betty feel helpless and stresses her because she wants to do something and cannot. The cause of Betty's stress is not just the mother calling, or the father yelling. It is more complicated. Her father grew up in a very abusive family and never learned to communicate calmly. Because her mother fears what the father would do if confronted, she tells Betty to do nothing, perpetuating a bad cycle indefinitely. The true cause of Betty's stress can be found among the many factors creating this difficult situation. After I helped Betty identify the causes more clearly, she succeeded in convincing her mom, together with another relative to confront the father. Both mother and daughter felt more confident with the third person involved, giving them the courage to challenge the father's hostility. Despite his protests, his behaviors did improve over time.

The Law of the Mechanism

This represents a fundamental cosmic principle that <u>everything</u> has a **mechanism**. In order for cause and effect to work, a *means* must exist. Just as the gears of a clock turn to show time, every function, from the smallest to the largest, has a system or a mechanism that makes it work. If you do not know what the mechanism is, you will not be able to fully use the system. On the other hand, understanding how something works enables one to utilize it effectively. This principle is universally true on all levels, from the cosmic down to the microscopic, especially with respect to the mechanisms of how the mind works. A simple example would be hearing, with all the tiny parts inside the ear connecting to nerves that lead to a specialized part of the brain. This mechanism takes the nerve signals generated by vibrations of air and interprets them into the sounds we hear. A complex example could be the panic mechanism, which perceives a threat and engages the entire body into the fight-or-flight reaction. A variety of strong physical sensations get turned on, like sweating, goose bumps, heart pounding, or butterflies in the stomach. These biological systems operate a vast number of separate mechanisms that produce changes in our organs, thinking, emotions, and actions.

The natural extension of the principle of mechanism is ***purpose***. The universe has a brilliant way of giving each mechanism a meaningful purpose for existing. That means that everything that works has a role in a larger scheme of cause and effect. The reason for each mechanism may not always be clear, but you can be sure it exists. There can easily be multiple reasons for one mechanism. The key is that every system has a purpose. When you identify it clearly, you gain better control of that mechanism. If you attribute the wrong purpose to some activity, you only create more problems. An example might be a person who encounters a "bad omen" (a black cat crossing his path) which makes him turn around and fail to reach his destination. The cat would not have in reality affected his visit to some friend or relative.

Illustrative example:

> Jack developed a dependence on alcohol to help him manage a very high pressure job. Every day after work, he would run to a local bar and have two or three hard drinks. That was his way to 'take the edge off' from his daily stress. My first question to him was how did drinking decrease his stress? He did not have an answer. After teaching him how to relax and let go, he gained better control of the stress at work. He also learned to shift his worries toward a greater sense of confidence. Shortly afterwards, his dependence on alcohol disappeared.

The Laws of Energy and Matter

This law represents a number of specific rules of how energy and matter behave and describes the curious relationship between them. Basically, matter is structure and energy is movement. What is amazing is that they are interchangeable. Based on Einstein's theory of relativity ($E=MC^2$), neither energy nor matter can be destroyed; they only transform into one another. All activity requires energy to flow and be utilized. What energy and matter have in common is ***vibration***. Even solid objects have a degree of vibration, whereas energy has a much higher amount of vibration.

Energy must be stored in matter like batteries, gasoline, springs, dynamite, calories, etc. It is up to us to develop the skills to master the process of storing and using energy well.

Part of our success in life depends on mastering the use of energy and maintaining the best structures to store it. These principles have tremendous relevance on all levels of reality, especially to people. We were all born very sensitive to the amount of energy we are expending compared to what we are receiving. When the exchange is in balance, everyone is happy; when it is not, then someone experiences stress. The reason for the stress is that energy is a very precious commodity to each of us, and so it is disturbing to feel an imbalance or its loss. Therefore, it is advisable to keep your body healthy and constantly charged up on good energy. The key is to respect energy, store it when possible, keep it flowing, and to use it, rather than hoard it.

Just as a light bulb illuminates a room because of the movement of electricity (electrons) through the wires, you may light up a room when you enter it because of your smile, the cheerful tone of your voice, the bounce in your step, and the good news you bring. All of these behaviors are various forms of movement or vibration. We are very quick to "read" people's energy, whether we like the way they move, sound, and express themselves or not. We often refer to this energy as the person's "vibration." I like to call it their "vibe" for short. On the material plane, all matter has its particular shape or structure, which automatically is either attractive to us or unappealing. This is how we pick colors, shapes, and objects we like or try to avoid.

Another curious aspect of the vibration of energy is its *resonance*. When two things vibrate in a similar way, they resonate. This reflects our

> *Vibe:* the either good or bad vibrations that person radiates by their actions or appearance.

personal preferences. When we come in contact with an event, a person, or even a thing whose energy vibrates in synch with our own, we are automatically attracted and feel comfortable. That is what we refer to as good energy. Similarly, when we observe something out of synch with us, we get uncomfortable and want to escape – what we might call "bad energy." Every person is sensitive to the resonance of vibrations around him or her, some more than others. This is part of our internal radar system that tells us when we are near pleasant or bad vibrations. The key is to learn to use this information in the most constructive manner possible.

The most important extension of these principles is **evolution**, the constant hierarchical re-organization of energy and matter into more refined patterns. This represents the progressive development of the cosmos, world, and ourselves. There are two forces acting upon all energy and matter. The force of evolution is **order**, promoting development and stability in opposition to the force of **chaos** that creates disorder and uncertainty. Any time something unexpected and unwanted occurs, it can generally be attributed to the forces of chaos. The key is that chaos is an ever-present factor in our world that we are constantly trying to minimize or avoid. There is always a mixture of evolution and chaos. Fortunately there is considerably more order on earth than uncertainty, but it remains impossible for anyone to know for sure which force will dominate at a given moment.

The desire for us to predict what will happen is only natural. Unfortunately, it is difficult for us to predict what the future will bring. Science and the rational approach claim to have the best tools to tell us what is most likely to happen. In contrast, those who follow the intuitive approach, along with astrologers, psychics, and others also claim to be able to predict the future. In reality, neither group has such a good track record. The truth is that the future is extremely difficult to foretell. Progress in life depends heavily upon our ability to make reasonable predictions about what will occur. Success in life depends on having contingency plans in the event our plans are changed. A troubling fact we must accept about the nature of life is that, it really cannot always be predicted. Paradoxically, that is what we can rely on the most. Do you like surprises?

The Laws of Prediction

The key to understanding these laws is to see the weaknesses of both systems. You can be the most logical, rational, intelligent, and knowledgeable person, with scientific predictions that you are extremely confident of, and yet all these predictions may be totally wrong. Similarly, no matter how intuitive and psychic some person is, even if he or she gets the strongest gut feeling about some prediction, he or she can still be completely wrong. Ultimately, the key is to learn to use both systems to

The Cosmic Connection by Yanusz Gliewicz

make predictions, but to be prepared with alternative plans all along the way if something unexpected happens. The key is that each decision we make remains to some degree a gamble. That's the uncertainty of life.

The 5 % Rule: *approximately plus or minus five percent of everything that happens will be chaos or unwanted. The rest of life should be rather orderly and predictable (about 95%).*

The issue of making plans refers back to the problem of chaos, which is a real force that creates uncertainty in our world on a constant basis. The key to understand chaos is that approximately +/- 5% of every day will be affected by some unpredicted disruption – uncertainty. Some days it may only be 1% with minor problems, like you can't find your keys. Other days it may be about 10% chaos where bad things keep happening all day long. Still the key to dealing with chaos is to be prepared for it, and remember that 99% of the time it is not very destructive. Usually, chaos is just disturbing, annoying, or frustrating. However, our history indicates that occasionally chaos is totally annihilating (like on 9-11) and nothing can be done about it. Most of the time there will be plenty of things we can do to minimize the chaos; like when your car is stolen, the police may retrieve it or you may have insurance and get another one.

Throughout history we have been trying to cope with uncertainty. The simple fact is we cannot be sure what will happen next; there are good and bad surprises all the time. There are wonderful miracles. There are horrible tragedies. This knowledge produces a great deal of anxiety in many people because that is the way their brains react to the uncertainty. Every one of us would like to have some sort of advance knowledge, a "future" radar or a crystal ball that will at least warn us about danger if it can't give us the numbers to the winning lottery ticket. Alas, there is nothing that reliable, neither scientific nor intuitive. The key is to accept this uncertainty, learn to deal with chaos by being prepared, and not let its presence disturb you emotionally. This will be explained in greater detail in the chapters on emotions and judgment.

The Laws of Abundance

The cosmic principle of ***abundance*** reflects that the universe creates plenty of everything with endless diversity. Our world is full of riches for all to enjoy. Whatever you want or need, you can find it. Abundance means that everyone can prosper in some way, whether it is materially, socially, spiritually, intellectually, or artistically, the list can be endless. The evolution of our universe has provided for a vast array of spectrums in every imaginable variety. Typically spectrums go from extremely small to gigantic, from very negative to totally positive, from very poor to extremely rich, from lowest to highest, and so on. The point here is that universal abundance appears in vast spectrums or dualities, usually with opposite polarities; that is just the nature of it.

The laws of abundance create several factors that we can either take advantage of or be burdened by. Some people enjoy the *diversity* in our world; others would prefer more similarity. An example could be all the different races or ethnic groups; there are people who appreciate the variety, and others who hold prejudices against it. The same applies to the duality of our world, the extreme *polarities* found in so many aspects of life. Some people accept these large differences, whereas others are tormented by them. The question is, what is the purpose of these polarities; are they there to bother or serve us? Since they are present everywhere in nature, then I think it is safe to assume that polarities are there to be useful to us. The question is how are polarities supposed to help?

The concept of polarities represents a fundamental aspect of the universe, that on every scale possible, you find opposites. From the cosmic level, such as day and night, high and low tides, the heat of summer and the cold of winter, or the magnetic (positive and negative) poles, all these describe polarities on a planetary level. When we consider people, we can appreciate many more polarities, as in where we live (seashore or high in the mountains), how we live (rural country or inner city), and what we do (very busy or totally lazy); all these polarities describe differences among us. Psychologically, there are many more important polarities in the way our minds work. Just as in nature, we observe countless polarities that continually change, we are uniquely empowered to choose the conditions in which we live. The point is that you are free to decide which side of the polarity you want to be on. Consequently, the idea of *shifting polarities* reflects our freedom to take advantage of the nature of our universe for our benefit. Polarities offer us the ability to take control of the diversity in which we live by shifting directions and moving where we prefer to be.

The Laws of Beingness

Among all the principles described, there exists invisible, immeasurable, and difficult to define factors that unite all the laws together. The previous laws all referred to concrete, measurable factors that compose the objective aspect of reality. The truth remains that there may be more than one reality, other dimensions, even other universes. That does not change the fact that we operate on the basis that we exist in only one *objective reality*. Whatever you perceive, there are ultimately two levels of your experience. The first is your *subjective reality* - the immediate impression that your senses and brain create for you of the world around you. The second is the *objective reality* - the logically analyzed, deduced sense of reality that we generate above and beyond the subjective one we first become aware of. This objective reality is often a more accurate and true representation of the universal reality we are living in. That is because our brains do not perceive information very accurately; rather the brain and our senses are frequently fooled by illusions, distortions, poor assumptions, and so on.

The point is that there has evolved a means for us to experience reality internally through the operation of our conscious awareness. This is how the principle of beingness, using our bodies and minds, constructs an image of objective reality.

> *Loomy:* *a person who illuminates us with facts, ideas, and valuable information that we should know, but despite it being obvious, strangely we can't find it or see it ourselves.*

These concepts reflect the philosophical laws of our universe. Consider the fact that we have evolved on this earth with countless abilities and even more potential. Yet, the brain's ability to perceive reality is limited, especially when it comes to human interactions. We are just not very good at sensing true reality. Unless we take the time to learn how to analyze and generate an objective image of reality, we will fall victim to the illusions, distortions, and false sense of subjective reality. This subjective reality is often the source or cause of our misery, pain, anxiety, anger, and our failure to achieve our true potentials. The laws of *beingness* exist to help us regain the internal awareness of what is truly real and what is not. Beingness requires consciousness to be experienced. Consciousness requires the rest of the universe to operate. You are conscious, therefore you exist. These principles would not exist if our universe were not human friendly. That means that, for some reason, <u>the universe created consciousness to allow us to discover reality</u>. I think that is amazing.

The principles associated with beingness cover a wide range of life. These laws reflect the right conditions in our universe to support *beingness* and all the other philosophical factors that unite all the other laws described above. One example is the principle of *perspective* that refers to our ability to escape our subjective view and seek an abstract, different, more objective viewpoint. This is also the bridge between the universal laws of nature and laws of human nature. The key is that reality has created plenty of room for us to experience beingness, and through it, we can become aware of the most objective reality.

> Our biggest problem as human beings
> is not knowing that we don't know.
> Virginia Satir

Summary – 13 Key points from this chapter.

Key 1

Every event has a cause and a consequence. Identify the correct causes and consequences and you may be able to gain better control of these events.

Key 2

Karma is the law of cause and effect in life. If you are mindful of your actions, it is possible to choose to do the right thing in order to produce good consequences in your life.

Key 3

There is an origin and a destiny for every event. We are free to make choices that determine what our futures will be. Recognizing our power and taking responsibility for our decisions are important actions.

Key 4

There is a mechanism for every cause. There is a purpose for each event. By understanding how something works and why it happens, we gain vital knowledge to deal with our world.

Key 5

The laws of energy and matter provide the basis for relativity. Good structures and positive energy have many advantages. Keep energy moving, constantly flowing, and when the exchange is balanced or positive, the results are rewarding.

Key 6

Become aware of resonance, that is, when two things are vibrating in harmony. Positive resonance indicates that you are in sync with another source of energy.

Key 7

The forces of evolution promote greater order and stability in your world.

Key 8

The forces of chaos create uncertainty, even destruction. Chaos is a constant, although minor, factor in daily events. By taking it into account, we can prepare for the unexpected and deal with it more effectively.

Key 9

We all wish to predict the future. The truth is that neither logic nor intuition can guarantee to make accurate predictions of what will be. There are no guarantees. It is wise to have contingency plans to be prepared for surprises.

Key 10

The laws of abundance provide amazing diversity, with large spectrums and extreme polarities in our world. This is the nature of our world. When we embrace these facts, we can take advantage of this abundance.

Key 11

The principle of polarities offers us the freedom to decide where we want to be on some spectrum – the key is to shift directions and explore the opposite pole of where you are.

Key 12

The laws of beingness were formed in the mysteries of the universe, giving us the ability to become subjectively aware and more importantly, internally conscious of objective reality.

Key 13

The principle of perspective requires that we escape our subjective experience and seek a greater, more objective reality through the faculties of our mind.

All you need is love, love

Love is all you need

Lennon & McCartney

Chapter 2

The Laws of Human Nature and Nurture

> We suffer primarily not from our vices or our weaknesses, but
> from our illusions. We are haunted, not by reality, but by those
> images we have put in their place.   Daniel Boorstin

The next three chapters reveal the vital knowledge regarding the structures and functions of the body and mind. What is the nature of being human and how is it nurtured? To begin, this is the continuation of the story of cosmic laws, the specific rules and conditions that explain who we are and how we are. Some of these details may be elementary to you; others complicated. This information is gathered from many brilliant minds who have shared insights about how it all works.(9) My concern is that I provide you with the essential information so that you will be able to unlock your limitations and maximize your potential. These are some of the tools you need to change directions to shift polarities. At the end of the chapter, you will find a summary of the keys presented here.

Which wins: Nature vs Nurture?

A preliminary issue is the question of nature versus nurture; a subject that has been debated for centuries. The focal point is whether we are more the product of our ancestors' genetic inheritance or more the result of our environmental experience. There is no doubt that we inherit a great deal from our parents; it is however, in the form of potentials and predispositions. Our experience, encountered throughout life, determines which of these potentials or predispositions are activated or realized. There are far fewer experts arguing that inheritance has the most effect on our lives. Many more experts strongly support that the environment or nurture is most responsible for what happens in our lives.(10)

There are many people who have a strange prejudice that they either inherited something bad or did not inherit anything good, so therefore they cannot be successful. That is absolutely nonsense. What we inherit can certainly be a burden, but it in no way has the power to limit what you can achieve in life. We are all born with some talents. It depends on you to find and develop them.

Illustrative Example:

> We have all heard stories about how someone overcame all the odds: Like Jack, whose father was an immigrant caught up in his old ways, could hardly speak English, and had a hard time adjusting to life in America. This probably made him feel insecure and weak. He was unable to get a good job, complained all the time, was depressed, and felt hopeless. He never gave Jack any encouragement. Instead, he constantly put Jack down for any efforts he made. Despite his struggle with his family, Jack went on to become a lawyer and earned himself a strong reputation for being a very assertive man. Jack did not follow in his father's footsteps; rather, he went in the opposite direction and achieved his own goals. That means he transformed all the criticism he heard into praise, changed the fears into confidence and built up his skills to assert himself.

The Laws of Identity: Who are you?

You are a product of the universe. Some people explain it as divine creation by God; others believe that it is the logical result of a natural progression. Whichever story is true, the universe gave us the materials, energy, and laws to exist. The laws of beingness enable us to experience ourselves, the world, and imagine almost anything. Self awareness or a sense of "Iness" is the most basic human experience. It is ***consciousness*** that makes everything possible. One view about consciousness is that it is a very complex process in the brain, integrating our senses and internal thoughts into a streaming multimedia experience of being alive. At the same time, the experience of consciousness in the mind is a very simple, transparent, automatic system that works constantly without much effort on our part. This reflects the obvious duality of consciousness between the brain's nervous system and the mind's experience of life.

The fundamental nature of being human can be described as ***constructive***. That means that we are constantly building our own experiences; we are not like a video camera that records a documentary of our life. Rather, we are always constructing the mental, physical, and emotional experiences that mobilize us to respond to the events around us. The most common problem with this process is that our constructions tend to be very subjective and can be inaccurate or even completely wrong, yet we believe they are right. How is that possible?

The reason we all get a bit overly sure of ourselves is that our experience of consciousness demands that we establish an ***identity***. It is our sense of identity, all of our personality traits together, which creates a stable image of our character. Being wrong or unsure of ourselves can generally be unpleasant because it threatens our stability, so we do what we can to avoid those situations. Consequently, it becomes our sense of identity that wants to be right all the time. We all know people who are completely stuck in that mentality; they cannot be wrong, no matter what. These people are insecure because being wrong somehow threatens their sense of selves. The key is to develop a very confident identity. Then it becomes easier to accept our own mistakes. Our identity is another example of the integration of the physical and psychological aspects.

Illustrative Example:

> The story about Jack's father describes how an insecure person could never accept being wrong. Consequently, his father became very controlling and even put down Jack's successes. If his father had developed a stronger sense of self-confidence, he would have identified with his son's achievements and felt proud, instead of having negative feelings.

> **Experience is not what happens to you; it is what you do with what happens to you.   Aldous Huxley**

The Laws of Consciousness

Our sense of reality, the experience of life, is the creation of consciousness, which is the product of the brain and mind. The brain refers to the nerves and complex wiring of the various processors that take our sensory input (like vision, hearing, touch, etc.) and integrate it into our experience of life. The mind refers to the psychological functions and experiences of life, such as feeling excited, happy, sad, or contemplating the meaning of love. The mind is the dynamic counterpart of the brain. While the brain is responsible for all our physical movements, mental skills like speaking, reading, mathematics, or even the expression of emotions, like fear or anger; the mind is the fertile valley where our personality blooms, where our preferences are rooted, where we decide which memories are more important, and so on. The mind gives us meaning to all that happens. These deeper psychological functions have not been identified as discrete, specialized areas of the brain despite many attempts to do so. The key is that our experience of life is based on the duality of the brain's perceptions and the mind's interpretations.

The rules of consciousness ultimately take everything else into effect. Conscious awareness is not a problem to solve or even to understand; it is a tool for us to gain maximum control of ourselves and the world we live in. The principles of judgment, emotions, energy, and patterns are all various aspects of conscious activity. The more conscious, alert, or objectively aware you are, the easier life gets because you can develop the means to master every situation you find yourself in. Self awareness has its own extremes, from none to superior. Shifting polarities in this case refers to recognizing the need to increase your self-awareness. When you begin using the keys to unlock many of the limitations we all have, your self-awareness will grow significantly. The main key is to learn how to direct attention most efficiently.

Self Awareness: what do you consider yourself – more analytical, constantly thinking, or more of the intuitive type who experiences life through feelings. All of us do both, but each of us leans more one way than the other.

The laws that drive us

A fair question is why were we designed with such a complex operating system that makes us so vulnerable to errors? The answer is that we are the results of abundance, providing us with greater diversity, even if this may produce problems for us. Another reason is the complexity makes it more difficult to compete for the available resources. Consequently, this complex system creates numerous ways to search for and satisfy our basic needs, as well as the most abstract and lofty needs that drive our activities. Our drives refer to what motivates us to take action and pursue goals; the "what" usually refers to our needs.

Our nature is very flexible because it's possible to satisfy our needs in many different ways. However, early on in our lives, we get into specific *patterns* of how we want to meet our needs. This reflects our predisposition to follow patterns, and often we become dependent on just one or two ways to satisfy our needs. This can be a problem because there may be better ways to reach our needs than the ones we rely on or are used to.

Human needs begin with survival and end somewhere among the Fortune 500 wealthiest people in the world. What drives us to achieve goals? The simple answer is our needs create an urge to do something. Then we gather the energy and develop a vision of how to meet our goals. Specifically, this begins with directing our conscious awareness to deal with opportunities or challenges in our environment. Those of us who develop superior skills in this process are able to achieve more than others. This skill of directing our awareness is based on two complex functions: sensitivity of our system and targeting control.

> Unfortunately, most of us are so run by our habits that we never change our behavior. We get stuck in our conditioned responses... Everything you think, say, and do needs to become intentional and aligned with your purpose, your values, and your goals.   Jack Canfield

How do we direct consciousness?

On the physical level, consciousness depends on the sensitivity of our sense organs, the speed at which we process this information, the number of associations we make, and how well we integrate all the details. Sensitivity also refers to how well we connect our perceptions with our memories. Some of us have an extremely effective system; others do not. On the psychological level, this is a matter of being alert, curious, spontaneous, receptive, assertive, inventive, and creative, just to mention a few factors.

The ability to target our *attention* is a skill anyone can improve given the training. In general, attention tends to get better in all of us as we become more experienced in some special area. Targeting refers to our ability to focus on a specific subject and avoid distractions, just as one might use a telescope mounted on a rifle to aim at a distant target and wait for the center to be in the cross hairs before pulling the trigger. Your ability to concentrate is of paramount importance throughout life. This skill first requires you to focus attention on just one thing, which is relatively easy for a brief period of time. The difficulty comes with sustained attention and concentration. To keep your attention focused and not be distracted by irrelevant events, is a difficult skill that takes a great deal of time and energy to learn. The key is to learn how to direct your attention more effectively so that you can concentrate and not be distracted easily.

Once we learn to direct our attention well enough to deal with the world, we tend to stop developing those skills any further. The truth is that what we learn very early in life is usually enough to obtain the basic needs we all must have, but not the higher needs. Abraham Maslow was a psychologist famous for being the first to establish and describe a hierarchy of needs.(11) He explained that our primary needs begin on the physical level, move up through the social level, and end on our need for self actualization. (See Table 2 for a description)

Table 2. Maslow's Hierarchy of Needs

Rank	Category of needs	Description of needs
5	**Self-Actualization**	ongoing activation of potentials, capacities, talents, with the intent to fulfill a mission that is driven by internal desires...
4	**Esteem**	self respect, competence, autonomy, confidence, pride...
3	**Love**	affection, intimacy, family, connections, relationships...
2	**Safety**	avoidance of pain, anxiety or any threat, security, comfort...
1	**Physiological**	hunger, thirst, sleep, sex, warmth, vision, hearing, touch...

Maslow believed that we all had to satisfy the primary (physiological and safety) needs before we could pursue the higher needs. He claimed that as a person satisfies all his or her lower needs, then he or she can attempt to meet their higher needs. At the top, the need for self-actualization allows the individual to achieve his or her highest potential, enjoy peak experiences, and a deep sense of fulfillment. His theory has not escaped criticism or alternative explanations. There have been many times when motivated individuals ignored their lower needs and achieved fantastic ones. The key is that needs are hierarchically organized, and the basic ones tend to demand our attention more than the higher ones. Each of us seeks ways to satisfy the needs we have. They become the drives we use to motivate action.

Anthony Robbins is an internationally recognized leader of peak performance training. He attributes his remarkable success to his ability to determine exactly what are the driving forces behind each individual's actions. His work demonstrates that by identifying what motivates a person to act, you can obtain the leverage to get him or her to change their behaviors and achieve their potential more easily. Robbins describes his psychological system with six different human needs that drive all behavior.(12) Refer to Table 3 for a list and description of these six needs.

Every person will attempt to satisfy at least some of the top four, which are universal needs, in his or her own way. First, every person has his or her personal way of prioritizing these four primary needs from most to least important. Secondly, everyone finds unique ways to meet each of these needs. Consequently, we can always identify which two needs are the primary driving forces for any individual. The last two needs are "spiritual," providing those who seek them a sense of fulfillment. As you review these six needs, reflect about which ones you consider most important to yourself. Number them in order of your preference in the "Rank" column.

Behind every decision we make is an attempt to meet one of these six human needs. The question is how do we try to do that? There is an infinite variety of ways to satisfy these needs; the differences are the consequences of what we do. The most important question is: are we able to satisfy our needs in a **sustainable** way? That means in a productive and positive manner. Robbins explains that ideally, *"A person will achieve his or her needs in a way that feels good, that is good for him or her, that is good for others, and that serves the greater good."* If a person meets his

Table 3. Anthony Robbins' Six Human Needs

Rank which are most important to you from 1 to 6.

Rank	Categories	Description of the needs
	Certainty - Comfort	security, safety, predictability, protection, stability, simple, easy
	Uncertainty - Variety	instability, change, suspense, variety, surprise, uniqueness, complexity
	Significance	sense of importance, uniqueness, feeling special, competitiveness, seeking power
	Connection - Love	feeling of closeness, unified, intimate, desire to relate, sharing, bonding
	Growth	expanding your capacity, need to develop emotionally, intellectually, spiritually
	Contribution	give to others, leadership, support, service, dedication, generosity, kindness

or her needs in a manner that produces stress, causes harm, disturbs the well-being of others or himself or herself, then it cannot be sustainable and should be changed. The key is for each individual to become aware of how she or he is satisfying his or her needs and seek ways that are productive and healthy for all concerned. Another key is that by knowing your primary needs or what brings you satisfaction, you will have more leverage to make changes in behavior to achieve your goals.

The Laws of Reward and Punishment

The issue of meeting our needs, or anything else for that matter, depends on our experience of reward or punishment. There is an endless assortment of nice rewards and unpleasant punishments that is different for each individual. Whatever you find rewarding reinforces behaviors that brought that experience. Conversely, anything that produces some form of punishment makes it more likely that you will avoid the activities that caused that experience. This relates to the process of **conditioning**, the gradual programming to repeat some behavior or avoid it depending on the consequences.   Unfortunately, we are all susceptible to conditioning because of the way our brain and mind work. Although it is possible to resist the conditioning process and accept the punishment or ignore the rewards, it is difficult and not many people can do it because it requires greater awareness and a very strong, independent will. The truth is that most people get very easily conditioned by either rewards or punishments.(13)

One of the biggest problems we all face is the universal appeal of *immediate gratification*.   We all know it well because everyone experiences it from birth countless times. However, the opposite factor, *delayed gratification*, is not as interesting, usually not as powerful; we do not have as much training or experience in it, and it often requires dealing with many hardships before we finally get rewarded. These facts make it simply very difficult for anyone to invest his or her time and energy in activities that promise rewards far off in the future. This requires a special approach; otherwise the journey will never get completed. The truth is we all enjoy instant gratification. It should not be surprising everyone loves immediate reinforcement with nice rewards. The key is that anyone can learn the special skills to indulge in delayed gratification as well.

Every person in the world must confront the battle between immediate and delayed gratification. Because the brain responds to rewards with the experience of pleasure or even better emotions, it makes us easily persuaded to engage in behaviors that produce rewards right away. Conversely, since it is very difficult to ignore punishment, struggle, discomfort, and to be patient, delayed gratification is one of the most challenging tasks for us to learn. The key is the rewards we wait for longer tend to be bigger or more important than immediate ones. Consequently, it is possible to achieve goals that may even be years away. Part of the secret is to learn how to create clear intentions and develop our patience. Our achievement depends on mastering these skills.

The Laws of Achievement

Naturally, there are individuals who develop superior skills of achievement that include the ability to delay gratification. These skills are difficult to master because of our inborn preference for easy and fast rewards. This is another example of how the brain is designed to make our life more challenging. Achievement does not depend on any one factor (including delayed gratification); rather, it is the sum of many skills, talents, and abilities. The most important factors for anyone to identify to accelerate his or her achievement are all his or her inborn talents. Those individuals who enjoy remarkable success are people who know what they are really great at and accumulate as much experience as possible doing it. To identify your talents is not always easy because you may never find out what you are really gifted in without seeking this information. It is also true that you can excel at skills that you are not very talented in with hard work. One task is to analyze yourself and find all the unique talents or special skills you have that the world needs.

Your achievement begins with finding all your strengths, educating yourself in that area and then amassing the experience to reach a level of excellence in performance. The world we live in is very competitive. In order to prove that your talents or skills are superior you must attain a certain level; most people consider anyone in the top 10% as excellent performers. Many people are trying to reach a level of outstanding achievement, like Olympic champions, movie stars, the super wealthy, all of whom belong to the top one ten thousandth of one percent (0.0001%). That kind of mega success is extremely rare by definition and super difficult to reach. The larger the achievement, the greater the effort usually is, and the more likely that person has exceptional talent in that area. The key is that if you perform your work in the top ten percent of people in your area, you are achieving excellence. You may still continue to improve your skills; just recognize that anyone in the upper ten percent is performing at a superior level.

The main issue is the outcome. Achieving superior performance, in comparison to others is the goal. This can come through inborn talent or just hard work with a positive attitude. Anyone observing will measure the results relative to how others did; it does not matter if the outcome is based on talent or practice. Although many people hope for outstanding

---

Improving Ourselves: Think about the last few years and go back to any major decisions you made that you later regretted. As you reflect, knowing how everything turned out, would you make a different choice if you had the possibility of going back in time to repeat that decision? What you may today call a mistake was the right choice back then. Consider the lesson, what was your decision based on?

achievement, that mega success is available to about one person out of a million. Those are odds that very few can conquer; however, it is possible for every person to reach some form of superior achievement and enjoy the satisfaction of true fulfillment.

It feels good to be accepted, and even better to be admired. We all love recognition, in all the forms in which we can obtain it. Most forms of achievement bring social approval and often praise. Indeed, praise is a powerful force to motivate better performance.

The most significant factor in measuring performance is the degree of experience. How much time and effort we put into accumulating relevant experience is the best measure of expertise. For example, who would you rather have fly a plane? Is it better to have an extremely well educated engineer who knows everything about airplanes, how all the systems work, but has never flown a plane, or would you prefer a person with two years of experience flying planes, but has no knowledge about how they work, fly you? The answer will always be the person with experience because we all appreciate the importance of practical know-how compared to the theoretical book knowledge.

Whatever the mind can conceive and believe, it can achieve.   Napoleon Hill

What are the 3 Spheres of Conscious Awareness?

Human nature can be divided into three general areas of activity that contain all of our inborn skills: talents, abilities, and traits. When we are young, we should be encouraged to try many things to see what we enjoy doing the most and what we are most talented in. Unfortunately, our educational system does not provide most students with enough opportunities to determine what they are really great at doing. Do you know what are your best talents, skills, gifts, and valuable traits?

The three spheres of conscious awareness refer to our physical, emotional, and analytical fields of behavior. I refer to them as spheres because, like a balloon, they can expand in every direction. Each sphere overlaps the other spheres to some degree depending on which one is dominant. Each sphere contains all the attributes that belong to each respective field. See Figure 1 and Table 4 on the next page to see a brief description of these spheres.

These spheres are the most basic common building blocks of awareness. This refers to the talents or strengths you have in each sphere. Some people are very physically aware and that might make them an athlete or dancer, depending on their body type. Those who are very emotionally aware may develop talents in the artistic field. Those who are more aware of their analytical abilities are most likely to develop their intellectual powers. The problem is: if you are not aware of what talents you have the greatest potential in, then regardless of what you do, it is unlikely you will ever achieve true success or enjoy fulfillment. The key is that our inner sense of fulfillment depends on doing something that we are very aware of and enjoy performing.

Figure 1. The 3 Spheres of Conscious Awareness

Inside each sphere are the talents and skills waiting to be developed to turn your potential into your mastery. Each sphere grows larger the more potential is actualized within it. When one aspect dominates another, that sphere overlaps a larger portion of the smaller one. The spheres are dynamic and constantly are expanding or contracting depending on the activity within each sphere. See the table below for examples of the contents. There is more information regarding these spheres and your talents on the website or in the Achievement Workbook.

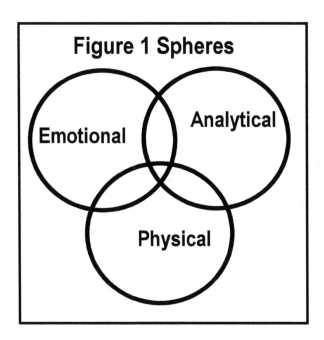

Table 4. Three Spheres of Conscious Awareness

Each sphere contains a large variety of traits, talents, predispositions, skills, abilities, qualities, and characteristics that can be cultivated and developed. As you go down each list, notice which sphere you have the most strength in. This is just a partial list.

Physical Sphere	Emotional Sphere	Analytical Sphere
Body	Temperament	Intellectual
height	stability	perceptive
weight	passion	imaginative
muscles	strength	deliberate
skin	love	patience
senses	sensuous	attention
vision	sexuality	rational
hearing	compassion	logical
voice	flexible	curious
taste	confident	creative
balance	secure	intuitive
movement	courageous	abstract
agility	charismatic	concrete
coordination	artistic	motivated
gracefulness	humorous	determined
attractiveness	happy	memory
endurance	sad	reading
sensitivity	angry	writing
strength	frustrated	mathematical
speed	envious	drawing
dexterity	anxious	musical
musicality	fearful	inventive
sports	irritable	organizing
athletic	guilty	obsessive

Every person who reviews the contents of these three spheres automatically will connect them to the traits they possess. The list of attributes in each of these spheres is just a sampling of traits and skills that each field of behavior contains. The importance of these spheres is to help you analyze and identify your best skills or strengths because those are the behaviors that will help you achieve greater excellence in your performance.

If you want to enjoy greater progress and success in life, you first must find what you are best at naturally. Your talents are the inborn predispositions to learn to do something better than others can. Better does not mean excellence unless you practice and train in the best ways possible. If you develop your talents or inborn skills, you can be certain that they will bring you a greater sense of fulfillment. The most important quality of a talent is that you enjoy working on it. This information is described in greater detail in the separate *Achievement Workbook*.

Your awareness of each sphere increases with greater experience. As your sphere expands through practice and training, it may overlap the other spheres to a larger degree. This process over time progressively makes a person an expert in his or her chosen field. Expertise automatically increases the conscious energy a person has in some specific area. The key is that increasing awareness of your inborn talents will accelerate the speed of your progress and increase the height of your achievement.

This material should be considered an introduction to achievement, the master key of achievement can be found in Chapter 16. The *Achievement Workbook* contains a step by step instruction manual to unlock your potential and maximize your achievement (see Appendix).

> This is the single most powerful investment we can ever make in life – investment in ourselves, in the only instrument we have with which to deal with life and to contribute.   Stephen Covey

Summary: 13 Key points from this chapter

Key 14

We all inherit traits, potential, and predispositions from our parents; then it remains up to each individual to actualize the positive possibilities through every means available; nurture is more important than our nature.

Key 15

We are a product of the universe; consciousness is our portal to experience ourselves and everything around us.

Key 16

The mind first constructs a subjective experience of our world that tends to be flawed until we reconstruct an objective reality with our conscious awareness.

Key 17

The reason we believe anything our subjective mind experiences is because the mind establishes a sense of identity that demands continuity, stability, and dependability. The more confident we become, the easier it is to accept differences between our first impression of reality and what it objectively is.

Key 18

There is a difference between the brain and mind. The separation of function creates a duality so that the brain's perceptions can be interpreted by the mind.

Key 19

To master every situation you must develop the power of the conscious mind to effectively direct your attention wherever it must focus.

Key 20

Our nature is to repeat patterns. The most important patterns are the ones that drive us into action to achieve goals as well as those patterns that stop us from doing so.

Key 21

Achievement depends on developing superior skills of concentration as well as shifting attention to the next important subject.

Key 22

Our needs are hierarchically organized: the lower physical and emotional needs tend to demand more attention than the abstract higher needs for self-actualization.

Key 23

When you identify what are your primary needs, you gain leverage to change patterns and achieve goals. This requires that you determine sustainable means to satisfy your needs.

Key 24

Delayed gratification is a vital skill to develop because we are all easily influenced by immediate rewards.

Key 25

Achievement requires us to identify our natural strengths, talents, skills, and abilities. These potentials must be cultivated, practiced, and developed to reach the level of excellence (top ten percent performance).

Key 26

Human nature is divided into three Spheres of activity: the physical, emotional, and analytical. By identifying all the best talents you have in each field, it is easy to build up your expertise and superior experience. Remember practical skills are better than theoretical ones.

Key 27

The greatest sense of fulfillment we can obtain is from doing things that we are naturally talented in and feel a superior sense of competency when performing; that can give us the experience of authentic happiness.

Chapter 3

How to Understand the Triplex Mind

> Brain researchers estimate that your unconscious database outweighs the conscious on an order exceeding ten million to one. This database is the source of your hidden, natural genius. In other words, a part of you is much smarter than you are. The wise people regularly consult that smart part.   Michael Gelb

The human brain is considered one of the most complex and amazing systems in the universe. It should not be surprising that it also causes the most problems for us. Curiously, most people don't suspect our brain to be the source of many of these problems; instead we blame other people, the world, injustice, or whatever. The unique contribution I am offering you is the explanation of what is wrong with your mind. I intend to describe the brain and how it works so that you can understand why it fails to work perfectly all the time. The key is to present you with a map of how the brain is organized into *different polarities* and explain why it works the way it does. This vital information will help you deal with the strange things the brain normally does, so that you can prevent many problems and achieve your potential. This chapter describes basic details of the brain's functions; the following chapter elaborates the more complex mental functions. At the end of each, you will find a summary of the keys discussed here.

The Triplex Mind refers to the three basic divisions of the brain. These represent structural and functional separations of the way the mind works. The three parts are *reflexive* at the bottom, the *automatic* in the middle, and *deliberate* at the top. Each part is specialized to deal with a certain aspect of our world. What is not commonly known are the limitations of each part of the brain. These limitations create the locks, and I will explain where to find the keys to unlock these problems. Each part of the mind has its own duality with a positive and negative polarity; however, the lower two parts have much more negativity than the upper part. This imbalance in the polarities causes most of our problems. Consequently, those who learn how to shift polarities open the locks and achieve more. Please look at Figure 2 to see a description of this map.

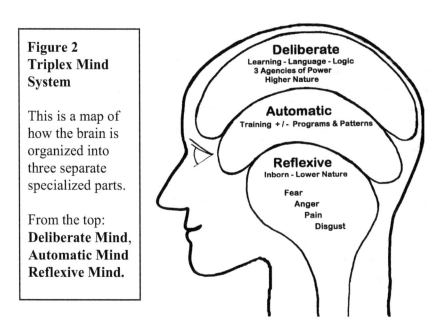

**Figure 2
Triplex Mind
System**

This is a map of how the brain is organized into three separate specialized parts.

From the top:
**Deliberate Mind,
Automatic Mind
Reflexive Mind.**

Deliberate
Learning - Language - Logic
3 Agencies of Power
Higher Nature

Automatic
Training + / - Programs & Patterns

Reflexive
Inborn - Lower Nature

Fear
Anger
Pain
Disgust

What is the Reflexive Part of the Triplex Mind?

The *Reflexive* part is "hard wired," meaning we are born with it. It is reflexive, like the knee jerk reaction to being hit below the knee. It requires no learning; all the things the reflexive part does are biologically built in from birth. It is also our main *radar system* designed to protect us from threats, and, hence, a big part of our intuition arises from here. It also controls our organic functions (respiration, digestion, cardiac activity, etc.) and the essential drives (hunger, sleep, and sex). The most important function of the reflexive mind is that it is the source of all fear, anger, pain and disgust, what I refer to as our "lower nature" - the primitive emotions.

The essential purpose of the reflexive system is survival. This is the central control of our biological functions and the instinctual emotions that are "negative" or unpleasant feelings. While the reflexive part does a good job keeping us alive, it very often oversteps its responsibilities and causes major emotional problems for us in the form of stress. Although there are positive aspects to the reflexive mind, its major activity is stress related; that is why I refer to it as our ***negative polarity***.

What is the Lower Nature?

The problem is found in the four principle negative emotions that are the source of our lower nature. These survival instincts are there to protect us, but they actually do more harm than good most of the time. The reason for this is there is a very significant imbalance in the function of these primitive emotions. We are all born with fear, anger, pain, and disgust. That means that no infant needs to learn these emotions; they are literally wired into the system. These four elements are actually distinct from each other. Although each of these negative emotions is unique, they give rise to many other lower nature feelings that belong to the same category, which evolve as we grow up. For example, fear generates all the similar emotions like worry, anxiety, tension, suspicion, paranoia, panic, terror, and so on. Each of these four negative emotions actually represents large categories or groups of lower feelings, any of which can cause us to experience stress. For a summarized list of the lower nature see Table 5, depicting the categories of these negative emotions.

Are we really dominated by our primitive instincts?

The significance of these primitive emotions is that they demonstrate that human nature is born more negative and is dominated by these instinctual emotions and our lower nature. To be clear, we are all born wired to be more prone to fear, anger, pain, and disgust than the opposite emotions. That may sound controversial; however, in a moment, I intend to offer you proof that this point is unfortunately true. These instinctual emotions are part of the autonomic nervous system, which is divided into two parts: one that turns on these survival feelings; the other part is designed to turn on the opposite emotions. Naturally, there is a higher nature with all our positive emotions. In fact, there are four principle positive emotions directly opposite the four negative ones. This higher nature is dominated by courage, acceptance, happiness, and love. This forms one of the most important polarities within the mind. The lower polarity protects us from threats, but causes stress, while the higher polarity helps us escape stress and feel good. Anything can be stressful. If something is difficult to deal with it can cause stress. The key is to reverse directions and shift polarities to escape stress. First you need to understand how the brain accesses these different emotions.

What is the difference between the stress and relaxation systems?

The two opposite parts of the autonomic nervous system are not equal. In fact there is a tremendous difference between them anatomically and functionally.(14) Although most systems in the body are divided equally, the *Stress* part of the autonomic nervous system is many times bigger and faster than the opposite *Relaxation* part. The reflexive stress system is automatic, instantaneous, goes everywhere in your body, has no "off" switch, and is at least twenty times bigger and faster than the opposite system. The stress part turns "on" the fight or flight response, which engages the entire body into action in response to anger or fear. And, it is also responsible for all the other levels of discomfort that we experience due to our negative emotions. Think  of the stress and relaxation systems like a see-saw: when one is up, the only way to bring it down it to raise up the other side. This is a matter of polarity shifting, reversing directions before we suffer the consequences of stress. The most general result of stress is that it speeds up your aging process.

The relaxation system is designed to turn off stress, to relax us and release the tension, but it only works if we learn how to use it. This part is not automatic; it takes time and effort to work; it goes everywhere in your body; it can be turned "off" at any time; and it is many times smaller and slower than the stress part. <u>The consequence is that we are biologically predisposed to feel more stress and tension than relaxation and feeling good</u>. The biggest problem is that the stress system is reflexive, while the relaxation part must be learned and exercised in order to work well. The result is that anything that threatens us triggers our radar and will make us jump into action. This is also the main reason for all the anger, hatred, violence, and conflict in the world. The reflexive system makes us much more vulnerable to stress, tension, and all the emotions of our lower nature. This system is responsible for all of our primitive animal instincts as described above. Below is Table 6 further documenting the dramatic differences between these two systems.

What are the consequences of stress?

The importance of this difference between stress and relaxation systems cannot be underestimated. The key point is that our response to stress is reflexive: it requires no thinking, it just happens. There are two phases to a stress reaction. The first (neurologic) is immediate; the second (chemical) is slower, starting after a few moments and may last hours. It affects every system in your body. Every person has his or her "weakest link," which refers to one system in the body that will break down first under stress. This leads to most of the problems that ail us. Stress can be responsible for minor or serious problems in any of the body's systems. Most commonly, it affects our digestive, respiratory, nervous, and circulatory systems. Two of the most respected physicians, Drs. Roizen and Oz, wrote in their recent book, *You, the Owner's Manual,* "Stress is the greatest ager of your body in general..."(15)

Table 5.

The Four Categories of the Lower Nature: The Negative Polarity

The first row contains the names of each category in bold and a brief scale of the emotions from mild to intense. The bottom row contains just a sample of related emotions from each category.

Fear	**Anger**	**Pain**	**Disgust**
Terror	Rage	Desperation	Hatred
Panic	Aggression	Suicidal	Repulsive
Scared	Angry	Depressed	Contempt
Anxiety	Annoyed	Hopeless	Boredom
Worried	Offensive	Agony	Apathy
Tension	Irritated	Sad	Ashamed
Doubts	Frustrated	Suffering	Inhibited
Nervous	Territorial	Misery	Pity
Trapped	Demanding	Grief	Disrespect
Paranoia	Screaming	Crying	Insulted
Weakness	Hostility	Guilt	Humiliated
Distrust	Vengeance	Anguish	Scorn
Frightened	Envy	Angst	Spite
Uptight	Jealousy	Awkward	Pessimism
Disturbed	Greed	Numb	Gloom
etc.	etc.	etc.	etc.

To view a color diagram of the nervous system that clearly shows the differences go to: www.ShiftingPolarities/ANS

Table 6. The Two Parts of the Autonomic Nervous System

Note the very big differences between the stress and relaxation systems.

The Reflexive: Stress - on system	The Relaxation: Stress - off system
1) It is automatic and reflexive	1) Must be turned on deliberately
2) It is instantaneous	2) Requires time and effort to engage
3) Goes everywhere in the body	3) Also goes everywhere
4) There is no off switch	4) It can be turned off anytime
5) It's at least 20 times bigger and faster than the relaxation system	5) It is many times smaller and slower than the stress system

Not all the consequences of stress are known. At low levels they can even be beneficial, in the form of motivation or excitement, but if stress goes too high or for too long, it becomes seriously toxic. I am certain that you have experienced some of the effects of stress first hand. The truth is that it affects each individual just a little differently. This is due in part to our diversity and the differences in our personal histories. Those who have had more intense stress and horrible experiences will tend to be more sensitive to future challenges unless they learn to compensate and cope better. This requires a polarity shift, reversing emotional directions. The key is developing your ability to relax and let go. This requires that each individual learns how to turn off stress by turning on relaxation. This is a simple process, but without direction and practice it will not be effective. Instead, most people reach for chemicals to deal with stress; they pop pills, smoke, and drink, whatever works to make them numb. Others will exhaust themselves so they have no strength to be stressed out. However, neither of these methods actually gets rid of the stress. The only effective means to stop stress and eliminate its effects is to use the internal relaxation system to replace tension with peace in your body. These skills are described in Chapter 8 and you will find a relaxation exercise in the Appendix as well.

These figures display the density of nerves inside the body. There are 20 - 30 times more stress nerves (darker figure on the left) than relaxation nerves (right lighter figure). Both systems are spread evenly over the body, but the stress system has millions of more nerves than the relaxation system.

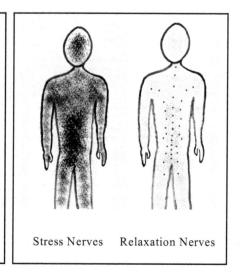

Stress Nerves   Relaxation Nerves

What is the Automatic Part of the Triplex System?

This is the part of the brain that is specialized in repeating *patterns*. The *automatic system*, located in the middle (see Figure 2), is designed to make all tasks, even complex ones, simple routines. This is an incredibly powerful part because it allows you to train your brain to do things automatically. This is where we develop all our habits, patterns, and mental programs. The problem is that most of these automatic activities are outside of our normal conscious awareness; hence we can not analyze or evaluate what we are doing effectively. This can be referred to as the "sub-conscious" mind, which does not operate under the spotlight of awareness. Consequently whatever is processed, good or bad, can become a new routine without the normal scrutiny of our minds. Curiously, this learning does not even require our intent to learn. Actually, many of our routines come about spontaneously through simple repetition.

The purpose of the automatic part is *simplification*. It takes things that require a major effort to perform and, with just a little training, they become automatic routines. Nearly every intentional behavior, both physical and mental, that we perform can become an automatic program. That means that this system specializes in memorizing and repeating whatever is experienced. The automatic system itself is an extremely complex network of interconnections in the brain.(16) It contains a high percentage of neurological loops or circular circuits that actually grow in size and power the more we use them. Any repeated pattern of activity, thinking, feelings, or behaviors becomes automatic, which makes it "wired" into the brain. That is why it is so difficult for us to change our patterns, and this becomes one of the major locks in this system. One of the keys is to identify our needs and what drives us, so that we can gain the leverage to change patterns we are not pleased with.

What are the advantages and problems?

New patterns are learned by repeating them a number of times. The more exactly we do so, the more easily they are learned. The automatic mind can make intentional behaviors or reflexive actions into new patterns. Consequently, they can be good or positive behaviors as well as bad or negative behaviors. For example, a musician may remember many songs stored in his or her automatic mind. A bad habit, like smoking, is also an automatic pattern that is difficult to break more for the habit than the addiction. Another problem is that the reflexive mind often creates one-trial-learning, which instantly becomes a new pattern. A typical case is when someone has a car accident, the trauma may establish a fear of driving or being near the location of the accident. In general, the automatic mind has a tendency to develop more destructive patterns than good ones, causing an imbalance. This is why it is essential that you learn the art of polarity shifting so that you can reverse any sabotaging programs into positive ones.

On one hand, the automatic system allows us to do many things without much effort or concentration, like driving a car and talking. But, if we get into a bad routine, like watching too much TV, or gambling, overeating, or anything that is not good for us, it becomes destructive to our progress. Patterns can be a major advantage simplifying life, or can become another lock that imprisons us. Obsessions are just patterns that we cannot escape. The worst problem is probably the negative self-talk we all get into. This is the source of our self-sabotage because if you get into a pattern of telling yourself that "you cannot do it," "you are worthless," "why bother, you won't finish anyway," then, in fact, that will be exactly what you are programming your life to be like. The key is to raise your awareness, become more objective, and filter out or completely replace the negative thoughts or patterns with positive ones in your automatic mind. This represents a polarity shift, changing directions from self-sabotage to asserting oneself.

What is the Deliberate System in the Triplex Mind?

The **Deliberate** mind is the ultimate control center. It sits at the top (see Figure 2) as the most developed part of the brain, also referred to as the **higher mind**. The deliberate system has many functions and responsibilities. To begin, this is the part of the mind with which you think because this is where the brain is specialized for language. The ability to learn, memorize, and process information is centered here as well. It is the processor of all sensory input and motor output. It is the system that assigns meaning to all our experiences. It provides us with our sense of I-ness, our individuality, because it is aware of time, which gives us a sense of continuity. The deliberate mind is the source of conscious awareness that enables us to enjoy the multimedia experience of life. All together these functions give us the ability to feel, think, and respond to demands as well as to act on our own intentions – that is the reason why this is called the deliberate mind. Finally, this part is the most positive polarity of the mind, as opposed to the two lower parts.

The primary purpose of the deliberate mind is **development**. This is achieved through our ability to direct attention to master our situation, adapt to it, or cope with the challenges before us. This is possible because learning language forced us to become somewhat logical as all languages are based on logical rules. Although the higher mind is capable of perfect logic, intelligent insights, and fantastic powers of reasoning, very few people develop these skills above what is necessary. It is possible for every person to improve these skills if he or she seeks the proper training and makes an effort. Whatever educational training you have had, it is unlikely that school did much to develop these skills for you. Most of what we learn is information: we gain knowledge, but we often lack the cognitive skills to be very creative or exceptionally rational. Without developing the power of the higher mind, we can anticipate more trouble dealing with the world around us.

What is most unique about the Higher Mind?

The most distinct quality of the deliberate mind is its ability to **learn**, in contrast to the reflexive part, whose functions are in-born, and the automatic part, which can only be trained to repeat something. In the higher mind, we not only constantly learn, we also invent, create, and develop new ideas that can improve our world. For instance, all inventions, works of art, systems, and organizations were developed by the higher mind. This is also the seat of the ***analytical*** part of our consciousness. This is where we are able to perceive, analyze, evaluate, compare, discriminate, make judgments, and decide what to do. The deliberate mind is where we collect our experiences, both good and bad, which can give us the motivation, determination and engage our ***will power*** to reach our intended goals. Our achievements are possible, then, because we can learn to direct our attention, focusing and concentrating on one thing or constantly shifting our awareness to the next important subject. Hence, we are able to be alert, deal constructively with our world, and make progress.

The deliberate mind is also the fertile territory to develop our ***higher nature*** and all the positive emotions. When we observe positive emotions in others, we begin to learn to identify them inside ourselves as well. The complex positive emotions like love, compassion, courage, optimism, respect, humor, and many others are acquired through learning; we are not born with these feelings. We may have the potential to experience these feelings, but they require years of practice before they progress from very plain to full and intense emotions. Some of the simple positive emotions evolve quickly from the right rewarding experiences. When we learn what makes us feel good, we may smile, laugh, feel satisfied, and perhaps even happy. But without the right experiences, we will not even learn these simple positive emotions. The point here is that our higher nature grows in this part of the mind. If we are exposed to positive experiences, we can develop these positive emotions to their fullest potentials. The idea of shifting polarities is about escaping from the lower parts of the mind and embracing these positive aspects of the higher mind. Although this part of the mind also contains some negative aspects, the great majority of the activity of the deliberate mind is positive.

The difference between a successful person and others is not a lack of strength, not a lack of knowledge, but rather a lack of will. Vince Lombardi

How does the Triplex Mind Work? (Who is in control?)

The Triplex Mind is really one integrated system. The three divisions all work together, although there is constant competition for control among these three levels. To be clear, each level is designed to control the other two whenever necessary. But, only the higher mind can take control away from the other two deliberately. The reflexive mind will become the leader whenever we are threatened; it spontaneously demands more control. The automatic mind often becomes the dominant system whenever we are engaged in a well established pattern. Everyone knows that trance-like state of doing something without paying any attention. A typical example is driving along when you suddenly realize it is your exit or street, and you come back from being "lost" in thought.

The ***deliberate mind*** is the only system that can wrestle control back intentionally from the other two parts. Being deliberate is not as easy as the automatic, or as fast as the reflexive parts, however, since it is much more refined and sophisticated; it can plan and execute very complex things that the others never could. Because it is not easy, the other two parts frequently interfere with our plans, goals, and ideas. The key is learning how to gain control of the deliberate mind so that our intentions can be realized. This brings us back to the concept of consciousness, because it is only through our awareness that we can direct our attention and energies successfully. Our progress depends on learning how to increase awareness to detect our illusions, distortions, or errors and correct them. When you recognize you are going the wrong way, make a ***polarity shift***, reverse direction, and head for more positive and rewarding goals. The details of this process are presented in section two.

Summary: 13 Key points from this chapter.

Key 28

To understand how the mind works, refer to the Triplex Mind Map, which is divided into three parts: the Reflexive, Automatic and Deliberate.

Key 29

The Reflexive part is our inborn, internal radar that is designed to protect us from threats.

Key 30

The four categories of instinctual emotions are fear, anger, pain, and disgust; together they represent our lower nature, which turns on stress.

Key 31

The stress system is significantly bigger, faster, and more dominant as compared to the relaxation system, which is much smaller, slower, and must be used deliberately in order to turn off stress.

Key 32

Stress has very serious consequences on our well being; if it is not limited, it will cause harm.

Key 33

The Automatic part of the mind simplifies any behaviors we repeat into internal patterns or programs that we perform subconsciously.

Key 34

The key is to raise your awareness of your automatic patterns to determine if any are not truly valuable, to transform them into more positive programs.

Key 35

The Deliberate part of the mind is the ultimate control center responsible for all development.

Key 36

The Deliberate mind is the seat of consciousness through which we experience and respond to the world by directing our attention more effectively.

Key 37

The Deliberate mind is the source of intentions, purposeful actions, and is home to our sense of Iness or identity, which is the reason we perform actions deliberately.

Key 38

The Analytical part of the mind is the source of our logic, ability to analyze, make judgments and decisions about our life, all of which occur in the deliberate mind.

Key 39

There are two forms of attention: 1) focused with concentration and 2) alert, but constantly shifting to the next important subject. These are the only directions our conscious attention can go in.

Key 40

All three parts of the mind compete for control of the other two; only the deliberate part can purposefully take control from the other two.

Key 41

The main key is that we learn to increase our awareness to identify the illusions, distortions, or errors our mind is making and correct them. Consciousness is the only vehicle that allows us to escape the lower subjective orbit and access a higher, potentially more objective, and real perspective.

Sometimes there are many aspects to a duality.

By Yanusz Gliewicz

Chapter 4

What Goes on Inside the Higher Mind?

The focus here is on how the Deliberate Mind works. First of all, this is the kingdom where consciousness rules in contrast to the reflexive and automatic parts. Consciousness is the ultimate gatekeeper; through it, we gain all experience, collect all the knowledge, build our memories, feel, think, and express ourselves. Through this portal, we develop all our special skills, wisdom, logic, our identity, and the colorful world of our higher nature. Our higher mind becomes the refuge for our sense of being, independence, freedom, power, wealth, happiness, and even altered states of consciousness. The higher mind is far above the other two parts, those that create patterns or instinctual emotions. This makes the higher mind the source of many of our positive polarities. Whenever we get caught in the lower negativity, those with the right keys can reverse directions and shift polarities.

How all this is possible is not easy to explain; let's start by describing what is going on inside the brain. Scientists estimate that there are over 100 billion neurons (cells) in the brain, and because each one has thousands of different connections with other neurons, there are over a quadrillion (10^{15}) possibilities. Just for perspective, the best computers now come with a 100 gigabyte hard drive, which can store an enormous amount of information; multiply that 100,000 times to get a quadrillion. The notion that we only use ten percent of our brain is another misconception. In reality, we use our entire brain at the lightning speed of about a quadrillion operations per second. Even the fastest super computer only does a trillion operations per second. The brain is wired for big business and can handle almost anything we throw at it.(17)

The higher mind is the most sophisticated system designed to process all this complex information, constantly learning, monitoring, memorizing, and responding to all the internal and external demands. The key is that sophistication creates simplicity. So simple, that you do not need to make any effort to integrate your senses into one continuous experience inside your head called consciousness. Despite the processing power, the higher mind still creates lots of distortions, illusions, mistakes and gives us plenty of reasons to feel stressed out. The key is to learn how to take advantage of this power and keep trouble under control. Just think about the sheer volume of activity, with so many connections happening every second; should it be any surprise that signals get crossed, lost, misdirected, stuck, or any number of other errors?

To better understand your deliberate or higher mind, it is necessary to examine the mechanisms by which it operates. The mechanisms described below are meant to be added to those already mentioned. They are the means by which the brain performs all the amazing things it can do. Naturally, each of these aspects has a positive and negative polarity. As with everything else, it is up to us to be aware of the direction in which our mind is going, and if it is the wrong way, to stop, shift polarities, and go in the right direction.

What are the Four Modalities of Experience?

What type of information do you prefer from the multi-media stream of events? Over time, we all develop subtle preferences for one form more than another. Typically, we break down these biases into four general categories or modalities of experience.

▸   **Visual:** perceived shapes, colors, sizes, contrasts, movement, brightness, hues...

▸   **Auditory:** perceived sounds, tones, pitch, loudness, rhythms, melodies...

▸   **Kinesthetic:** perceived body sensations, touch, taste, smell, movement...

▸   **Cerebral:** perceived mental information, thoughts, abstract concepts, ideas, rationalizing...

Every healthy person uses all four of these modalities, and yet each of us develops a preference to process information in one modality just a little better than the others. Sometimes the differences are very subtle; other times they can be quite profound; it depends on the individual. What do you think is your preference? Which modality of information is your favorite or easiest to deal with, and which is most difficult?

These modalities were listed in order of popularity. Most people are visually dominant. That means they prefer to deal with visual information and can process it more effectively than something else. This bias applies to the internal thinking process as much as it does to external reality. Consequently, visually dominant individuals also tend to process words or thoughts that refer to pictorial or visual imagery more efficiently. This refers to sayings like "Can you see what I mean" vs. "Do you know what I mean." The first statement's modality is visual or more familiar; the second is cerebral. There is considerable evidence that these modalities have a significant impact on communication success.(18)

Each modality represents a major path by which the brain obtains and processes information. When you are dealing with your preferred modality, it is familiar to you, and it should give you an advantage to perform better. Conversely, be aware that dealing with modalities that are uncomfortable for you may make you more vulnerable for mistakes.

Illustrative Example:

> Two writers may have very different styles of taking notes. The auditory dominant writer may keep notes on a tape recorder, while a visually dominant writer may take notes on index cards. Each writer's style makes it easier for him to achieve his goals.

> **Man's desires are limited by his perceptions; none can desire what he has not perceived.   William Blake**

What are the three Agencies of Power?

In society, an *agency* refers to a large group of people who work together to plan and execute special tasks much like travel or insurance agencies do. In the deliberate mind, this term describes well established and organized operating systems. There are three major agencies of the higher mind. These agencies use different systems within the brain. Each agency provides an independent source of power to perform complex tasks. Every person has all three agencies serving his or her needs. Depending on our experience in life, we all develop the power of each agency to a different degree. In every person, one agency becomes most powerful, and there is a middle one and the third one is the weakest. Which of these three powers is least developed in you?

▸ *Power of Perception* - observation, five senses, speed of information processing, awareness, understanding, and comprehension...

▸ *Power of Judgment* - logical or intuitive analysis, comparisons, and making decisions, making predictions, good recall...

▸ *Will Power* - intention, being deliberate, determination, passion, motivation, achievement, and being connected to your true desires...

Perception refers to our ability to observe, identify, categorize, and comprehend whatever is in reality as well as our imagination. These can be the concrete objects; what we see, hear, taste, etc. or the abstract concepts we only think about. The power of perception allows us to grasp the reality of a situation quickly, preferably in its entirety. For example, you look down a street and immediately can tell what kind of neighborhood it is; you may recognize the architecture, the types of cars, the age of the houses, and so on. This agency is responsible for our subjective impressions of any situation, event, person, problem, and so forth. There is also a natural bias with respect to the type of information we process. Depending on what is your preferred modality, it may help you "see" more or "hear" more than someone else.

As with each agency, perception depends on our consciousness to process information, the more alert, the more you perceive. Through experience, certain aspects of our perception develop more than others, determining how powerfully it works for us.

Judgment is our ability to evaluate what we perceive and decide what we think is best. This skill, in essence, is analytical thinking or intuitive sensing and making up your mind. Most people find making decisions very challenging. First, you must rely on your skills of collecting information accurately (Perception). Then you must analyze, evaluate, compare, and predict outcomes that are likely. Then, finally, you are in position to decide on one direction opposed to the other possibilities.

Everyone makes decisions based on their personal judgment. This may rely on a logical analysis of a situation or getting an intuition about it, or both. The information we collect should make our judgment easier, but not always. Usually, our judgments are just not very well thought out. Some people have more trouble with the actual analyzing part; others cannot seem to make the final choice.(19) This certainly can be considered one of the biggest problems we all face. We all have made plenty of mistakes because of poor judgment on occasion. The key is to develop these skills and take advantage of our power to discriminate and make good decisions.

What does it mean to be deliberate?

Our *will power* begins with directing our attention and ends by achieving our intentions. At first, it works by focusing the spotlight of awareness on our observations and then on the analysis of this information we get. After we have made a decision, it is up to our will to summon the energy to achieve our selected goals. The agency of will power is the most important function of the higher mind, and it is one of the *hidden keys* to unlock our potentials.

Being deliberate means to direct with intent, purpose, and specific goals in mind. When you are deliberate, you must engage your will power to achieve the goals or intentions in mind. This self-direction starts to develop during infancy and continues through life. Most people do not have a strong will, although everyone can develop the power of each agency. The point here is that the success of your intentions depends on your will power. As an agency, will power provides the fundamental engine to accomplish all our desired goals. Without it, we are like corks in the sea, at the mercy of which way the winds blow or currents pull us.

Those individuals who have strong will power are seen by others as motivated, driven, ambitious, stubborn, determined, and usually clear about what they want. The power of the will arises from deep inside the deliberate mind, where we talk to ourselves, listen to our thoughts, and construct very clear instructions about what it is we intend to do. The secret is intention. The more clearly you can describe what you plan to do, the easier it is to execute the action.

What is above the Higher Mind?

The question really is: who is in control of the three agencies? The answer is the *higher self*, the inner sense of *identity.* This returns us to the notion of your consciousness, the fact that you wake up each morning clearly aware that it is "you" opening your eyes. The concept of the higher self reflects this sense of "Iness" that we all know. This inner sense of self, your *conscious awareness,* is precisely what or who directs the power of perception, judgment, and will power. The higher self is the *crown* of the deliberate mind, the source of inner direction.

In contrast, the lower self is responsible for all the other aspects of your personality, including how you react with your lower nature and the style of your automatic patterns. This "normal" self reflects all the regular attributes of our identity: your name, address, features, basically how most people recognize you. The higher self is the permanent, essential, deeper core identity. When you feel really in charge and are controlling events, then this is the "higher self" working. If you feel enslaved by the reflexive or automatic parts, then this is the "lower self" participating. Normally, we do not spend that much time directing our lives from the higher self. The reason for this is that we are not often acting deliberately. The higher self is the place from where we give the orders to act with intention, purpose, and consciously. The higher self instructs you to shift polarities, so that when you are heading in the wrong direction, you can move to the positive one.

The higher self is the doorway for the most important experiences in life. When you connect to the higher self, it becomes easier to experience emotions like love, triumph, courage, compassion, empathy, and confidence more intensely. When a person has extraordinary experiences, like religious, spiritual, mystical ones or if he or she enters an altered state of consciousness, it is through the higher self. The key is to be aware of your level of consciousness and whether you are at that highest point of self-awareness where you can be more objective and deliberate. The higher self can direct your will power with full awareness and purpose by relying on a set of criteria that promotes the most objective perceptions, judgments, and actions.

Illustrative Example:

> When a journalist asked Nelson Mandela what he was thinking about for 26 years in prison before becoming president of South Africa, he answered that he was preparing to die as a martyr or gain freedom to lead his country. This is an excellent example of the higher self speaking with clear intent on what is the right course of action.

Imagination is more important than Knowledge.   Albert Einstein

What are the Five Institutes?

There are many mysteries about what really goes on inside the deliberate mind. Recall the Three Spheres (physical, emotional, and analytical). Each represents an arena of specific potential that some of us can achieve. The higher mind contains *five institutes* that make this possible. I employ this term because "institutes," as in our society, represent academic centers of excellence and higher learning. They are depositories of knowledge and power that continue to improve themselves. They are considerably different from those agencies that rely on a small set of skills and do not change much over time. The *institutes* imply a highly organized and purposeful system that continue to build upon the mind's experience and improve its performance. Every single person has these institutes to some degree, but only with a serious effort will they reach their full potentials. The role of each institute is introduced here briefly so that later you can understand what they do with respect to the four JEEP factors.

The Five Institutes:

▸ *Memory* - the efficient storage and retrieval of information

▸ *Imagination* - mental images of abstract ideas or sensory experiences

▸ *Passion* - physical and emotional energy to motivate and drive the will

▸ *Curiosity* - desire to know, learn, analyze, take risks, and understand

▸ *Creativity* - desire and skill or talent to create or transform things

It does not take any more energy to create a big dream than it does to create a little one. General Wesley Clark

The institute of *memory* is perhaps the most mysterious of all. Memory is like gravity; we know it exists for countless reasons, but we have no idea how it works. As described previously, there are a number of theories about memory, although none have been fully embraced. Most definitely, our memory is directly tied to specific structures of the brain and individual cells or neurons in the brain. The mechanism by which memory works remains unknown. However, we do know how to use it very well.

Whatever is perceived, physically, intellectually, or emotionally can be encoded through the neurological system and stored somewhere inside the brain and body.

The most remarkable aspect of memory is that whenever we experience something very important, it gets stored automatically and actually is harder to forget. Conversely, if you are trying to memorize something that is not really important, it can be a difficult task requiring much work. The key is to develop the skills to encode or store information and retrieve or recall it very effectively. This skill can be easily improved with practice; however, there are people with an excellent memory who need no practice.

The institute of ***imagination*** is closely related to memory. The definition of 'to imagine' is to hold in the mind, to have a mental representation of any thing or any experience, real, abstract, or concrete. If you can perceive something with your senses, then the mind must be able to imagine this experience. Every memory you have depends on your imagination to recreate the experience. The imagination also has the unique ability to create things that cannot even be found in reality (i.e. science-fiction).

It takes a very small effort to imagine; though sometimes the effort is to stop our imagination. That is when we create frightening images in our mind and we begin to worry even if they are extremely remote, like some terrible accident occurring. Every mind can imagine in at least one modality, usually in several, if not all four. This again is where your awareness of your strongest modality makes it easier to imagine about, visual, auditory, sensory, or just mental things. The key is that you are always in control of what you have in your imagination. If something is bothering you, just shift to another thought or image. If that is difficult, you are not alone, but certainly you are able to improve these skills with practice.

The third institute is ***passion***, which reflects the physical and emotional energy available for you to invest in some activity. On the physical level, there are all the bodily energy, strength, endurance, and skills that enable us to exert our intentions effectively. On the emotional level, passion represents the intensity of the feelings you have doing some activity. These can be good or bad feelings, those that motivate, inspire, and propel you into action. Passion is independent from the other institutes because it adds energy to any activity you are engaged in. It is rare that we put our fullest passion into what we are doing. How often do you feel intense ambition, enthusiasm, excitement, or internal drive to keep going? Obstacles in life exist everywhere; only if we have the energy (passion) to confront these and fight for what we believe will we be able to move forward.

Passion itself is not an emotion; it is the energy, intensity, and power behind the feelings or actions we are performing or experiencing. Passion can be expressed in an infinite number of degrees from extremely mild to wild and intense. It can be applied to any activity, be it emotional, physical, or intellectual. Passion turns up the volume, brightens the colors, and also makes things much more memorable. Even on the intellectual level, passion inspires, liberates, gives confidence, builds faith and energy to continue working on your project until you reach success. The key is to know how to produce passionate energy wherever you need it or want it.

Another unique institute is the sense of *curiosity*. Those who know this feeling enjoy a hunger to know more, discover the unknown, and experience as much as it is humanly possible. Curiosity can be directed towards anything – a person, a thought, a place. Certainly it can bring risks, but it can also generate valuable knowledge. Curiosity is the reason we have discovered so much about life, ourselves, and this universe.

Why do some people want to know so much? Why aren't we satisfied with less? Instead, we want more and more! Curiosity rules because it often generates little rewards of *ah-ha!* In fact, it is your curiosity that has motivated you to read this book about the mysteries of how the mind works. This institute exists in every single person, although what we are curious about is personal and the degree of our curiosity ranges from low to very high. Where do you rank your curiosity and what are you most interested in? The key is to nurture your curiosity; let it help you learn what interests you.

The most amazing institute is *creativity*. Being creative can be very simple or incredibly complex, but usually it's something in between. On some level, everything that comes from our mind is an act of creativity because it did not exist previously. Even reconstructing memories is a creative act. The mundane level of creativity may be preparing food, making a bed, or answering a questionnaire. Things like writing a love letter, designing a house, or painting a scene can be considered more sophisticated levels of creativity. The operational definition of creativity is any act that brings into existence something that was not there previously. That is a very broad concept. When this process is united with the highest part of our imagination, then it is possible that such creative acts improve the world in some way, aesthetically, socially, economically, or intellectually; the list is really endless. Ultimately, when others are impressed by such forms of creativity, these become the most rewarded and appreciated things in society.

This institute has no limits; with a good imagination, literally anything can be invented, as is quite evident in all the fictional stories and movies being produced. The machines, gadgets, tools, and the constant development of higher technology are all examples of creativity. The enormous amount of art, music, and dance is constantly being expressed in so many different ways. And yet, in my opinion, despite the abundance of creativity in our world, there could be and should be a great deal more of it! Past research indicates that most people do not consider themselves very creative. Why not? Is not being creative the most natural activity? Think of children; their nature is to be creative, to play or pretend, and what fun they have. The key is to embrace the creative impulse we have inside us and allow it to express itself in some original way. There is an extraordinary book by Michael Gelb, *How to Think Like Leonardo da Vinci*, that describes seven aspects of genius which parallel many of the points I am making here.

What is the Higher Nature?

The deliberate mind contains the most valuable human emotions, attitudes, and beliefs. The higher nature is home to these positive emotions, those that are often considered spiritual, noble, sophisticated, and are admired socially. This higher nature is the polar opposite to our lower nature. As described in the reflexive mind, there are four basic groups of negative, lower emotions (fear, anger, pain, and disgust). The higher nature contains the four groups of opposite, positive emotions, courage, acceptance, happiness, and love, which correspond to the four lower emotions respectively. See Table 7 to view a brief list of this higher nature.

The most important difference about the higher nature is that it is not in-born; it is not biologically "hard-wired" as is the lower nature. Most of these emotions must be learned, although a small group of these positive emotions can be evoked without learning by the right experiences, but still require nurturing to fully develop. Perhaps one could say that the higher nature is "soft-wired," so some potential exists. There are simple innate pleasure centers that help us develop and express positive emotions, yet they require practice. The higher nature does not fully develop in most people. If you do not observe these positive emotions in others and are not encouraged to express them yourself, then these virtues will remain as a "sleeping" potential within you.(20)

Table 7. Partial List of the Higher Nature: The Positive Polarity

The names in bold label each category. The top row of emotions is the primary group, followed by the secondary list. These positive emotions are only an example from each category, with a suggested ranking from low to more intense at the top. At the bottom are the four opposite categories of negative, lower emotions. (Also see Table 17 on page 297.)

Courage	**Accepting**	**Happiness**	**Love**
Strong	Compassion	Blissful	Bonded
Confident	Tolerance	Celebrating	Respect
Secure	Patience	Balanced	Admiration
Ambitious	Peaceful	Harmony	Pride
Bold	Assertive	Healthy	Interesting
Excited	Understand	Relief	Rapture
Tough	Flexible	Calm	Ecstasy
Stamina	Positive	Innocent	Humor
Pleased	Powerful	Faith	Fun
Relaxed	Forgiving	Hopeful	Beautiful
Satisfied	Kindness	Comfortable	Loyalty
Content...	Generous...	Active...	Optimistic...
⇵ ⇵ ⇵ ⇵	⇵ ⇵ ⇵ ⇵	⇵ ⇵ ⇵ ⇵	⇵ ⇵ ⇵ ⇵
Fear	**Anger**	**Pain**	**Disgust**

The emotions opposite fear and anger are nearly completely dependent on instruction and practice to be experienced. These are the categories of courage and acceptance, along with all the similar positive emotions under each group. In comparison, the emotions opposite pain and disgust are easier to evoke and learn. These are the categories of happiness and love;

there are some basic biological drives to make these feelings more easily experienced. Feeling calm, for instance, is a natural state of leisure and comfort. Similarly, feeling blissful, healthy, admiration, or rapture are also inherent potentials. Love is the complex issue. Certainly the simpler feelings of love, such as bonding, attachment, and affection are wired from birth. However, the more complex aspects of love require learning in order to develop. This refers to romantic love and aesthetic love of art, music, literature, and so on, that reflect a deeper sense of appreciation. The deeper, more mysterious levels of love certainly need instruction and rich experiences to evolve fully. There does not seem to be a limit to the depth that love can evolve to, given the time, desire, and opportunity.

Our higher nature is the gateway to experience and expresses our humanity. This is an important aspect of our positive polarity. *These positive emotions and attitudes represent the most successful ways to adapt to difficulties and cope with stress.* They also enable civilization to flourish by promoting a sense of unity among people, the spirit of cooperation, and support of one another in reaching mutual goals. This makes the higher nature the most valuable aspect of the deliberate mind, without which we would be reduced to the instinctual, animalistic, and primitive behaviors we commonly see in the wild. The truth is that many people become victims of this primitive instinctual nature and react with violence or fear. You are very fortunate to have the higher nature because it is the key to your virtues, mastering your environment, or adapting to problems.

> **Prodaptive:** *the ability to adapt to life in a very positive and productive manner, especially when things are difficult.*

Are You Mastering or Adapting to Life?

To live, we must either master our environment, or if we fail at this task, we must cope with our problems. So life is a constant battle to either gain control and enjoy success or to deal with the mess. The higher mind has miraculously evolved to do both these tasks. Truthfully, not all of us are that good at this game. However, most of us are good enough to survive. Luckily, there are people around us who are exceptionally skilled at this game and have helped the rest of us thrive, constantly raising the standard of excellence. The major benefit of the deliberate mind is its ability to harness available resources to win at the game of life.

The deliberate mind sets the intentions and then acts on them. The success of this process depends on all the factors described above. Once you know the vital information and develop the required skills, you can confidently proceed toward achieving your dreams and goals; you are equipped with the keys to master most situations. Perhaps you easily reach your goals. If yes, celebrate! If you do not achieve your goals, stress levels rise, and you are forced to resolve the problems; then you can try again. Those who learn how to *adapt* to life find creative ways to take advantage of every situation, including those where goals were not attained. This is a form of polarity shifting, reversing any negative outcome into a positive one.

This is the art of polarity shifting, learning to deal with the duality of life. Whenever you determine you are in the wrong zone, you figure out a way to reverse direction and move into a good zone. To do this consistently, requires the master keys described in this book. Once you learn the skills needed, this process becomes easy for you to do. The last reminder here is that the main key is to be conscious, raise your awareness to an objective level, and work from the higher nature so that you have the positive power, insight, and determination to direct your attention and be the master of your destiny. You can also refer to the page 284 to see a summary of the JEEP system and how to shift polarities towards the positive direction.

Summary: 13 Key points from this chapter.

Key 42

The Deliberate, or higher mind, is the source of all our noble, healthy, positive attitudes and emotions, like love, freedom, justice, optimism, courage, resilience, acceptance, and so on.

Key 43

The brain is designed with astronomical power to serve our needs, but it remains very easily fooled, caught in illusions, distortions, jumping to wrong conclusions, and is the cause of our stress.

Key 44

There are four modalities of communication: visual, auditory, kinesthetic, and cerebral. Each of us has subtle preferences for dealing with one type of information over another, which helps us communicate more effectively.

Key 45

There are three agencies: the power of perception, the power of judgment, and will power. Each agency utilizes many skills to enable us to perform the three basic tasks.

Key 46

The powers of perception are based on the skills and knowledge of observing and recognizing the important features for you to master the situation.

Key 47

The powers of judgment are based on the skills and knowledge of analyzing, comparing, evaluating, and predicting outcomes so as to make a decision about what is best.

Key 48

Will power is based on recruiting the energy and passion to increase the motivation, ambition, determination, endurance, patience, and whatever else is required to achieve your goals.

Key 49

The key to being deliberate is found in following the steps through the three agencies of power and by clearly establishing your intentions, with all the details necessary to realize them.

Key 50

The owner of your deliberate mind is the conscious higher self. This is your core identity, essence, and continuous sense of "Iness," which directs all the other parts from within the higher mind.

Key 51

The higher mind operates using the resources from our five institutes. Each concept refers to the internal work the mind does to achieve any task, beginning with memory, then imagination, passion, curiosity, and ultimately creativity.

Key 52

The higher nature contains all the positive emotions that are the polar opposites to the lower nature. Courage, acceptance, happiness, and love form the major categories. (See Table 7)

Key 53

Most of the positive emotions in the higher nature must be learned; they are not in-born. Only with the appropriate instructions and experiences are we able to express these healthy emotions.

Key 54

The higher mind gives us the vision, passion, desires, and skills to play the game of life. If we learn to shift polarities to express our positive emotions rather than the lower ones, we will be able to enjoy the game and avoid stress.

Key 55

The deliberate mind can always harness the power of consciousness to raise your awareness and see a bigger perspective. This allows you to reverse directions, escape the lower nature, overcome negative patterns, and shift polarities to embrace your higher nature and to direct your life meaningfully.

Neither fire nor wind, birth nor death can erase our good deeds.

Buddha

The symbol OM represents

the cosmic sound of the universe.

Chapter 5

Locks and Jails or Keys and Freedom?

> There may be some substitute for hard facts, but if there is, I have no idea what it can be.   J. Paul Getty

Normally, we do not pay much attention to all the things that are wrong with us, but we sure do notice all the problems around us. There is a constant stream of annoying troubles that affect us on a daily basis. Wouldn't it be nice to flip a switch to stop these problems from annoying us? Well, that is precisely what I intend to show you how to do. Except that it is not just one switch. There are many that you can develop control of – just learn how to use the keys.

The difficulty we have in turning off the stress and grief in life is an example of the many problems with how our minds work. In this chapter, I explain how the "locks" imprison us and the "keys" give us freedom. Locks usually set our direction downward toward the unwanted results and the negative polarity. Keys give us the skills to reverse directions and move in the ***positive direction***. I also briefly describe the consequences of stress, a common result of our locks. The first problem is to determine just how free are you really? There is a summary of the locks and keys described here at the end.

What is the Quest for Freedom?

Are you really free? In America, we are particularly aware of our freedoms. We can go anywhere, do anything (legal), say anything, believe whatever we choose, and that is just the top of a long list. Consider for a moment whether you really enjoy the same freedom inside your head? Can you think about anything the way you want to? The answer, unfortunately, is no! The reason is that we react to the events, people, weather; literally everything can have an effect on us. We cannot just think the way we want to because we are programmed to react in some way; even just rain can make us angry if we were planning to go out. People may say things that anger us, offend us, disappoint us; even if you don't react to them, you still experience the disturbing feelings inside. You cannot ignore things you wish you could, and you may wish to pay more attention to things that you end up ignoring. We are slaves of the Triplex Mind and all its built-in weaknesses. We may want freedom, but it is normal to be stuck in some prison our mind or body has created.

The first goal of this book is to demonstrate how to prevent problems. By realizing the various ways your body or mind locks you up, the easier you will learn how to open these locks and gain more freedom. There are many factors that take away our freedom, limit it, block it, or just cause suffering regarding it. Another way to explain this is that we get caught in the wrong polarity and experience pain, misery, stress, frustration, or whatever until we do a polarity shift and go in the opposite, ***positive direction***. This reflects the ultimate duality of life that we must deal with.

Illustrative Example:

> Neurotic is a term to describe people, who despite a wide variety of possibilities, feel compelled to always do things only one way. If anything were to interfere with their routines, they would become extremely agitated and anxious. A typical example of this is the person who must clean up everything after eating regardless of the circumstances. Sally and her husband invited their friends to celebrate her birthday and even hired two people to help with dinner and cleaning. Despite being the VIP for the evening, Sally could not leave the kitchen until everything was clean and put away. Anyone who tried to pull her away felt her anger and anxiety about not finishing. That's a neurotic prison.

What are Locks?

Locks can be anything that limit us physically, emotionally, intellectually, socially, or block our freedom in some way. Locks may vary from minor to major. They can be temporary or permanent. Locks can range from simple to very complex, or concrete and real to abstract and illusionary. There are many possible locks; each creates a problem for us by causing either us or others grief, stress, or pain. In general, locks push us down toward the negative polarity and unwanted consequences.

These locks can appear as physical problems, such as stomach aches, ulcers, headaches, or allergies. Emotionally, these locks can give you anxiety attacks, interfere with love, cause conflicts in relationships, or make you depressed and miserable. On the mental level, locks can cause confusion, bad choices, poor attention or you may become very critical and judgmental.

The source of most of your locks is the Triplex Mind, specifically the reflexive, automatic, and deliberate parts. Each part offers valuable advantages and also contributes serious problems. The locks we have can come from just one part, two or even a combination of all three. These locks can be biological, as in the wiring of the brain, or they can be psychological, as in the way we learn to behave. There are even cosmic locks that affect the way we think or what we believe. For example, if you believe in a predetermined destiny, then you will not be motivated to make changes in your life because you believe it is out of your control.

Each lock we have has a direct effect on one or more of the four basic psychological factors that affect everything we do: judgment, emotions, energy, and patterns. Below is a general list of the types of problems, the illusions, or distortions that we all encounter on a daily basis from different extremes.

Lack of ...	Too much of ...
Ignoring, indecisive ...	Too rigid, excessive pressure ...
Blocked by, slow ...	Going too fast, impulsive ...
Under reacting ...	Over reacting ...
Misperceptions ...	Not seeing at all ...
Submissive ego ...	Domineering ego ...
Confused, lazy...	Obsessed, stubborn...
Inattentive, distracted...	Too focused, no perspective...

As you can see from this list, the locks indicate an **imbalance** that is potentially harmful to yourself or others. They are caused by either the brain's wiring or the psychological programs that we have learned through life. These bad programs are caused by many reasons. In general, they are because of a lack of vital knowledge or the failure to learn required skills; these are the keys contained in this book. The biological problems can also be corrected by exercising the deliberate mind to gain greater control over the inherent inadequacies of the brain and nervous system. This is another example of the need of polarity shifting. For example, if you experience a large imbalance of energy in a relationship, such as the person you love does not love you back as much, this creates a great deal of stress and discomfort for you because there is an unequal exchange of energy. If you cannot shift the other person's feelings to be more loving, you will not be able to remain in that relationship for very long. This is another example of the duality of life.

Why do we end up in jail?

The idea of getting arrested and being thrown in jail is not comforting to anyone. Actually, many people live in a psychological prison without ever having been arrested. They get there innocently because they got caught by one of the psychological traps in life. The locks being described here often create a self imposed limitation on what you can do in life. This limits your freedom. If you are not as free as you could be, then you are in jail.

Illustrative Example:

> Zack's father died when he was twelve years old; since then, he has been very close to his mother. She is a very demanding and critical individual whom Zack has always made an effort to please in part because he believed he had to - taking the place of his father. Zack recently turned fifty and still has not been able to find a lady friend whom his mother would approve. It has become the running joke among his friends that he has to clone his mother in order for her to approve his getting married. He came to me to review beliefs about his life and finally confronted the program in his head about pleasing his mother in selecting a wife. With just a few new keys that helped him look at life more objectively, he realized that even his mother's disapproval was not absolute. Finally, he has been able to get married despite his mother's doubts. Last I heard, everyone was happy.

What are the most common jails?

There are many different jails. Social jails are easiest to understand. We live with many expectations, obligations, and duties, like when we join some club only to realize that we are expected to do things we did not want to do. Like when Jerry joined the army and had to get up at dawn to run 10 miles through mud up to his ankles every morning. A common social jail is simple poverty. Without financial resources, it is very hard to get the training, education, or tools to get a better paying job. Poverty creates a variety of prisons, physical (housing), emotional (feeling poor), and intellectual (underachievement) among others. The worst prison is "poverty thinking" – that regardless of how much money you actually have, it never feels like enough.

The body can become our prison as well. Obesity, lack of exercise, or bad habits like smoking or addiction to drugs or alcohol create limitations on our normal freedoms. If you experience chronic pain, a lack of vitality, fatigue, allergies, or any number of ailments, this too places you into a prison.

The mind is actually the master craftsman of jails. If you become overwhelmed by the reflexive mind and the lower nature (fear, anger, pain, and disgust), you may feel tremendous limitations on what you can do. Fear causes paralysis, stopping us from moving forward. Similarly, the automatic mind can impose horrific limitations on our freedoms. When we embrace any negative routines or self-destructive patterns, we lock ourselves in a cell with bars. Even the deliberate mind can believe that some dubious religious cult is our true salvation, and we willingly sign over all our worldly possessions to an unscrupulous individual. There are many ways that we end up in a prison, looking out the barred window not even aware of what freedom we are missing. That is the most frightening part of the story. Without the right perspective and inner awareness, you may spend a life time in jail and never know it because you were never actually arrested.

Everyone experiences some limitation of his or her freedoms. Depending on how constricted you feel, this may give you the impression of being locked up in some sort of jail. This also causes you stress. No one wants to sit in a prison, but without the right keys, you may not be able to escape.

Illustrative Example:

> Mary grew up under very harsh conditions. Her mother abused her and criticized her constantly. Her parents got divorced when she was only four. She never got the support or encouragement that a young girl needs to feel good about herself. Although she is an attractive and intelligent young woman now, she feels terribly

insecure about herself. This caused her stress that affected her digestive system and gave her irritable bowel syndrome. She came to me after living for years with these severe physical and emotional burdens. After obtaining a few keys, she was able to escape her stress and insecurity, and go on living a fulfilling life. The prison she was in was physical and emotional, which arose from her mind. The keys that liberated her rebuilt a healthy self image and taught her to transform her anxieties into relaxed confidence.

What is stress?

Stress is often misunderstood. It can be anything that affects our life, positive or negative. Even getting married (presumably a happy event) is considered almost as stressful as the death of a family member. If we do not eat enough or eat too much, it can cause our body stress. Your body is constantly trying to keep all the internal processes working in balance. If we are hot, we perspire; if cold, we shiver. There are thousands of similar programs running in your body. Anything that pushes our systems out of balance is considered stressful and requires time, energy, and effort to correct. This is as true biologically as it is psychologically. That means that whatever we believe is our normal psychological balance - anything that disturbs us – becomes stressful and must be dealt with. The major, universal consequence of stress, regardless of what it is, can be summarized as - *speeding up the aging process*. I have never met anyone who told me they were in a hurry to grow old. However, high levels of stress cause us to grow old faster, spinning the hour hand of our biological clock hundreds of times per actual hour. So if you want to stay young, you better develop your abilities to decrease stress in your life. The point is that stress is actually a struggle to return to some level of balance and comfort.(21)

What are the consequences of stress?

So we react with stress, why is it a big deal? Every person experiences stress; it is normal until it gets to be too intense for too long. The problem, as mentioned earlier, is that we all have our "weakest link," one system inside of us that is weaker than the others. Whenever we get stressed out, that system starts to break down. Over time, our *weakest link* will give us trouble. There are seven major systems in our body: nervous, digestive, skin, respiratory, endocrine, cardiovascular, and skeletal. Under stress, one or more of these will age faster and cause illness.

The term "psychosomatic medicine" represents the field of study of how psychology affects the body. For example, asthma, allergies, acne, eczema, psoriasis, then all the gastrointestinal disorders like ulcers, colitis, irritable bowel syndrome, and even the cardiovascular group beginning with hypertension and going all the way to heart attacks or strokes are among many other disorders that have been shown to have a major stress component. The tragic consequences of cancer are attributable to a large degree to stress as well. We know that even among identical twins, if one gets cancer the other twin has less than a 50% chance of getting the same cancer despite a predisposition to it; the reason for that is that stress and environmental factors play a huge role. Drs. Roizen and Oz, two major authorities on medicine claim that: "Three major life events or sets of unfinished tasks can make your real age more than thirty-two years older." In short, stress causes us to age much faster.

Illustrative Example:

> I had a friend who lived with a great deal of stress. She developed a chronic case of acid reflux. Despite the fact that she was herself a physician, she did not take care of this problem. Finally, it became cancerous and took her life. The stress of life became her murderer. She never learned to shift polarities and escape the sources of her stress.

The consequences of stress can be minimal, dramatic or even deadly. The locks being described cause problems on many different levels; when they persist, we eventually experience physical stress. If we experience stress day after day without time to recuperate, then eventually it will take away our well being and freedom.

What are the two types of locking mechanisms?

There are two varieties of locking mechanisms. One you are born with. The other you develop through experience. There are major differences between these two types of locks, yet both have dramatic effects on the mind, body, and behavior. Each lock has its negative side along with its positive polarity. The problem with the locks is that we are all prone, and more susceptible, to the negative troubles dominating our life. Without the keys, these locks will cause terrible imbalances in your life. For example, you certainly remember the most frightening event you experienced or what made you most angry in your life, don't you? These experiences are unforgettable because bad events in our life will evoke very intense emotions and cause stress that is hard to escape. When you learn to shift polarities, it becomes possible for you to escape stress much more easily by moving to the positive side of some duality.

What are the locks you were born with?

The most important weakness we are all born with is the **reflexive mind** that which controls our emotions. This is the lowest and most primitive part of the triplex mind and the source of the lower nature and all our *fear, anger, pain, or disgust*. These negative feelings are responsible for much of our stress. Recall the fact that our (reflexive) stress system is about twenty times (20x) bigger and faster than our relaxation system so it is much easier to turn on stress, than to turn it off. That is a serious disadvantage. This fact makes us very vulnerable to experience negative feelings much more easily than the positive emotions. This refers to those survival instincts we are born with that dominate our life. The specific locks are all part of our *lower nature emotions* within the lower nature.(See Table 5) In addition, the problem with the reflexive system is that it works outside our awareness, so it is hard to monitor.

Illustrative Example:

> Leanne was a tall, strong gal who was extremely sensitive to any criticism and had a very short temper. If anyone said something suggesting she was wrong, Leanne would scream with protest. This was her way of defending herself, but it was also destroying her relationships. With the right keys, Leanne was able to shift polarities, escape her impulsive emotions and enjoy better relations. The keys enabled her to transform questions into requests for verification that she was able to respond to peacefully. She also learned to relax and change her anger into compassion, something she has always wanted herself and never got enough of.

The other lock we are born with is our **automatic mind**, which is ready to make a routine pattern out of any behavior, regardless whether it is good or bad for us. This part of the triplex mind creates subconscious routines from any source; it can be a physical, emotional or an intellectual program that becomes an ***automatic pattern***. The brain is "wired" to take any intense experience and create an automatic response to it, or the brain will convert any deliberate act, repeated several times, into a routine pattern of behavior. *Illustrative Example:*

> Tina was from a European country that idolized men at the expense of women. Tina was never allowed to protest the abusive behaviors of men in her community. Even when one molested her as a young girl, she was unable to complain to anyone. This established a terrible pattern of abusive relationships that Tina went through because it was her program not to protest, just to accept men's behaviors, whatever they were. Once she was given the right keys, she liberated herself from this pattern and has begun searching for a healthy partnership. The key was to establish a new pattern based on what she really wanted and also to change her fear of rejection into confidence to assert her desires.

These are the two basic locks we are all born with. They represent the ***Emotions*** and ***Patterns*** of the four JEEP factors. They are also the lower two parts of the triplex mind system. These locks are "hard wired" into our bodies and create a large variety of secondary problems, or locks, for people.

What are the learned locks?

There are many locks that develop because of the experiences we go through. Yet we would not develop these locks if our bodies and minds were not pre-designed with certain weaknesses. Every person creates his or her own unique locks because each of us has had different experiences. What is the same for everybody is that the consequences of these locks can affect any area of life.

These locks are very simple to learn. In part, the reason these lessons are easily learned is because our system is designed to memorize negative experiences much more than positive ones. That is why we slip towards the negative polarity so quickly. The most significant locks we learn are those that disturb our ***energy*** balance, distort our ***perceptions***, and/or affect the ***deliberate mind***. These locks develop within the deliberate mind of the triplex mind system. Even the source of our strength and awareness can learn to think or feel or believe the wrong things. More specifically, we learn to have difficulties with our *higher nature emotions, judgment*, and *will power*.

Normally, these factors must be learned and developed through experience, practice, and reflection. Everyone is familiar with how easy it is to experience an imbalance in the exchange of energy or realize how wrong certain perceptions are that we initially felt were clear. Then later, we may conclude that it was not what we thought. The higher emotions are not inborn; if we do not learn them correctly, we will have confusion or conflict rather than positive emotions. Similarly, if we do not learn how to analyze situations and make good choices, we will suffer from poor judgment and the bad consequences. Finally, will power is an extremely important force in our lives, but if not used properly, which we must learn to do, it can cause massive hardship for us and others. The major learned locks (from the four JEEP factors) are *Judgment* and *Energy*; additionally, there are *perceptions*, all of our *higher nature emotions*, and our *will power*.

Illustrative Example:

> Politicians are notorious for distorting perceptions, coming to erroneous judgments, and standing by their bad decisions with stubborn determination. Their inability to be wrong makes them rely on their will power to assert their opinions. These are the most unlikely people to ever get counseling or experience the desire to change their personalities.

What do Locks do?

Locks limit your freedom. Locks interfere with achieving your goals. Locks cause conflicts, arguments, stress, and misery. In the section above, I describe seven general categories of locks. In reality, there are many different types of locks that must be deal with. There are many locks, big ones and small ones; some are easily opened, while others require a great effort to unlock. Some locks arise from the cosmic or philosophical level, like beliefs that lead to hatred, depression or even war. All locks put you in some sort of prison.

Most locks are found within the triplex mind system. These locks can be the result of what we were born with, the wrong or mistaken knowledge we acquire, or a lack of vital information. A summary of these major locks is described in Table 8, which reveals the basic positive and negative aspects of each factor. The keys to open these locks are among the vital knowledge and the required skills. These keys develop within the deliberate mind if we have the right experiences and learn the lessons. Remember, it is much easier to learn the "bad" lessons than the "good" ones. In Table 9, you can find a more detailed list of the locks with which we all commonly deal. If you like, you can go through this list and indicate which locks you deal with yourself, or with others in your life. All of these locks can be opened using the keys listed throughout the book.

Illustrative Example:

> I recall Debbie, an anxious and insecure young girl who was very pretty. She grew up with unrealistic expectations and decided to cope by over eating, slowly gaining weight, until she became obese. Until she obtained the right keys to restructure her world, food replaced her unreachable dreams. Over time, she created a new set of realistic goals that rewarded her progress changing the bad patterns of over-eating into a healthy way of achieving her desires in small easy steps. She learned to reverse negative directions and shift to positive polarities.

Table 8 briefly describes the basic duality of the psychological factors and their positive and negative aspects. As you review the categories ask yourself which aspects give you the most trouble in life. Notice that the locks cause stress and sabotage our life, while the opposite keys remove the difficulties and help us progress.

Table 9 contains a list of common locks we all experience. As you review the different locks, ask yourself which ones give you the most trouble and indicate with an "S" for "self" or an "O" for "other," if you have to deal with people that act in that way. This can help you become more aware of the locks that you need the most help with yourself or with others.

Table 8. The Major Dualities of the Mind – The Consequences of Positive and Negative Aspects on Life.

Aspect	Negative - Locks	Positive - Keys
Reflexive Mind **Emotions**	Lower nature: fear, anger, pain, and disgust - Stress	Intuition, passion, protection, (fight - flight response) - Relax
Automatic Mind **Patterns**	Sabotaging patterns (mental, physical, emotional)	Adaptive positive patterns, simplifying life
Higher Mind **Perceptions**	illusions, distortions, lack of perspective	clear vivid observations, details and larger perspective
Energy	lacking, losing, stealing, leaking, greedy	power, passion, stamina, sharing, exchanging, generous
Emotions	must be learned & developed, expressed falsely, unjustly	noble virtues, courage, love, acceptance, happiness, truth
Judgment	irrational, prejudiced, lacking analysis, poor choices	accurate, analytical, comparing, good decisions
Will Power	stubborn, obsessive, hostile, or weak, undisciplined	assertive, powerful, achieving, intentional

Locks of all types imprison us or at least limit our freedom.

Table 9. The General List of Locks that we all experience.

Problems or Locks:	S/O	Problems or Locks:	S/O
Inattention		Jealous, envy, vengeance	
no focus, easily distracted		bad urges, temptations	
Lack of concentration		Obsessive, compulsive	
Misperceptions, illusions		Hypersensitive, distrust	
Misunderstood, distortion		Irresponsible	
False beliefs, assumptions		Hypocritical, two-faced	
Forgetful, poor memory		Egocentric, conceited	
Disorganized, confusion		Selfish, rude	
Impulsivity, impatience		Critical, judgmental	
Irritable, inflexible		Unsupportive, neglectful	
Lack of motivation, lazy		Insensitive, obnoxious	
Negative, pessimistic		Dishonest, cheat, steal	
Worthlessness, no esteem		Manipulative, disloyal	
Embarrassed, inhibited		Exaggerating	
Anxiety, nervous		Ignore, minimizing	
Fears, phobias, paranoia		Intrusive, no boundaries	
Depressed, sad, lonely		Complaining, whining	
Hopeless, very depressed		Projecting, blaming	
Disgusted, guilty		Denial, distortion	
Hatred, prejudice		Addictions, bad habits	
Anger, frustration, tension		Sloppy, dirty, filthy	
Rage, screaming		Poverty, life	
Abrasive, offensive		Superficial, boring	
Hostile, territorial		Ambivalent, indecisive	

What does all this mean?

The question is why is this long list so familiar to you and everybody else? Because it is much easier for anyone to experience the negative side than the positive one. These negative experiences are simply much more intense and more easily learned. Consequently, our tendency is to get stuck in the lower nature (fear, anger, pain, or disgust) and the destructive patterns of our automatic minds. Our brains are wired to make negative behaviors more intense, faster and easier to experience, and very difficult to escape.

This list of specific locks demonstrates the wide range of problems that we are subjected to by the faulty function of our brain or a lack of knowledge about our own world. We can suffer all of these terrible locks and live in a prison, or we can search for the keys to unlock these problems and escape to freedom. All of the locks described here can be opened, and the problems corrected. All that needs to be done is to identify what the specific issues are and then apply the right keys to regain your freedom. This is the process of shifting polarities and changing directions, that anyone can learn.

Expect trouble as an inevitable part of life, and when it comes, hold your head high, look it squarely in the eye and say, 'I will be bigger than you. You cannot defeat me.' Then repeat to yourself the most comforting words of all, 'this too will pass.'   Ann Landers

What are the Keys?

The keys that I have been describing are the **vital knowledge** and **required skills** that can correct the problems we encounter. Keys unlock jail doors so that we can escape to freedom. The keys described so far began with a basic understanding of the natural laws of the universe and then continue with how the triplex mind works. The first four chapters provide you with the knowledge to understand why we do the things we do. Part of this perspective explains how our brains undermine our efforts to stay healthy and happy. That is because we must constantly combat the natural tendencies we are born with to get stressed out very easily or become stuck in unwanted patterns. The only way to fight stress and regain balance is by using the powers of the deliberate mind. In fact, the deliberate mind holds most of the keys to the locks that imprison us and give us stress, conflicts, problems, and grief.

The knowledge is the information you need to understand the basic laws of nature, including how your mind works. Without these vital facts, you are very likely to make major mistakes that will cause stress or stick you in a prison of some kind. The most essential knowledge is about the deliberate mind, which harbors the tools to reverse the negative imbalances we are born with.

The required skills are specific things you must do to open any of the locks that cause stress, bad patterns, poor choices, or some form of misery. Each key helps you correct part of the natural imbalance we all deal with. The skills described are simple exercises for the mind or body to train you to escape the unwanted tendencies and regain a healthy positive balance. This is what I refer to as *polarity shifting*, changing directions to escape the stressful part of some duality and head towards the positive side.

These skills are described in the next section in greater detail with respect to the specific locks. These are very simple exercises that anyone can perform. Each skill is designed to train the mind to counter any imbalance that may exist.

How do the Keys Keep us in Balance?

The JEEP factors represent the four basic psychological systems we use to deal with life. The most important words to remember are *polarity shifting*; like in a balance, it can swing one way or another. Whichever factor you consider, judgment, emotions, energy, or patterns, each one has a positive, good polarity and each has a negative or bad polarity. The biological and psychological faults in our brain or body cause us to always tip over into the negative sides of these factors. The keys are the knowledge and skills to tip the balance back toward the positive and good polarity. The most important direction to remember is *upward*, to go from the lower reflexive mind, or automatic mind, up to the deliberate mind to gain control. The key concept is to *Think Up!*

Thuppo: *the act of thinking up and in the opposite direction of any negativity in order to master the situation.*

The locks represent bad wiring in the brain, or faulty thinking in the mind, which makes us swing into the dark, negative polarity that causes stress and misery. As we grow, every experience we have stimulates the brain to grow new connections or enhance the ones that are already there. This neurological process cements either good or bad behaviors. The keys rely on increasing your awareness of the power of your deliberate mind to wrestle away control from these vulnerable systems and regain balance, harmony, health, and happiness, and promote fulfillment. To *Think Up* means to focus attention on the deliberate mind and to use awareness to go to the opposite polarity of any negative experience.

The idea of polarity shifting is not a new concept; those who embrace this idea live a better life. When His Holiness the Dalai Lama was asked if his exile helped him, he replied: "Oh yes! Without a doubt. I can try to tell you why. When, at some point in our lives, we meet a real tragedy - which could happen to any one of us - we can react in two ways. Obviously we can lose hope, let ourselves slip into discouragement, into alcohol, drugs, unending sadness. Or else we can wake ourselves up, discover in ourselves an energy that was hidden there, and act with more clarity, more force." The Dalai Lama uses polarity shifting too!

What about Psychological Defenses?

The natural ways we all defend ourselves against stress and conflict are not very effective. The most common ways are to repress, deny, ignore, and try to avoid unwanted elements in our life. These approaches may be helpful, but they do not eliminate all the stress or correct the problems. Other times, the ways we cope just add more pressure and trouble to the situation.

Illustrative Example:

> Ralph grew up in the streets of Brooklyn as one tough guy. Trouble was always a normal part of his life, so was drinking, arguing, fighting, and high levels of stress. His job added a lot of pressure and responsibilities; consequently his favorite way to "unwind" after work was to get drunk. This would follow with arguments with his girlfriend, and eventually gave him an ulcer. He explained to me that he was very good at handling stress and could deal with anything, when in fact, the only thing he actually did to cope was drink alcohol. He easily learned to relax and

change stress into his sense of tolerance, which made him feel strong. He also realized that his need for certainty in life created unnecessary pressure on him. By embracing the uncertainty of life a bit more, he was able to accept his situation much more easily. Once he was given the right keys to shift polarities and escape stress more effectively, his entire life changed for the better.

Why does normal coping fail?

The truth is, we all struggle to cope the best we can. The way we cope depends on how we learn to deal with problems in life. Normally, we simply learn to put up with difficulties – accepting the stress, pressure, hardship, and their consequences. The way we cope with life is limited to the skills we already possess. If you never learn superior coping skills, then you must rely on the inferior ways, that do not really help as much. These are the natural coping mechanisms we all use.

The reason our common coping skills fail is because they are developed through our faulty thinking, false beliefs, poor strategies, and fears. These coping mechanisms were first described by Freud a century ago. They were all we had to rely on for decades, but not any more. They are not adequate to deal with the ever increasing amount of information we must digest every day. The mounting pressure and complexity of life are raising the levels of stress. One of the main reasons for this problem is the growing pressure in our society to do more in less time, creating a constant sense of being rushed. We grow up in such a hurry that most people learn to put up with life rather than find brilliant ways to cope more effectively.

Which system is better: the internal or external coping?

Consider the state of health in our society; despite the flood of self help books, medical and psychological specialists, there has never been as much frustration, anxiety and stress. The use of drugs, either prescribed or illicit, has never been higher. The amount of violence in the world has also been increasing; even among children which is appalling. Gambling, addictions, and chronic insomnia are more prevalent than ever before and reflect mounting levels of stress. All of these facts point to our foolish search for fast solutions from external sources, rather than relying on developing internal resources to cope more effectively.

The information presented above is strong evidence that our traditional ways of coping are not working, and are causing a major imbalance in our lives. To return to balance, I propose that we develop better coping skills to deal with our challenging world much more effectively. The *required skills* describe the most powerful techniques to cope with life. Some of these keys rely on scientific methods; others depend on the more subjective and intuitive approaches to life. Together they create a variety of superior strategies to adapt much more successfully to the challenges we face. This approach is based in part, on the new field of Positive Psychology, begun by Martin Seligman, Ph.D. as you can read in his exceptional book *Authentic Happiness*. Positive psychology focuses on all the qualities, characteristics, virtues, attitudes and so on, that develop the most admirable personality and satisfying experience of life.

What are the normal coping strategies?

We all learn to use the normal coping mechanisms as we grow up. These are the standard, psychological defenses that are just to help us cope; they make the problems manageable, so we do not become totally overwhelmed. In Table 10, The Psychological Defenses, illustrate an outline of basic coping mechanisms that we commonly rely on. There are only about twenty defense mechanisms that we normally use. Most people will recognize these coping tools and remember experiencing at least some of them. (22)

Many people rely on pills to decrease anxiety, alleviate depression, or minimize stress. These pills often have significant cost factors with respect to side effects, effectiveness, expense, and unwanted long-term effects. Most physicians, especially the psychiatrists, do not teach their clients improved coping skills; instead, they just prescribe drugs to remove unwanted symptoms. This may be a quicker form of treatment, but it rarely is permanent. Rather it suppresses the symptoms, but never gets rid of the causes of the problems or stress.

Actually much of psychology and all of psychiatry pathologize the normal experiences we all must go through. The official psychiatric diagnostic manual (DSM 4) contains hundreds of behaviors or feelings that are considered "abnormal" when in fact, every human being has many of them. Psychology is in the business of "fixing the abnormalities" with various forms of therapy. Some approaches work much better and faster than others. Most of all, it is not the approach, rather the individual and the quality of the relationship between the therapist and client that has proven to make the biggest difference helping people.

I have a great deal of respect for many schools of psychology. The most powerful approaches include techniques I have utilized in writing this book. For example, neurolinguistic programming (NLP), Ericksonian hypnosis, integrative psychology, and cognitive psychotherapy usually teach additional coping skills to people. The most profound source of wisdom comes from the ancient schools of the East. They do not pathologize what we do or experience, rather they offer a holistic approach to help people adapt more effectively. The more intelligent techniques can make a significant difference in resolving the conflicts or stress we deal with. There is plenty of evidence that by learning how to cope more effectively people will not only overcome difficulties, but also prevent them in the future. (23)

It is my intention to introduce you to a new psychology with new strategies, and a new perspective that together will prepare anyone to deal with anything more comfortably – ***shifting polarities***. Although, this book is in the category of "self-help," that should not imply that you have to be suffering some sort of psychological problem. To the contrary, I am addressing the normal troubles of life we all deal with. The point is that it is completely normal for us to swing from one polarity to the other. It simply is not healthy to spend much time or lose much energy on the negative side of the equation.

Table 10 - Psychological Defense Systems

These are the common ways we deal with stress or conflict, however, you can see that these defenses do not usually promote greater health.

Defense Mechanism	Normal Psychological Function
Anticipation	prepare to deal with conflict
Affiliation	deal with conflict by recruiting help from others
Altruism	deal with conflict by self sacrifice
Humor	deal with stress through amusement
Self assertion	expressing your thoughts or feelings
Self observation	reflecting on internal events

Sublimation	channeling bad feelings into acceptable activities
Suppression	intentionally avoiding bad feelings
Repression	unwanted conflicts are kept out of awareness subconsciously
Denial	refusing to acknowledge conflict
Tolerance	coping or enduring challenges
Dissociation	separating from normal awareness
Displacement	transferring bad feelings onto "safer" substitute
Fantasy	gratifying frustrated desires by imagining goals
Projection	attributing conflict unto others
Rationalization	justifying conflicts by illogical or immoral means, coming up with poor excuses
Ignorance	not knowing how to deal with consequences
illogical thinking	assumptions that are not logical or realistic
Faulty attributions	assigning meaning to the wrong factors
False belief systems	making unrealistic and unprovable theories, rules for life
Passive-aggression	using a facade of compliance to mask hostility, with anger and resentment
Acting-out	reducing anxiety by allowing to express forbidden desires
delusions & psychosis	loss of reality testing skills and entering an internal reality

Summary: 16 Key points from this chapter.

Key 56

The locks represent the inherent problems in the universe, the brain, or the way your mind works, which imprison you and often cause stress and misery.

Key 57

The keys represent the vital knowledge and required skills that will correct and even prevent the natural problems that all the locks cause and will minimize our stress levels.

Key 58

Our freedom is limited by the faulty way our Triplex mind works. There are locks on all three levels of the mind that require specific keys to unlock them. There are also cosmic locks that affect the ways we think about life.

Key 59

The locks can be any limitation on our freedom be it physical, emotional, intellectual, social, economic, or anything else that causes grief.

Key 60

Every person has a different set of locks that have a direct effect on one or more of the four basic psychological factors that affect everything we do: judgment, emotions, energy, and patterns.

Key 61

The locks can cause poor judgments, floods of negative emotions, blockage or loss of energy, and destructive patterns that interfere with our life.

Key 62

There are many different jails that represent the loss of freedom to do what is best for us or others and leads to some form of destructive actions.

Keys 63

Most people do not realize that they are in any type of prison; however, if you experience any lack of freedom to pursue your goals, happiness, or deal with stress or grief, then you are locked up.

Key 64

Stress is any situation that causes your mind or body to struggle to regain balance, comfort or a sense of control. The degree to which you experience stress speeds up your aging process.

Key 65

The consequences of stress can be minor or even deadly. They can affect every area of life. In the body stress will begin to cause bad effects on one or more physical systems.

Key 66

The reflexive mind is the source of our lower nature emotions with which we are born. The categories of fear, anger, pain and disgust are about 20x easier to experience than positive emotions.

Key 67

The automatic mind is the source of our negative patterns and programs that we can learn very easily. We are all born with this ability to create physical, emotional or intellectual routines.

Key 68

Through our experience, we learn the other locks: energy imbalance, distorted perceptions, and misdirected efforts of our deliberate minds.

Key 69

The locks we develop within the deliberate mind cause confusion, interfere with our judgment, derail our will power, and evoke the wrong higher emotions.

Key 70

Each key offers the information or skill you need to regain balance in your mind or body. The general rule is to think "up," raising your awareness from the lower reflexive, or automatic minds, up to the deliberate mind to regain control.

Key 71

The psychological defenses we normally rely on primarily help us to cope and do not correct the problems, eliminate the stress, or make us feel much better.

Key 72

The principle of polarity shifting means that if you experience unwanted, negative events, you must reverse directions and go to the polar opposite to escape stress and enjoy success.

You may be disappointed if you fail, but you are doomed if you don't try.   Beverly Sills

Chapter 6

What is Our Quest for Fulfillment?

You have to find something that you love enough to be able to take risks, jump over the hurdles and break through the brick walls that are always going to be placed in front of you. If you don't have that kind of feeling for what it is you are doing, you'll stop at the first giant hurdle. George Lucas

What Do We Really Want?

The simple answer is to be happy because that means we got what we wanted. What if you cannot have what you want or the struggle to get it is not worth it? That is when life begins to get complex. Recall from chapter two Maslow's hierarchy of needs and Robbins' six human needs? There are things that everybody wants and needs (safety, food, shelter, social contact, meaning in their lives, and so on). The key is to know *exactly what you want*; then it is easier to obtain it and be happy.

Naturally, we want health, happiness, prosperity and a positive flow of energy! These can be acquired in countless ways. In fact, that is what makes the pursuit great and complex. There are many roads to the "good life." Finding the one that makes you happy can be tricky. There are many separate paths; one is happiness and the second is fulfillment. I refer to happiness as that spontaneous, giddy, joyful feeling that usually makes us laugh and smile. One of the simple *secrets to happiness* is you must search for it and *discover it yourself*. If other people tell you what is supposed to make you happy, it is unlikely to make you feel good, no matter what. This is the number one reason for so much frustration in our modern society, because few people actually make the effort to create happiness for themselves. Do you know what really makes you happy? If you do not, by the end of this book, I promise you will.

What is the Ladder of Fulfillment?

What is that "good life" we are truly searching for? It cannot be money alone; certainly just being healthy is not enough, and nobody can be constantly happy. I refer to this "good life" as ***our quest for fulfillment***. It cannot be a single goal; rather, it is the sum of our wishes, accomplishments, and all the good things that happen during life. I refer to fulfillment as that deeper sense of satisfaction from reaching multiple goals, or that occasional excited jumping, yelling expression of achievement upon attaining an important goal.

Somewhere deep inside we all have "score" sheets that keep a tally of how far up the ladder of fulfillment we have climbed. The keys that help us climb that ladder higher, faster, and easier, are the most important ones you can find. You will not find these keys outside yourself. The most valuable keys are the mechanisms within the mind, which anyone can learn for free. It does not matter how intelligent you are or how much money you have. And it has nothing to do with how much you even know. With the right keys, every person can enjoy some degree of satisfaction and positive meaning. That is how you can gain a sense of fulfillment, even when the circumstances of life are not meeting your expectations or desires.

With the right attitude and a focused plan, we can remain positive and find fulfillment, despite even very challenging situations. That means that you can have a good life without being constantly happy. There are many examples of people who surprise us with positive attitudes that allow them to make the most out of misfortune. The individuals who survived unjust imprisonment, like Nelson Mandela or the author Victor Frankl, are good examples of mind-over-circumstances.

Our quest for fulfillment can be simple or complex, tiny or tremendous; it all depends on you. There are no limits on what you can achieve. Those individuals who focus their efforts exclusively on the stereotypical social expectations that are created by much of the media like wealth, power, and fame will often experience greater struggles and disappointment. There are in fact, a very wide variety of things that each of us may be able to achieve. Recognizing your potential is the first step in your journey towards success.

The other reason for unhappiness is the failure of our mind to think right. Instead, many people experience envy, jealousy, greed, and desire for what someone else has. These are mechanisms in your brain that make you squirm when your neighbor drives up in a brand new car. This sense of envy is really a form of anger; unless you make a polarity shift, this experience will result in stress and unpleasant emotions.

Those people who make bigger, daily efforts seeking satisfaction from life usually climb higher up the ladder than those who are waiting for some special far off goal. Fulfillment and happiness do not have any special requirements; rather, it depends on each individual to find what he or she can achieve that will be satisfying. The key is to maintain a positive and realistic frame of mind that promotes balance and harmony in the face of the normal troubles of life. As Winston Churchill said, "Never, never, never give up!"

> **If only people who worry about their liabilities would think about the riches they do possess, they would stop worrying.   Dale Carnegie**

How do you measure fulfillment?

Since you were born, you have been on your quest for fulfillment. How high up the ladder have you climbed so far? Has your quest been satisfying? This search for that sense of accomplishment can be described in two categories. The first part is how you see yourself. The second part is how you think others perceive you. What you believe the answers are to the following questions is more important than whether they are true or not.

See Table 11. Answer the following questions with a checkmark in the box that indicates your response: very little -- some -- very much. To calculate your score, count all the check marks and give yourself 1 point for each mark in the very little column, 2 points for the some column, and 3 points for each mark in the very much column. Add up all your points for a total score. This is a simple self-analysis just to make you more aware.

See the Appendix, page 312 for an explanation of this table.

> **Thousands of candles can be lighted from a single candle, and the life of the candle will not be shortened.   Happiness never decreases by being shared.   Buddha**

Table 11.

The quest for fulfillment - Self Analysis	Very Little	Some	Very Much
Do you like yourself, and your life in general?			
Do you feel proud of your accomplishments?			
Are you confident that you can handle anything?			
Have you been achieving most of your goals?			
	1	2	3
Do you think most people like you and enjoy your company?			
Do you think others respect and admire your accomplishments?			
How many people consider you a strong and healthy individual?			
How many others would agree that you do something exceptionally well?			

Honestly, these are complicated questions, but I am certain that nearly everyone keeps some form of score in his or her head. So, what do you think? The deeper question is, are your responses accurate, or did you minimize, making yourself worse than reality, or perhaps, you exaggerated making yourself better than you are. This may reflect a problem with your scoring system rather than with your life. That means the way your mind and body work may be making it difficult for you to measure yourself accurately. Curiously, if we lie to ourselves, somewhere deep inside we know it. Consequently, if you discover the internal keys to operate the mind and body better, you will be able to enjoy greater fulfillment and open the pathways to reach more of your potentials. There is always more that you can accomplish. The most important goal now is to get all the keys - the vital knowledge and required skills to make your journey through life easier.

Success follows doing what you want to do. There is no other way to be successful.   Malcolm Forbes

How to be Wealthy?

What is prosperity? The definition of prosperity is enjoying an abundance of something valuable to you. Prosperity is not just meeting your essential needs; it is going beyond them to enjoy the good life; whatever that means to you. Life offers us an endless variety of resources. It is up to each of us to decide what we want and then find ways to get it. Everyone wants to prosper in his or her own way. Throughout life we make some kind of effort to acquire various forms of *wealth* that are important to us. They may be concrete or abstract, short-lived or permanent; they also may bring us pleasure and pain. Below, in Table 12, is a short list of a few different categories of wealth. Among them, you must be able to find something you have or want more of. Prioritize the categories you are interested in gaining wealth in by numbering them. (Some people give tie scores to two items because they are equally important. Rank them from 1 to 21.)

Table 12. A brief list of what makes us feel wealthy

Category	*Rank*	*Category*	*Rank*	*Category*	*Rank*
Material		Intellectual		Spirituality	
Political		Knowledge		Love	
Power		Creativity		Family	
Money		Artistic		Children	
Fame		Beauty		Security	
Prestige		Sports		Health	
Valuables		Skills		Meaning	

From this brief list, you can see that I consider wealth much more than just money. Not everyone can have millions of dollars, but every single person can enjoy unlimited wealth because there are thousands of categories of prosperity other than cash. Unfortunately, many people have been convinced by the media that financial wealth is the only type that matters. That concept is not supported by reality, where countless people enjoy some other form of prosperity. What you must ***reach is a sense of abundance about something you value***. It can be anything that you already have or can acquire or develop and definitely enjoy possessing.

The question is how do we accumulate the things we want and avoid the ones we don't want? This quest should be simple, and yet, a great majority of us do not feel wealthy, worry about the future, and are often frustrated with life. The list above is just a sample of common things that give people a sense of wealth. Some are easier to acquire than others. Knowing what your priorities are or your highest values are an important key. This relates to the concept of polarity shifting. When you identify priorities for yourself, then you can acquire a greater abundance of those things – first with your intentions and then in life. The key is never to go in the direction of poverty or lacking, but if you find yourself in that negativity, make a polarity shift to seek abundance and prosperity.

Everyone can be wealthy; it is just a matter of synchronizing your inherent talents and abilities with the opportunities around you. This is a matter of your potentials. First you must identify your personal strengths or talents; then you must set out to develop these qualities and improve them as much as possible. Remember achieving superior success is being in the top 10% of performers doing what you are really good at. Whatever that is universally brings you a degree of personal satisfaction and a respectable income. When it is a skill high in demand in our society, it may also bring a tremendous amount of wealth. In the third section of this book, I offer you the tools to identify your talents and find ways to maximize your potential for success and wealth.

> **Success is to be measured not so much by the position that one has reached in life as by the obstacles which he has overcome while succeeding.   Wise old saying.**

What about falling off the ladder?

Climbing up the ladder of success has its risks; not climbing has even more. Failure does exist for those who give up or refuse to take the necessary risks to achieve their goals. There are many people who have much more potential than they have realized because they did not make the right efforts or take the worthwhile risks. Consider the cost of failure. You never achieve the dreams and goals you have secretly held inside. You may experience happiness occasionally, but you never reach a sense of fulfillment. As you grow older, achievement becomes more difficult, risks harder to take, and ultimately, even if you succeed, you have less time in life to enjoy the fulfillment. I have met many older individuals who have never gotten a sense of fulfillment; they tend to be depressed, bitter, resentful, frustrated, and suffering from all sorts of stress induced physical problems.

Become aware of the risks and make your calculations about what you are willing to do. The risk of failure should not bother anyone who is determined to keep trying; then it is not failure, just a learning experience. The cost of failure should be clearly and carefully calculated in terms of what you are prepared to do to avoid it. Your will power and motivation to push as hard as possible for success is a great defense against the cost of failure.

In summary, if you know what gives you the feeling of abundance, then you can enjoy a sense of wealth; that makes you among the most happy and conscious people alive. Do you want to join them? Then you must learn the keys offered here and use them. The workbook on *Achievement* discusses how to apply knowledge and passion along with your personal talents and strengths to gain greater success. Following this path will bring you closer to that elusive sense of prosperity. These are just some of the goals you can achieve.

Keep away from people who try to belittle your ambitions. Small people always do that, but the really great make you feel that you, too, can become great.

Mark Twain

Summary: 8 Key points from this chapter.

Key 73

The key to happiness is to search and discover it personally. Once you know exactly what you want, then it is easier to obtain it and be happy.

Key 74

The key to find fulfillment in life is to maintain a positive and realistic attitude that promotes balance and harmony in the face of the normal troubles of life.

Key 75

We all keep score sheets in our heads about our fulfillment; the better we get at noticing and counting our successes, the faster, higher, and more easily we climb the ladder of fulfillment.

Key 76

It is important to evaluate your life objectively, first how you see yourself and secondly, how you think others see you. Together, this information can give a better measure of fulfillment.

Key 77

Jealousy and envy are negative emotions from the reflexive mind. To fight these sensations, you must shift polarities and go in the opposite direction and seek your own abundance and happiness.

Key 78

The first key to prosperity is to recognize what you have or can easily acquire an abundance of. Then you work at developing those special talents until you reach a level of excellence. Knowing that you are really competent (top 10%) gives you a feeling of achievement, wealth, and fulfillment.

Key 79

Remember, feeling wealthy or prospering in life is not reducible to money; there are countless ways to experience a rewarding sense of abundance in life.

Key 80

Calculate your risks carefully; the cost of failure is limited to a learning experience so long as you are determined to keep trying until you succeed.

Do you want to find your Master Keys?

SECTION II THE REQUIRED SKILLS

Positive Directions

Master Keys

JEEP Factors

Chapter 7

The Psychology of Master Keys

**There is always room in your life for thinking bigger, pushing
limits, and imagining the impossible.**

Anthony Robbins

This begins the detailed description of the major locks and the master keys
as they relate to the four JEEP factors. The locks (problems) may originate
on any level of the Triplex mind or out in the world. In essence, anytime
you are being pulled or pushed in a negative, unwanted direction, you must
make a polarity shift to escape the stress and go where you want to. These
locks or psychological problems are the typical errors, mistakes, distortions,
illusions, and misunderstandings we experience. Although there are many
possible problems to deal with, for the sake of simplicity, I have separated
them into four basic categories, or JEEP factors. You can only go in one
direction at a time, down towards the negative problems or up and forward
to positive solutions. This is the basic nature of the duality of life. There
is a separate chapter for each psychological factor that contains the top ten
most common locks. Each factor is described with ten examples of what
goes wrong and exactly how you can correct it with step by step
instructions.

Psychology has been struggling to understand and change behavior. There
have been many authors who described a variety of complex theories about
the mind and behavior.(24) Most of these theories have had limited success
in helping people eliminate stress and resolve their problems. The Triplex
mind system I have been describing is easy to understand and utilize to
make significant changes in your life. In order to change anything in your
life, you must first identify the problem clearly, and secondly, you must
follow a series of specific steps to reverse polarities or directions to
succeed.

The strategy I have developed groups most behaviors into one of the four fundamental psychological factors. These four categories of behavior are the JEEP factors: judgment, emotions, energy, and patterns, respectively. Each factor represents a very specific group of activities or behavior. Within each group, there are many different behaviors, but there are only a few locks and keys for each group. For each factor you can only make several different types of mistakes or distortions, and you only need a few master keys to correct these errors. Consequently, the following chapters explain most of the typical mistakes we make and how to resolve them or prevent them with the right keys.

What are the Universal Rules?

There are several universal rules that apply to this system. The first universal rule is that all four factors stretch across a wide range of duality from extreme negativity to the polar opposite positivity. Unfortunately, our inborn tendencies are to slip into the negative direction. Most of the keys described are designed to keep you alert about where you are in that spectrum and give you the steps to reverse direction and to go toward the positive polarity. I refer to this process as ***Polarity Shifting*** - *changing the negative into positive.* It is a simple formula to follow and will work nearly every time you use this technique. For example, the polar opposite of greediness is generosity. Please note that I do not claim that being dragged into the negative direction or into a subjective impression is wrong or abnormal; it is the most common thing for all of us to do. The key is that being stuck going in one direction will never serve you, and that is what usually happens. Hence, polarity shifting is about changing directions to help yourself and/or others. This is how we can better deal with the duality of life. The Shifting JEEP Polarities table on page 284 summarizes this.

Illustrative example:

> When confronted by challenging situations (their home burns down, or they get fired, or their car gets stolen), most people react to such events with a mixture of strong emotions. Some individuals will react with anxiety, fear, or even an occasional panic attack; others will get angry, become infuriated, demanding, critical, abusive, or even aggressive; still others become withdrawn, hopeless, depressed, and isolated. Everyone has his or her own way to deal with difficult events, but because of our inborn tendencies, nearly every person gets entangled in these negative experiences. Wouldn't it be great if you had a technique to escape these problems easily?

The second universal rule is that everything you do is controlled by your subjectivity. In order to escape your subjective perspective, you must develop special skills to be more objective. The two most important skills are reaching *your own higher self-awareness* and then directing your attention from a better perspective. This is important because the subjective mind has a natural tendency to make serious errors in observation, judgment, and expression. Only by raising your conscious awareness of what is going on, can you prevent problems or resolve them quickly when they occur. I refer to this process as *monitoring the mindmatics.* That means returning to an *objective perspective* of the deliberate mind or the higher self, which is able to advise you about reality much better than other parts of the mind can. Mindmatics refer to the three parts of the triplex mind that operate reflexively, auto<u>matically</u> or impulsively, without reflection.

Subjectivity is a normal perspective we all maintain. To reach your higher self-awareness you must be able to stop automatic processing and expand your perspective to imagine how others would think or feel about some situation. For example, when Madeline, who used to be a famous actress, could not find work for several years, her subjective self perspective caused her to feel depressed and worthless. Only after she began considering how others still respected and admired her did she regain a more objective and healthy perspective with more energy. This led her to move her career in a new direction.

The third universal rule requires that you learn to direct your intentions with very *strong will power*. This is the *Hidden Key* I mentioned earlier; will power is the invisible force that does all the work. Will power is a complex set of skills. Those individuals who achieve the most in life have great control of their attention and also have extremely strong wills to follow through with their intentions. I refer to this skill as *being deliberate*, exercising complete control of your attention and will power to reach your goals. There is no better guarantee of success than to have a very strong will to achieve your goals. This is a skill you are all born with, yet if it is not encouraged, rewarded, and practiced, you will not develop its full potential. It is always possible to improve these skills and utilize them more effectively. Especially when we are confronted by challenges, it is our will power that helps us overcome difficulties and change directions towards our goals.

These are among the special required skills that will be discussed with respect to each of the JEEP factors. The explanations begin with patterns, then continue with energy, emotions, and end with judgment. In each case, I describe the top ten examples for each of these factors. First, I must explain what the master keys are, along with all the other keys you will use to resolve your problems.

> If people knew how hard I had to work to gain my mastery, it wouldn't seem wonderful at all.   Michaelangelo

The Psychology of the Master Keys

The master keys represent the most important skills to deal with life. I have observed and studied behavior all of my career and have noticed very clear patterns, especially among the most successful and most burdened individuals. The keys I am describing are not just my idea. They are the proven techniques used by the healthiest, happiest, and most successful individuals I have encountered. The people who rely on the old fashioned coping mechanisms instead of these skills are more stressed, unhappy, frustrated, and anxious about their lives. These master keys are simple skills that anyone can learn to use. They may take a bit of time and effort to get good at, but I assure you, it is absolutely worth it!

These techniques can be considered superior strategies that are often relied on by the most creative, intelligent, and emotionally well balanced individuals. Many of the people who use these master keys developed these strategies through decades of trial and error. The instructions provided here will save you an enormous amount of time and effort because they are the tried, tested, and proven techniques that do work in most situations. So, allow me to reveal to you what I refer to as the "Master Keys" because they are the best strategies, skills, and techniques for reversing the negative effects of the four JEEP factors. At the end of Chapter 17 you will find a summary list of the master keys.

What are the Nine Master Keys?

The master keys are a group of nine basic strategies with a number of specific instructions on exactly what to do when confronted by challenges in life. In the following chapters I describe each of the JEEP factors and give ten common examples of how to use these master keys to deal with problems under a variety of circumstances. Just as the locks create blockages, limitations, distortions, etc., the master keys open the locks and reverse these effects, giving you more freedom and making life easier. Naturally, there are more than just nine key strategies, but these nine master keys are the most important and powerful tools to utilize.

Each master key refers to a set of instructions that should be followed in order to gain the greatest benefit from these techniques. These are the most powerful tools that I have discovered.

If you frequently feel burdened by life, struggle to reach your dreams, and have a lot of stress, then these master keys are the required skills to deal with life more effectively. If you are ambitious and desire to achieve more in life, then these master keys will empower you to overcome any limitations and reach your true potential. I refer to these master keys as the *required skills*; however, they are also the superior strategies that the most successful and healthy individuals use to maintain a competitive edge. With these special keys you are like a master locksmith who is always able to open the door to escape the prisons of stress and unlock the vaults holding your treasures. This list briefly defines the nine master keys. The following chapters describe the specific instructions for using each key.

The Nine Master Keys

> **Attention (concentration & shifting)**
> **Perception (awareness & knowledge)**
> **Higher Self (objectivity & direction)**
> **Passion (energy & motivation)**
> **Will Power (stamina & patience)**
> **Judgment (rational & intuitive thinking)**
> **Replacing patterns (positive programming)**
> **Transformation (negative into positive)**
> **Achieving Peak Potential (talents & goals)**

What effect do Modalities have?

There are several universal rules that apply to all of the keys. The first point is that you must determine what is your *preferred modality*: visual, auditory, physical (touch, taste, smell), or cerebral (thinking, analytical). (See page 82 for a detailed description of modalities.) Order these four modalities from your strongest, most utilized to the least preferred. This is a completely subjective matter, but it is important for you to know which modality is naturally preferred by you. This has nothing to do with intelligence or occupation. It is purely a personal choice.

List the four modalities in order of your preference, numbering them from 1 through 4. Usually the differences are very subtle.

_____ *Visual* _____*Auditory* _____*Physical* _____*Cerebral*

Keep in mind that these modalities are your subjective preference for gathering and understanding information. This usually means that the number one form of information is easier for you to digest than the others. Most of us can process through all of these modalities, but each of us also has a slight prejudice towards one modality over others. Knowing what your least preferred modalities are can help you prevent making mistakes because you can pay more attention to those forms of experience. The key is to use your number one and two preferred modalities to help you deal with your third and fourth preferred modalities.

Each modality uses a different area of the brain to process information. Since each area of the brain is connected, the more modalities you use, the more your brain is stimulated making it easier for you to learn and remember these events. To promote the fastest and most efficient learning it is advisable to rely on as many modalities as you can.

> Hear something once, forget it; see something once, and remember it; do something and understand it.   Chinese Proverb

What is the benefit of a Live Workshop?

Another universal rule is the power of a multimedia presentation and the unfortunate weakness of a single media source, such as this book you are reading. When you read, information is processed mostly in a visual format because you are seeing the words, unless you read out loud, which I suggest you do when you reach areas important to you. The reason for this is that when we experience life in several modalities at once it is always more powerful and memorable. For this reason you will find some of the exercises described here in a recorded auditory format available from my website (www.ShiftingPolarities.com). I would urge you to try these special tools because they can help you access more processing areas in your brain making your experience more intense and memorable.

In addition, this book creates a foundation for a series of live workshops that you can attend to further develop these master key skills and improve your life. During a multimedia presentation that is specifically organized to stimulate all of your senses and be very memorable, it is easy for you to maximize learning through that experience. The workshops deliver advanced content, along with a variety of experiential exercises that help you learn and develop the power of the tools being described here. More detailed information about these workshops and recorded programs are available in the Appendix.

> **Success is going from failure to failure without a loss of enthusiasm.   Anonymous**

Balance requires continuous work.

Chapter 8

Master Key 1 The Power of Directing Attention

> Each player must accept the cards life deals him. But once they are in hand, he alone must decide how to play the cards in order to win the game.   Voltaire

Attention is a natural, principle life skill that every person uses. Do you know the two types of attention? The brain engages in these two different tasks automatically and all the time, but how good are you at directing attention where you want it to go? The ability to direct attention is a skill that can be learned and improved. The master key of attention is based on developing control of the direction of our awareness.

Attention can go in only two directions. Either you focus on one subject, or you expand your attention to every subject around you, constantly shifting your focus to the next item. The first part requires prolonged concentration with the ability to ignore (let go of) unimportant distractions. The second part depends on your ability to constantly shift attention while letting go of every, individual focal point. Instead of directing your attention on one focal point, you must be able to keep moving your attention to notice the next thing in your surroundings. These are the two directions our attention and awareness can go in - ultimately an extreme focus or a totally open awareness of everything around you; both skills are equally important. Another related skill is learning to "Let Go" or release and ignore whatever becomes not important. Once you shift away, you do not return to the previous focus.

Obviously we all know how to pay attention. However, there are tremendous differences between people's ability to pay attention, some of whom can do it better than others. Those who have superior skills of attention utilize one or more of the principal skills described below. Our attention also works automatically because our brains are biologically programmed to react to certain events in set ways, like loud noises that startle us or monotonous and repetitive tasks that make us drowsy. The instructions given here are to increase the power of your self developed attention. Be certain that the more you practice these skills, the better you get at them.

The skill we do not develop automatically is **letting go**, or selecting what to ignore, dropping things from our attention. This is obviously a skill we all learn to perform with varying degrees of ability. The more you exercise this skill, the better you become at concentrating because you improve your ability to ignore distractions. More importantly, there will be things that become the focus of your attention that you need to forget and cannot. Letting go or releasing these things from your attention is an essential skill to keep your sanity. Every person experiences events that get "stuck on a loop" replaying over and over. Many of my clients have come to me seeking peace from a bad relationship that ended years ago, a traumatic accident, or even a stupid nuisance like weeds growing in their garden. If you keep thinking about anything annoying or painful, it will drive you crazy. The key is to learn how to let go, forget and forgive if necessary.

Principal Skills - Focused Attention:

▸ **How to develop the power of *intention*?** Analyze your situation and establish a clear plan of what you intend to do or achieve, announce to yourself what you want to focus on, and be specific; it helps to write things down. For more details, refer to creating intentions in the section on judgment.

▸ **How to develop the power of your *imagination*?** Create multiple images of what you must focus on in your mind using all four modalities starting with your preferred (visual, auditory, physical, or cerebral) mode of processing information. Imagine yourself paying focused attention on your plan.

▸ **How to develop the power of *narration*?** Engage your voice to begin describing exactly what you intend on doing or paying attention to. This requires you to speak, out loud, in a whisper, or silently, everything that you do and what you want to focus on. Practice this vocally first. Then as you improve this skill you will be able to do it sub-vocally just as well. Narrating what you are doing really helps you keep your focus at peak performance.

▸ **How to develop the power of *distraction-negation*?** This requires you to establish a set of criteria about what event could possibly pull your attention away from your focus. If the distraction is not important then negate it, ignore it, let go of it, and immediately return to your task. The criteria for getting distracted should be clear, for example, only your boss or a real emergency. See *Letting Go* described in more detail below.

▸ **How to develop the power of *concentration*?** This refers to your ability to maintain focus on a selected matter observing and responding appropriately to the situation. Create a clear set of goals about your desired results from what you are focused on. Be aware of all the details you are focusing on. As you narrate your activity, cycle around a few main points of your focus, and try to keep it under five elements. As you continue to concentrate, congratulate yourself on being focused. Keep moving your awareness through the main points around your focus in the same order and note any changes. Practice does improve this skill.

▸ **How to develop the power of *prediction*?** Be aware of your progress. Be clear about the rewards you will obtain for focusing successfully and be certain of the consequences (punishment, failure, etc.) if you stop paying attention. When you can clearly describe what to expect, it increases your motivation to succeed and not be distracted.

▸ **How to develop the power of *pacing*?** As you practice concentrating, build up your stamina progressively to become better at focusing for longer periods of time. Be also aware of your limitations; plan and take breaks when your ability to be attentive begins to weaken. Pacing requires you to know how long you can concentrate on any given subject and how often to take short breaks to refresh your mind. When you become tense, it interferes with you ability to pay attention, so remember to remain relaxed.

Power of Relaxing & Letting Go:

To effectively deal with unwanted, annoying, or painful experiences you must be able to physically and mentally escape them. That means sometimes you will find yourself paying attention to the wrong stuff. You may also just find it difficult to focus on the right stuff. Either way you must be able to redirect your attention.

The ability to relax and let go quickly is important because it is vital to both concentration and shifting attention, as well as removing undesirable distractions from your mind. There are two parts to this process: relaxing the body and letting go of the mental focus.

The purpose of relaxing is to change your physical state. Remember when anyone is confronted by a difficult challenge, the natural reaction is to become tense with either more anger or anxiety. If this tension goes over a certain level of stress, it will do more harm than good. Tension and anxiety have a paralyzing effect. Similarly, anger causes mental fogging and impulsiveness. Remaining alert and on-task are the preferred constant goals. Doing this effectively requires you not to get very tense, but rather for you to remain relaxed and comfortable. To maintain mental clarity, you must be able to let go and ignore whatever distractions are not relevant.

The ability to relax physically is a simple skill that many people need to develop. Sure, most people are able to rest well enough, but are you able to relax at any time, anywhere? When something is turning on the alarms in you or someone is pushing all your panic buttons, this is when you especially need to be able to relax, releasing any tension while focusing on the matter.

The ability to mentally let go of problems is equally important because your attention is limited. If you have the wrong stuff in your head, you obviously will not have enough room to deal with the right stuff. The skill to let go, release the focus of your attention, to forget it and to put it out of your mind takes time to develop. Letting go means to stop thinking about what you would objectively categorize as a distraction. In general, these distractions can be events that hold your attention despite your desire to not think about them. Distractions come in many varieties. They can be very important events or people, as well as silly, stupid, or completely irrelevant items that monopolize your attention. The key is to be able to first identify what is a "distraction" and then learn to ignore it. Together, relaxing and letting go give you the superior ability to deal with difficulties in life.

Principal Skills:

▸ **How to develop the power of *relaxation*?** Get comfortable, become aware of your body, then progressively instruct your body to release all the tension and allow yourself to relax. Become aware of your breathing; slow it down, making it deeper and smoother. Visualize, imagine, or just think about a beautiful, peaceful place that you would feel very safe and comfortable in. Drain your body of all tension, physical, emotional, and mental. Give yourself a few minutes to relax, and notice the physical changes in your body. (In the Appendix see a description of the *Relaxation Program,* which is also a recorded exercise available on CD or on the Internet for those interested in experiencing these tools.)

▸ **How to develop the power of *open awareness*?** This requires you remain alert and very calm as you rely on all your senses to observe the world around you. The key is to constantly let go of every focus, keep shifting and expanding your awareness. This can evolve to the art of transcendence, being deeply connected with the object or event you perceive, but not becoming attached.

▸ **How to develop the power of *releasing*?** Learning to "*Let Go*" of all thoughts, images, feelings, memories, events, people, or items that you decide are distractions is an exercise of your deliberate mind. This is the process of quickly deciding that something is a distraction and not relevant. It is necessary to have a clear set of criteria of what is important versus what is a distraction. Then you can make a decision to release or remove it from your mind. Once you begin to practice this skill, it may help to repeat the vocal command, "I am letting go of ____." This is the process of letting go, of transcending, forgetting, forgiving, ignoring, or removing from the mind and releasing. This is the same skill you use to stop thinking about something as well as applying it to distraction-negation or focus-negation, so that you can better direct your attention. (In the Appendix see a description of the *Letting Go Program,* which is also a recorded exercise available on CD or on the Internet for those interested in experiencing these tools.)

▸ **How to improve your ability to relax and let go?** Start with simple and easy situations that you have the most control over. Practice relaxing at the first sign of tension and then clearly decide what you consider a distraction and make a mental effort to release it and to refocus on what is important. Every time you exercise this skill you will become better and quicker at relaxing and letting go of unwanted matters.

Principal Skills - Shifting Attention:

▸ **How to develop the power of *shifting attention*?** Analyze your situation and establish a clear plan of how you intend to direct your awareness. Determine how slowly or quickly you need to shift your attention and move in the direction you wish to. The most common level of shifting attention is being prepared, receptive, and responsive to a quickly changing environment, much like shopping in a supermarket.

▸ **How to utilize the power of *narration*?**   Engage your voice to at least sub-vocally begin describing exactly what you are doing, constantly shifting attention to something new. This requires you to speak out loud, in a whisper, or silently, everything that you do or whatever goes through your mind.

▸ **How to develop the power of *focus-negation*?**   This requires you to resist keeping anything in your mind for more than a moment. This is accomplished by creating a clear set of criteria about what not to focus on. Do not concentrate on any one subject; instead, keep shifting your awareness to the next item. Unless something really important appears, ignore it completely. This is the skill of focus-negation or open attention that requires you to constantly let go.

▸ **How to utilize the power of *releasing*?**   As you develop your power to shift attention, it also helps you improve your skill of letting go. Carefully select what to pay attention to and what to ignore. Then practice mentally detaching from your observations through a deliberate effort to make quick decisions and focus on the next matter. This skill is also required if you need to stop obsessing about something. (In the Appendix see a description of the *Letting Go Program*)

▸ **How to utilize the skill of *shifting focus*?**   This is an alert state of attention during which your awareness uses all your senses and is spread out over everything in your environment. This is a heightened awareness of where you are, what you are doing, and what is happening around you. Rather than focus on any event, constantly move your attention to the next item. The key is to have a clear set of criteria of what is important versus what is a distraction, and then make it your intention to keep shifting your awareness. Do not focus on any matter for more than a brief moment; remain prepared to deal with each new experience, but do not get stuck. Keep your attention alert, receptive, and forward seeking. Narrate your activity, and be ready for each new experience. Determine the speed and direction of your awareness and embrace the growing overall consciousness. As you proceed, congratulate yourself for being alert and attentive.

▸ **How to develop the power of *expectation*?**   As you develop more experience repeating this exercise, you will be better able to visualize what to expect. Be aware of your progress. Be clear about the rewards you will obtain for remaining alert, shifting your awareness, and be certain of the consequences (punishment, failure, etc.) if you stop shifting and focus on an irrelevant matter. Notice how much you can actually hold in your awareness at any given moment. The ability to predict helps you achieve more and determine the degree of your success.

▸ **How to utilize the power of *pacing*?** As you practice this exercise, build up your stamina progressively to become better at shifting focus for longer periods of time. Be also aware of your limitations. Plan and take breaks when your ability to direct attention begins to weaken. Pacing requires you to know how long you can direct your attention in that open manner. An important key is to breathe slowly, deeply, and deliberately through this process. Learn to take short breaks to refresh your mind.

▸ **How to develop the power of your *open awareness*?** The ultimate destination of wide-open awareness is a heightened, transcendental state of expanded consciousness. Become aware of all that is going on inside your body and all that is around you. Remain alert; constantly change the focus of your attention, expanding it across a very large variety of items and levels. You do not need to respond to any situation; instead, develop your ability not to get attached to any thing, person, event, feeling, or memory. The goal is not to hold anything in your attention for more than a moment. Expand your awareness without keeping anything in focus. Just keep shifting your attention to everything around you. Relying on your senses, notice all the things you can see, hear, feel, taste, or smell. Use your imagination to create images of whatever is around you, the building, your neighborhood, the area, even your part of the world. Equally, go inward to become aware of what is inside of you, your organs, muscles, bones, cells, and so on. This is an exceptional state of awareness that takes time and effort to reach; the rewards are equally remarkable. (In the appendix see a description of the *Open Visualization,* which is also a recorded exercise available on CD.)

In summary, directing attention effectively requires three special skills. *Concentration*, during which you focus your awareness on one narrow area. *Shifting Attention*, during which you remain alert and open your awareness to all that is around you, constantly shifting the focus of your attention. *Relaxing and Letting Go* of unnecessary distractions gives you the power to concentrate better and shift attention more effectively. When you read about the JEEP factors, you will be given specific examples of how valuable these forms of attention are.

Light, like a person must be born;

darkness always exists.

Janusz Kapusta

Chapter 9

Master Key 2   Power of Perception

The intellect has little to do on the road to discovery. There comes a leap in consciousness, call it intuition or what you will, and the solution comes to you, and you don't know how or why.   Albert Einstein

Perception naturally refers to what you pay attention to when observing your world. The senses are portals to various modes of information we all perceive. Every person learns to rely on his or her perceptions, yet there remains a tremendous difference between the quantity and quality of what each of us perceives. The reason we all perceive in a different way is due to what we have inherited and then what we have experienced. Some people are just better at observing than others. The key is to know how to improve your skills of perception which will ultimately increase your awareness and knowledge.

The power of perception represents the multiple skills of acquiring information, integrating it in your mind, and assigning meaning to it. This is knowledge. Although we all do this spontaneously, there are countless differences between us in how we process all this information. That means that any two people perceiving the same event do not have an identical experience of it. This may be obvious; however, the point here is that it is possible to describe what makes your perceptions unique. If you develop the skills of perception you will be able to notice more of what is available in the world around you.

The *Master Key of Perception* is designed to counteract the inherent weaknesses of how your brain actually processes your observations. As described earlier, the brain constructs your sense of reality from all the impressions it perceives. Very often, you do not notice what is really important, or you misunderstand something, or perhaps you create a false impression of an event. This requires that you increase the power of your perception and seek a more objective perspective to correct what may have been mistakes.

How to increase your power of observation?

Consider what specific aspects of your perception make it unique to you. First, remember which modalities you prefer to rely on. Think of how your perceptions would change if you had to use the other modalities (visual, auditory, physical or cerebral). Remember being blindfolded and trying to determine what was before you with your hands? This is an example of relying on a different modality than what you normally use to perceive. Can you increase the power of your perception? It is certainly possible. If you simply increase your attention and focus on something, it will become more vivid and clear to you. If you increase the intensity of what you are observing, it should also become brighter, louder, larger, etc. Most of all, if you expand your awareness of the various dimensions you pay attention to, you will increase your objectivity and improve the power of observation.

The power of your perception depends on the number of sources from which you collect information and how well you pay attention. The better the system works, the more knowledge you collect to serve your needs. Below are several principal skills that can increase your capacity to observe the world around you.

Principal Skills of Perception:

▸   **How to develop the *power of senses*?**   Consider each sensory experience separately and determine how each sense contributes to the perceptions you have.

▸ **How to develop the power of all your *modalities*?** Cycle through all the modalities to expand and strengthen the impressions you perceive. See Table 13 Multiple Modalities below for a list of all the various modalities you might consider. (In the Appendix see a description of the *Exploring Modalities program,* which is also a recorded exercise available on CD or on the internet for those interested in experiencing these tools.)

▸ **How to increase the power of your *thinking*?** Develop your rational, logical thinking skills, and learn to question your observations. (See the Judgment section below for a detailed description.)

▸ **How to develop the power of your *intuition*?** Heighten the sensitivity of your intuitive impressions. Learn when to rely on your gut feelings. (See the Judgment section below for a detailed description.)

▸ **How to expand your perspective?** Develop your sense of objectivity and seek ways to widen the horizons of your perspective. Objectivity requires that you escape your subjective prejudice and search for a more universal understanding. By accessing your higher self, you tend to see a more objective perspective. (See the Higher Self section below for a detailed description.)

▸ **How to consider many different dimensions?** Your perception depends on your approach in gathering information. The more various dimensions you think about, the greater the number of impressions you will collect. Dimensions can be on the physical, concrete, or mental and abstract levels. Refer to Table 14, which contains a brief list of different dimensions upon which we can expand our perceptions. These generally reflect the polarities that exist in our world.

▸ **How to develop the *power* of perception?** Continually make an effort to expand your skills of observation, and do not accept the first impressions. Do not trust your senses without verification. Develop the power of your judgment to better evaluate your perceptions.

In summary, the key to increasing the power of your perception is to expand the sources of your information, especially from your higher mind where you can expect to access a more objective view of reality. The various modalities and dimensions described offer additional ideas of what to "look" for when you are analyzing a situation. The more of these rules you apply, the more you will perceive.

John Ryder, Ph.D.

Table 13. Multiple Modalities of Perception:

Core Senses	Submodalities
Visual:	eyes, visual acuity, depth, color, sensitivity, hues, contrast, brightness...
Auditory:	ears, positional sense, sound, tone, pitch, volume, timbre, harmonics, voice recognition, pressure, emotions
Physical:	**Touch:** body, pressure, vibration, temperature, itch, weight, movement...
	Taste: tongue, mouth, temperature, sweet, salty, bitter, pungent, spicy...
	Smell: nose, aromas, sweet, spicy, arid, moist, noxious...
Cerebral:	brain, thinking logically, analytically, serial or parallel processing, reasoning, imagination - abstract and concrete, levels of alertness ...

Everything is Connected: *Sitting, raise your right foot and turn it in clockwise circle. At the same time, raise your right hand a draw the number six in the air. Why does your foot change directions? Try this, it is strange.*

Table 14. Multiple Dimensions or Spectrums of Perception. Many behaviors are on a continuum from one polarity to the opposite polarity. Below is a variety of different dimensions or dualities. The more dimensions you consider while perceiving your world, the more diverse and balanced your perspective will be. As you review this list, ask yourself, 'how often do you get entangled at one end at the expense of the other?'

logical vs intuitive	universal vs local
focused vs diffused	infinite vs finite
objective vs subjective	whole vs part
important vs unimportant	general vs specific
resonating vs antagonistic	unique vs common
concrete vs abstract	free vs limited
real vs illusion	deliberate vs accidental
direct vs indirect	obvious vs concealed
powerful vs weak	order vs chaos
dull vs exciting	absolute vs relative
independent vs dependent	increasing vs decreasing
reward vs punishment	simple vs difficult
attractive vs repulsive	new vs old
positive vs negative	open vs closed
developed vs inborn	present vs past
spiritual vs materialistic	present vs future

Chapter 10

Master Key 3   Power of the Higher Self

> Experience is not what happens to a man. It is what a man does
> with what happens to him.   Aldous Huxley

There is a regular self-image or identity that contains all of your normal subjective thoughts and feelings. When you access the higher self you get power to be more objective and have a deeper awareness of your true individuality. This part is also in charge of planning your intentions, directing your will power, and monitoring your progress. This higher self can direct your attention to observe what you deem relevant and store those perceptions for later use.

The higher self is an elevated perspective of a more objective reality. It also represents the most intimate self-awareness. When you strip yourself of all your physical, social, and personality traits, what is left is that inner, core essence of your higher self. The word "higher" refers to the self that remains above the influences of the lower parts of the mind and is closely connected to the ultimate nature of humanity. Taken concretely, this represents your morality, compassion, empathy, and all the noble or desirable virtues. Taken more spiritually, (for those who believe) this refers to your spirit, the soul, the immortal aspect that is experiencing life. This is the seat or deepest aspect of your consciousness.

The power of the higher self is in its ability to be free of influences from negative emotions, automatic patterns, or misperceptions. This is achieved by learning to enter that state of higher awareness and by following the criteria to establish the most objective perspective possible.

To enter your higher self you must first think "up," become deliberate, and separate yourself from any lower nature emotions, negative patterns, even the ego and attachments. Then increase awareness of what you are experiencing until you are directly connected to the source of the information. Then embrace this core of being; be present in the moment, and experience the sense of Iness from deep within.

Principal Skills of the Higher Self:

▸ **How to *access* your Higher Self?** First, think "up" (to the top of your deliberate mind) to directly experience your conscious awareness, and then become very purposeful in carefully directing your attention. This is how you become deliberate in your actions. Acknowledge that you are "in" your higher self and free from the influence of the lower, negative emotions or destructive patterns. Now you are within the core part of your being, your essence, the one that knows, directs, decides, and experiences life.

▸ **What do you *achieve* in the Higher Self?** Entering higher self-awareness instantly places you in charge and control of all the other systems. From the higher self, you can direct your attention, perceptions, passion, will power, judgment, make decisions, acquire knowledge, transform negative polarities into positive ones, and achieve your potentials.

▸ **How is the *higher self* more objective?** Whenever you act from the higher self, your actions are automatically more objective because you are not under the influence of the other parts of the mind. Secondly, you can instruct yourself to follow very objective criteria to be even more certain to avoid your subjective nature, which is prone to distortions and prejudice. This frame of reference allows you to think about the world in abstract terms so that you can go outside your own experience.

▸ **How do you become most *objective* in your actions?** The higher self can establish a set of criteria that clearly determine how to think, perceive, and respond objectively. In order to be objective, you can ask the following questions with respect to some planned action:

1. How would others experience this action if I do it my way?
2. What would others do, feel, or think if I do this action my way?
3. If someone else did this action to me, what would I experience?
4. What will be short and long term consequences if I do this action?
5. Am I taking everything into consideration before taking this action?

▸ **How does the higher self *make decisions*?** The main advantage of the higher self is the possibility of achieving a wider perspective where you can consider all the knowledge, facts, intuitive feelings, and predictions to make a clear judgment. Once you have completed your analysis and prioritized your alternatives, a decision is much easier to make. This is when you hear yourself say "I have decided ____."

▸ **How does the higher self *create intentions*?** There are big differences between an urge, a craving, or an impulse and what you decide you really want to achieve. An intention arises from the higher self. After you have analyzed a situation and made your judgments, then you are ready to make a decision about your desired goals. When you take the time to think about and decide what you want, that becomes your true intention; these are your plans that you can achieve.

▸ **How can the higher self access *altered states of consciousness*?** The mind is capable of many states of awareness. The most important doorway is through the higher self. It gives you access to every possible level of consciousness, even the mystical states of higher cosmic awareness.

In summary, the higher self is the ultimate director of your awareness. It makes decisions and enforces your intentions by directing your will power. It promotes objectivity because it can assume an abstract perspective and raise and answer questions so you can verify your subjective perceptions.

Your Higher Self is the conductor of your life.

Chapter 11

Master Key 4   The Power of Passionate Energy

> I do the very best I know how - the very best I can; and I mean to
> keep on doing it until the end.   Abraham Lincoln

We are all born with an internal radar that constantly measures the amount of energy inside of us and around us. No one requires instructions to understand energy or to feel it. In fact, it is rather difficult to describe it. Passion is one form of energy that you utilize every day to some degree. It is the higher self that can demand your body to generate more or less of this energy. In life, energy is the principal commodity that keeps you alive and functioning.

Energy is movement, as opposed to matter, which is stationary. All activity requires energy to flow and be utilized. What energy and matter have in common is *vibration*. Even solid objects have a degree of vibration, whereas energy has a much higher amount of vibration. Energy must be stored in matter like batteries, gasoline, springs, dynamite, calories, etc. Every human is able to gather, store, and use energy well, but how many people master these skills? This is not a question of your diet. Although you do obtain energy from the nutrients in food, you get far more from the world around us if you know how to absorb it.

Among people, energy is most commonly experienced in emotions, more specifically, the tone of voice, the brightness of a smile, the firmness of a handshake, or the strength of an embrace. Literally every movement you make relates the amount of energy you are expressing. We are all very sensitive to the amount of energy we are expending compared to what we are receiving. When the exchange is in balance, everyone is happy; when it is not, then someone experiences stress. The reason for the stress is that energy is a very precious commodity to each of us, and so it is disturbing to feel an imbalance or its loss. Part of our success in life depends on mastering the use of energy and maintaining the best structures to store it. Therefore, it is advisable to keep your body healthy and constantly charge up on good energy.

We are very quick to "read" a person's energy, whether or not we like the way he or she moves, sounds, and/or expresses him or herself. We often refer to this energy as the person's vibration. I like to call it his or her **"vibe"** for short. This describes another curious aspect of the vibration of energy, its *resonance*. When two things vibrate in a similar way, they resonate (like two notes on a piano an octave apart). This reflects our personal preferences because when we come in contact with an event, a person, or even a thing whose energy vibrates in synch with our own, we are automatically attracted and feel comfortable. That is what we refer to as good energy. Similarly, when we observe something out of sync with us, we get uncomfortable and want to avoid it, what we might call bad energy. Every person is sensitive to the resonance of vibrations around him or her, some more than others. This is part of our internal radar system that tells us when we are near pleasant or bad vibrations. This radar is a positive part of the reflexive mind.

Passion itself is not an emotion; it is the energy, intensity, and power behind the feelings we experience or actions we perform. Passion can be expressed in an infinite number of degrees from extremely mild to very wild and intense. It can be applied to any activity, be it emotional, physical, or intellectual. Passion turns up the volume, brightens the colors, and also makes things much more memorable. Whatever you do, when you do it passionately, you simply put more energy into it than is required. The degree to which you put more energy than required is the degree of your passion.

What are the three levels of conscious energy?

Our life activities can be divided into three basic levels of energy. These reflect the three most common states of consciousness. Our normal state of energy is **passive** awareness. That means that we are awake, observing what is going on, ready to respond, but remain idle, or we are performing a routine that requires little deliberate action. Any sort of simple, robotic task, like peeling potatoes, or as more commonly seen in the couch potato squeezing a remote control. The next level of energy is **active** awareness, where you are acting deliberately with specific intentions and doing so with a degree of motivation and passion – like writing a business letter or assembling a new computer system. The highest level is **energized** awareness, usually brief periods during which you are extremely alert, deliberate, creative, absorbed in your task, focused, determined, and actually molding events around yourself. These rare moments are the most memorable events of your life. They can be very natural, like giving birth for a woman, or very deliberate, like a soldier running out into a battle field to rescue a comrade under fire.

Passion represents the amount of energy flowing: in, out, and around you. Passion can refer to what you are putting into your internal or external activities. It is also what you pick up from others and events around you, like your favorite singer performing a concert or driving your dream car. Passion is the energy you receive, create, hold, and spend. Energy, in general, appears in many forms. Money is obviously a form of energy as well. You learn to gather it, store it, and use it; most of all you enjoy it when energy flows abundantly.

Principal Skills for Passionate Energy:

▸ **How to develop your power to *read energy* better?** First, become aware of the different sources or types of energy; and then consider how it impacts you. Does the energy affect you in a personal, social, economic, environmental, or even a cosmic way? As you begin to identify the type of energy you are dealing with, then you can quantify it - how much is there?

▸ **How do you develop the power to *measure energy* better?** We all have an internal radar that automatically measures energy levels, but you can perform this task deliberately. When you take the time to analyze the level of passion you feel, you are receiving, or you are expressing, you will always get a specific reading (low, medium or high), whatever it really is. Imagine a scale that goes from 0 – 100 so that you can rank the amount of energy you observe more objectively. Repeat this process deliberately so that you develop better awareness of the amount of passion.

▸ **How to better *acknowledge* the level of passion around you?** The key to keep the energy flowing is to always notice it and at least acknowledge your awareness of the movement. Usually, most people just react to energy. You can choose to respond to it as well, return it, or reciprocate in some way. Make it clearly known to yourself and others that you are aware of the energy flowing and whether you want to approach it or avoid it. If pleasant, express your gratitude.

▸ **How to determine which energy is *resonating* with you?** Most of the time the answer is rather obvious; either the energy is attracting or repelling. When you are confused whether the energy is resonating with you or not, make an attempt to connect with the source and notice what the dominant mode the energy is in. The passion you are experiencing may be either visual, auditory, physical, or in the cerebral modalities. That may be in sync with your preferred modality or not. If it is not in sync, then you may experience a modality mis-match, a grinding of gears, or a clash of some sort. Resonance is an experience of harmony and closeness.

▸ **How to *connect* with the passionate energy?** There is always an abundance of energy around you at all times. The question is how do you connect to this flow of energy? The answer is to tune yourself to the energy you would like to receive. Notice the source of energy; and then adjust your own passion to be in harmony with the vibration surrounding you. You may need to turn your passion down, or crank it up, depending on the situation.

▸ **What to do to *create passionate energy*?** The key to producing more energy rests upon having a strong healthy body, being in sync with your environment, not feeling stressed, and expressing complete confidence while performing at your peak ability. Whatever you do requires energy. To do the same action with tremendous passionate energy only takes a little more physical strength, but a lot more psychological power. The ability to focus, direct your attention, and feel the excitement of performing something you love to do, are all natural experiences. Practicing being passionate about your activities builds strength and confidence to achieve your goals with greater energy. (In the Appendix you will find information about live workshops that address this subject with exercises to enhance your connection to passion and create more of it; see the ***Power Move***.)

▸ **How to keep the passion of *energy flowing*?** The most natural state for energy is to flow. If you do not block it, it will continue to flow. Make it your intention to read, measure, acknowledge, connect to the energy, and create more of it generously. Passion does not have a price. It is our freedom to express as much passionate energy as we desire. The more we create, the more energy will flow. It is also important to observe others; when you notice others blocking or letting energy drain, offer your assistance. It is possible for every person to become more mindful of the energy flowing around him or her.

▸ **How to promote the *flow of prosperity*?** The world is full of energy. If you acknowledge the presence of passion around us, you will promote its flow. Prosperity depends on the continuous exchange of energy; the more energy flows among us, the more prosperity it brings. This may be in any form – spiritual, artistic, love, prizes, goals, wealth, and of course, money. To keep the power of prosperity flowing, connect to sources of such energy with appreciation. Do what you can to utilize the energy and pass it on.

In summary, the key to managing energy is to be aware of how and where it is flowing. We all realize that everything around us has a vibration or vibe. When you resonate with that energy it is likely to flow more effectively. If you do not resonate with that vibe, the energy will not flow as easily. If you make an effort to be aware of the energy moving, you can promote a better exchange of it.

Think & Up

Chapter 12

Master Key 5   Will Power

> Nothing in the world can take the place of persistence. Talent will not;
> nothing is more common than unsuccessful men with talent. Genius will
> not; unrewarded genius is almost a proverb. Education will not; the world
> is full of educated derelicts. Persistence and determination alone are
> omnipotent.   Calvin Coolidge

This is the ultimate master key in my opinion. When you consider all the
things that challenge you throughout life, your will power is probably the
single most vital skill to utilize in overcoming obstacles and reaching your
goals. The will is the driving force of your deliberate mind to fulfill your
intentions. It gives you stamina and patience to persevere even when
everything else is telling you to quit or give up.

Will power is a deeply rooted natural skill we are all born with. In essence,
this begins as our urge to live, to survive, to eat, sleep, to explore, and so
on. Every person learns to use his or her will power to accomplish his or
her intentions every day. However, not everyone can apply his or her will
power to achieve all his or her intentions the same way. We all recognize
the tremendous differences between individuals and the differing degrees
of will power each of us has. These differences can be found in the normal
limitations of how the mind works and the lack of skills people have in
applying their will power to achieve desired ends.

Typically, most people consider will power to be the ability to resist a
temptation, or stubbornness, or someone imposing his/her will on others.
In reality, will power is much more. It represents a complex set of skills
that gives the individual the greatest amount of control over his or her
actions. The key factor is to determine what your intentions are. Once
your higher self decides your intentions, then you must learn to direct your
will power to achieve those plans.

Principal Skills of Will Power:

▸ **How to clearly *identify will power*?**   You must align your intentions with your passion and relentless determination to make something happen, to experience will power. For example, connect to a basic urge, like feeling very hungry, and then become aware of what you do to obtain food. Most likely, you decide what you want to eat; then you go get the food, and happily place it in your mouth. Following similar steps, establish a very clear, specific intention, then call up your passion to obtain this intention, and pursue it with total determination. The experience of your special effort to complete this task is your will power. The key is to be aware of the "muscle" of your will power working to reach your goals.

▸ **How do you *develop* your will power?**   The power of your will depends on the following skills:

1. Enter your higher self awareness, focus on what you personally desire. Establish very clear intentions, plans, and a detailed vision of your goals.

2. Exercise your imagination to visualize, verbalize, and write out your intentions along with the strategies, schedules, goals, deadlines, rewards and be aware of what the cost of failure would be.

3. Mobilize your passion by raising energy levels of your motivation to peak levels.

4. Focus your attention. Become very deliberate, and monitor your progress carefully.

5. Raise your convictions to obtain rewards from your ultimate success.

6. Be prepared to carry any burdens, face any challenge, fight any force.

7. Affirm your determination to reach your goals regardless of all obstacles.

▸ **How to *direct* your will power most effectively?**   Think up! Go to your higher self, clearly identify your intentions, and determine a plan to accomplish these goals. Visualize the steps you must take to reach success. Now, call up your passion, energize your will power and begin working on your plans.

▸ **How do you *maximize the strength* of your will power?**   First, you must be very clear about your plans and goals. You must raise your motivation to its peak levels, focus your attention on the required steps, and begin narrating your progress. Pace yourself, building up your stamina, to reach your desired goals. The strength of your will power is ultimately measured by your determination when confronted by growing challenges. Follow rule number one: never give up!

▸ **How does will power give you *self-control*?** Once your higher self has decided your intentions, then you can direct your will power to realize these goals; they may be physical, mental, abstract, or concrete. You can use will power to actualize any type of goal – it may be something to achieve or avoid. This is your self-control – being able to overcome either internal desires or external pressures to make you do something you have decided not to do, or forcing yourself to do something aligned with your intentions. You can instruct your will to stop you from giving into a temptation, or have it push you to reach difficult goals.

▸ **What is the difference between *stubbornness* and will power?** Stubbornness refers to a person's refusal to go along with someone else's will, which may not be an exercise of will power or personal intentions, just a matter of ego. When the matter is a choice between two people, a fair relationship is based on some degree of reciprocity, going along with another person's desires. The other case of stubbornness is in foolish defeat. When your plans cannot be successful due to overwhelming odds, it is wiser to change directions than fail to make progress.

▸ **When are we supposed to *surrender* our will?** There are times when we realize that our intentions are not immediately possible. When our efforts are met with obstacles much greater than the resources we command, then it may be wise to surrender our intentions or at least reorganize our plans to minimize the waste of time and energy on intentions that definitely cannot be realized.

In summary, you are in position to direct your behavior in countless ways. When you decide on a specific intention, then you can recruit your will power to achieve these goals very deliberately. This gives you the most control over your activities. Those individuals who argue that will power is an illusion are right; they have not learned how to be deliberate. These are skills anyone can master if he or she learns the steps and practices.

> **If you don't get what you want, it is a sign either that you did not seriously want it, or that you tried to bargain over the price. Rudyard Kipling**

Chapter 13

Master Key 6   The Power of Judgment

A man's most valuable trait is a judicious sense of what not to believe.

Euripides

Thinking is a fundamental activity; how well we do it varies tremendously. Judgment refers to the ability to think clearly or intuit sensibly, analyze situations, and make good decisions. Those decisions that promote progress can be called "good." Those that cause trouble or stress is not good. There are rules about thinking, sensing, evaluating, discriminating, and making choices. If you follow these rules, your judgment improves; if you do not, you become more likely to make bad decisions. There are many reasons that we make poor choices, mainly because judgment is dependent on all the other master keys mentioned. If any of those keys are not working well, then our judgment will suffer. In addition, the reflexive and automatic parts of the mind can result in extremely bad decisions. Finally, there are cultural influences or prejudices that can make judgments unjust. Consequently, superior judgment is the product of an exceedingly well-developed, open mind that contains vital knowledge and required skills to think clearly.

This master key is meant to alert you to the various levels of thinking and the skills necessary to improve your judgment. This is the most complex key to develop because it involves so many different abilities. Most of us are born with the ability to think rationally, yet we hear of more people doing stupid things than brilliant ones. All of us occasionally do something idiotic or brilliant; wouldn't it be good to avoid stupidity and spend more time being brilliant?

Judgment most specifically relates to the process of comparing alternatives and selecting the best one to follow. This act is in fact a very complex process that relies on numerous other factors. Judgment requires the ability to juggle abstract concepts in the mind. This means imagining different possibilities and figuring out which one is the best, smartest, and most advantageous. However, even the most superior judgment can be mistaken. The reason for the failure of even the most intelligent judgments is that we cannot always accurately predict what will happen. This is why history is full of very bad decisions. Despite the difficulty of making good, intelligent judgments, there is a simple set of criteria that you can follow to promote the best judgment possible.

What do you need to improve your judgment?

To begin, your judgment depends on developing the power of each of the master keys described (directing attention, accurate perception, higher self awareness, passionate energy, and strong will power). Second, you need to obtain vital knowledge (laws about the universe, cause and effect, energy, and so on), storing it in your memory for quick recall and comparison. Third, you must learn to make predictions and check results. Finally, you must develop and exercise the power of your judgment to make decisions. This means you need to implement a "thinking system."

Making *predictions* requires you to imagine or work-out in your mind what could happen if you follow one path versus another. This skill is primarily dependent on experience; the more of it you have, the easier it is for you to predict what will be, but because of uncertainty in our world, you can never be sure. There is always that possibility that something strange will occur that no one could have predicted. That is a simple fact of life. Evaluating your results and comparing them to what you predicted is the other half of this skill. This process constantly adds valuable information to your bank of experience. Effectively predicting what will happen promotes superior judgment.

What are the two basic ways we think?

As mentioned in the introduction, there are two approaches to making judgments, besides flipping a coin – the rational and the intuitive. The **rational approach** is the logical system of thinking that relies on facts and details. The **intuitive approach** is based on the feelings we experience or vibrations around us. Both approaches give us information. The first is more objective; the second is more subjective. Either one can help us determine the best choice. However, either one or both can also be wrong. That is the reality we must accept; no matter how intelligent you are or how much you know, even if you work out every possible logical detail perfectly, you can be totally wrong. Similarly, you may have the most powerful intuition, be ready to bet your life on a feeling and still be completely mistaken.

If you are ready to <u>accept the uncertainty of life</u>, then you can arm yourself with the most powerful weapons to defeat an uncertain future and achieve greater success. We are not born logical or with the ability to think rationally. As we learn to speak, we develop the ability to think rationally because all languages follow logical rules. This is the basic, rational thinking process we all develop growing up, which allows us to make sense of the world and understand what is going on around us. This thinking process enables us to gain knowledge and improve our thinking, but equally it is vulnerable to distort reality, ignore relevant things, and even defend our stupidity, ignorance, or insanity.

The fundamental ability to think allows us to learn and accumulate knowledge. Learning is unlimited. What you learn and how much you learn is up to you. The thinking skills you acquire from language are enough to make anyone a genius, but it is easier to be passive, lazy, apathetic, and not to make the effort to learn more. If you make an effort, it is relatively easy to learn the skills to think more effectively, relying on rules of logic, thinking more scientifically, and even to experience moments of brilliant insight or creativity.

Rational thinking naturally evolves from instruction through common sense, to more analytical logical reasoning. Rational thinking is most suited to effectively deal with objective facts, details, organizing, prioritizing agendas, measuring, and building in the material world. The rational approach provides an excellent system to evaluate, analyze, and determine which options are best when dealing with concrete matters like technical, mechanical, economic, medical, educational processes, and so on. See Table 15 *Different Levels of Thinking* for a description of the spectrum.

On the other hand, we are all born with some sort of internal intuitive radar. Whatever intuition is, we all experience feelings that something is either safe or dangerous, something to approach or avoid. These feelings are very simple, but extremely valuable. An intuition can be a sudden physical experience – a "gut feeling" that is difficult to explain logically, but may offer important information. It may also be instant knowledge, a pre-cognition, a message, or an image of some sort. Intuitions are those internal flashes of insight that urge a person to do one thing more than another. Intuition can work on the concrete factual details or the abstract emotional energy.

Your intuition is constantly working, providing you with information about what kind of vibrations or energy are around you. This information is usually more valuable in our human matters, dealing with the emotional life, relationships, family issues, art, music, career directions, and so on. These are very subjective questions that often only your intuition can offer you any insight. See Table 16 *The Intuition and Messages it Sends*. This table explains the more common intuitions that we experience.

What are your choices when you make decisions?

The process of making a decision can be impulsive, thoughtless, poorly evaluated, or is just a reaction to circumstances you may be in. Those decisions most often bring regret and dissatisfaction because you actually did not make a decision and the results were rarely what you really wished for. To review all the information about the choices you have requires time and effort. Use your higher self to direct your attention to observe all the relevant information, to carefully analyze your predictions, compare possibilities, and then you can come to a conclusion. That conclusion can be based on rational analysis, intuitive feelings, or both approaches to give you the most comfort deep inside as you make your decision. The selection of what you believe to be the best choice ideally is made by your higher self and then initiated by your will into action.

> Two things are infinite: the universe and human stupidity; and I'm not sure about the universe.   Albert Einstein

To make progress you must decide which way to go.

Janusz Kapusta

Table 15. Different Levels of Thinking

Thinking	*Description of thought processes*	*Examples*
Genius	exceptional insight into our world's reality	Einstein
Creative	contributing with special talents to improve the quality of life for all artistically, scientifically, etc...	Lennon & McCartney
Scientific	generating theories, evidence, and eventually proving the nature of our reality	Crick & Watson
Critical	analyzing, comparing, investigating, eliminating, calculating, and determining what works	Thomas Edison
Logical	analytical, pragmatic, objective observation, research, prediction, reliable, reproducible, factual information that is empirically verifiable	some people
Common Sense	experiential awareness of how things work, understanding cause and effect	many people
Rational	sensible interpretation of meaning, reasonable understanding of the world, able to work and play	**all people**
Robotic	concrete following of regulations, slips-of-the-tongue, bad patterns, very simplistic	all people
Stupidity	repeating mistakes, unable to learn, obvious errors, narrow minded, unaware of the world or consequences, illogical	most of us Homer Simpson
Primitive	ignorant, uneducated, lack experience,	some of us
Madness	weird, ridiculous, irrational, paranoid, distressed insane, deranged, fanatical, obsessed, irrational	Hitler
Psychotic	schizophrenic, irrational, delusions, hallucinations	very few
Retarded	brain damaged, extremely limited thinking	very few

Table 16. The Intuition and Messages It Sends

Experience	Description of sensations
Vivid Images	mental picture of a person or event, can be positive urging you to approach or negative to be avoided
Sensations	gut feelings that either attracts you or repels you
Premonition	a distinct image or story of what is to happen
Deja vu	feeling you've been somewhere, or seen something that you know you have not visited or seen before
Psychic	mental or intuitive perceptions of people or events
Clairvoyance	insights into spiritual matters, life beyond death
ESP, 6th sense	extra-sensory perception, knowledge without learning, instant awareness of something
Telepathy	ability to read others thoughts or to project ideas
Dreams	nocturnal visions, stories, and experiences that may have significant meaning about the past or future
Awareness	vibrations of surrounding environment or people
Inkling	subtle sense of something attracting or repelling you, a gentle intuitive feeling
Faint Whisper	sense of a message sent to you telling a story, an inner voice telling you to do something
Instincts	sudden alarm warning to be prepared for an intense event, fight or flight system, your radar

The intuitive mind is a sacred gift and the rational mind is a faithful servant. We have created a society that honors the servant and has forgotten the gift.

Albert Einstein

Principal Skills for Judgment:

▸ **How to *prepare* to make judgments?** Begin by engaging your higher self awareness. Direct your attention to perceive all the details around you, gather up your passionate energy, and finally focus your will to evaluate, compare, and make a judgment.

▸ **Did you *identify* exactly what is the problem?** Clarity of the issue is important to start collecting information. The problem may be concrete or abstract, but it is necessary for you to put it into easy-to-understand language so that your intentions to solve the issue can be equally as clear. Make an effort to describe the problem in the most objective and descriptive terms possible.

▸ **How *significant* is your decision?** Do not forget to evaluate how important the issue you are working on is to you and others.   The consequences of your choices require you to imagine what will happen if you follow one path versus another.

▸ **Can you determine if you *know* enough to make a decision?** Often the information you need to obtain before making a decision is hidden or not apparent. As you analyze your situation, you must ask whether there is additional information that needs to be uncovered before you make a choice. If you realize that you do not have enough information, avoid a decision and try to gather more details.

▸ **Are the *causes and effects* clearly established?** This is a matter to determine if X-event can cause Y-consequence. Even the most brilliant scientists have a difficult time with this issue sometimes because it may be very tricky to figure out exactly what causes what. Below are several questions you should be able to consider:

1. What is the simplest explanation you can find to this problem?
2. Are you certain that X-event is sufficient to cause Y-effect on its own?
3. Are you certain that X-event is necessary to produce Y-effect?
4. When you observe X-event does it always produce Y-effect?

▸ **What do the *rational and intuitive* factors indicate?** The rational, or objective information, offers valuable details about concrete facts, while intuition, or subjective information, provides important insights about impressions, feelings, and human matters. Do not ignore either source of information. If you can combine these two factors, they should help you reach a better decision. If there is a conflict between the rational and intuitive, review everything more carefully, measuring the strength of the objective and subjective evidence before making a decision.

▸ **How to *analyze* all available information?** The process of reviewing, investigating, and calculating what is important is a complex series of steps that literally occur in the abstract dimension of your imagination. If possible, write down your ideas. One of the keys is to rely on your preferred mode (i.e., visual or verbal) to make your search more meaningful. Analyzing requires that you check both the subjective and objective information and find appropriate ways to prioritize your findings based on what is most significant. Use multiple modalities to increase the amount of information you think about.

▸ **How to make *predictions* based on what you discovered?** As you analyze your observations, you can begin to imagine what will happen in the future if this or that event occurs. Predicting outcomes is a simple exercise that creates stories about what you are likely to experience. As you imagine these future events, consider their consequences for yourself and others.

▸ **How to make *comparisons* between different ideas?** The key is to imagine the various predictions you have been considering and make direct comparisons between them. First, you must establish a set of criteria (what you want) to measure each prediction. The more choices you have, the more complex this task becomes, so as you compare possibilities, drop any that do not meet your criteria. The comparisons must ultimately lead to a short list of the top two or three choices. If you have difficulty doing this in your mind, write the alternatives down in columns to see and compare your options.

▸ **How to determine *what to avoid* before making a decision?** If you do not want to make a mistake, it is important to consider what you should avoid. How would your decision affect others? Is it possible your actions will be harmful, destructive, irritating, disturbing, invasive, rude, or troubling in some other way to yourself or others? This requires you to consider more objectively how your decisions will be seen by others.

▸ **What will *clarify* your choices if you remain uncertain about your decision?** There is a simple question you can always answer that will provide you with an additional perspective. The clarity question is: ___*can you afford to make this mistake?*___ That is, if you choose this path, can you afford the costs of the trouble if it turns out to be the wrong decision? This gives you a concrete measure of what will happen if your choice does not lead where you want it to. The opposite question may also be valuable: *can you afford not to take action?* What are the likely results if you do not make a decision and leave things the way they are?

▸ **How to calculate your level of *confidence*?** Most decisions we make are relatively simple, but when they get both complex and important, then you want an extra gauge to measure your own certainty. The level of confidence is an indication of how sure you can be about the choice you want to make. This measure is dependent on experience; the more of it you accumulate, the easier it becomes for you to determine what level of certainty you feel regarding some choice.

▸ **How to make *judgments* that you are comfortable with?** The key to making good decisions is to take the time to carefully analyze the situation, prioritize the alternatives intelligently, and then consider what the consequences will be. If you engage the higher self, then you are already more objective and will have a better perspective. When the issue you are trying to determine is a concrete, yes or no decision, you will either be right or have to learn from the experience. Questions that have a large "grey-zone" mean it is important to consider the long-term consequences to avoid short-term benefits that eventually can become regrets. The judgment you are making can either serve your higher mind's interests or something of the lower mind. When you "think up," the decision is most likely to come from your higher nature, which means your choice will be based on the virtues, noble values, and intelligent principles of life that give a greater degree of confidence and comfort. The key is to have a positive attitude about your judgments so that you know that you are always learning and moving forward with your life regardless of the consequences of your decisions.

▸ **How to be comfortable with *uncertainty* of your judgments?** Uncertainty is a fact of life. It does not depend on your judgment, intelligence, wisdom, or experience; it is ever present. Knowing that, offers a universal comfort about all the choices we make in life. You can be certain that uncertainty is likely to appear when least expected, or that chaos will change things in an unpredictable way. Therefore you prepare, brace yourself, and acknowledge that you understand the nature of uncertainty, the laws of cause and effect, and whatever else matters. This is the best comfort you can have; nothing can take it away.

▶ **What happens when your *judgment* is clear and on time?** The skills of making good judgments rely on a variety of factors. When everything falls into place, you are able to make a clear choice, and you can initiate your action with confidence. Your higher self directs your will power to achieve the decisions you have made. You experience the sense of being deliberate, directing your life with meaning and purpose, and driving it towards your goals. This also generates a heightened awareness of being in control of your life and reduces stress.

In summary, judgment is about thinking clearly and making decisions that help you progress in life. The skills required to make good judgments are many and complex. However, if you simply apply some of these rules to making decisions, your life will surely improve. You do not need to be a scientist to make intelligent choices. In fact, it does not matter how smart you are because everyone has the skills necessary to make good judgments if one applies the skills described here. The truth is that we all make bad judgments and extremely poor decisions sometimes. These experiences, of acting stupidly, are there to help you learn how to make better judgments in the future. Due to the way your mind works, you are unfortunately much more prone to make stupid mistakes in life, but any of us can equally rise up and be creative, or even be a genius, for a moment.

Stupidity is always astounding; no matter how often one encounters it.
Jean Cocteau

Chapter 14

Master Key 7 The Power of Replacing Patterns

> **Man's mind, stretched to a new idea, never goes back to its original dimension.   Oliver Wendell Holmes**

We are definitely creatures of habit. The automatic mind (as described in Chapter 3) is responsible for all the good and destructive patterns we engage in. This system is so effective that any behavior you repeat a few times becomes an internal, automatic pattern or program. These patterns can be any kind of routine activity that we train the brain to repeat. In general, patterns simplify our lives because we can learn to do things automatically, which conserves our energy and frees our minds to be busy with other matters. However, this also makes the destructive patterns we repeat our greatest challenge to change because they are deeply programmed into our brains' function. Consequently, the power of this master key is about how to replace unwanted patterns with desirable ones.

The problem with changing patterns is that these programs are outside our normal conscious awareness, so it is very difficult for us to know what we are doing. Patterns or programs that we continually repeat are operating from the automatic mind and not the deliberate mind. How can you change a pattern that you are not conscious of? Well, the answer is that you must direct your awareness to the automatic patterns, and then you can evaluate which ones are worth keeping and which ones are causing sabotage and must be replaced.

How are patterns created?

The ability to train new patterns is inborn; everyone can do it. The more often you repeat a new pattern deliberately and precisely the same way, the faster it becomes a new routine. A new program always brings some form of reward because it satisfies one of our principal needs. Even if the pattern is destructive, it still usually meets one of our major needs: that is what motivates us to repeat it despite its potential sabotage. Consider all the routines that fill your everyday life. Useful patterns are similar to driving a car, typing, signing your name, or the way you laugh at jokes. Similarly, bad patterns are like overeating, constantly getting distracted, becoming very irritable, or any bad habit, which you just accept as part of your life. The truth is that if you do not like the pattern you are in, you can change it. This is another form of polarity shifting because once you identify the programs you do not want to repeat, you can replace them with new patterns that are valuable.

How do we Train New Patterns?

The first step is to ***think UP.*** That means that you must raise your awareness from the lower two parts of the mind to the top of the deliberate mind. Become aware of your higher self and gain a better perspective of your behaviors, both internal (thinking or feelings) and external (activities). Now direct your attention to analyze all of your routines or automatic programs. This requires an effort of objective self-awareness. Vocalize, visualize, and/or write down any negative patterns that could be causing sabotage. The worst of these destructive programs is your negative self-talk. When you think to yourselves that "I am not good enough; I am stupid; I will never succeed; nobody respects me; or it is not worth my trouble" such self-sabotage will effectively paralyze your growth. By clearly identifying negative patterns, you can deliberately write the opposite, positive affirmations to replace the sabotage. Then you must repeat those positive patterns until they become firmly rooted in the automatic mind.

These sabotaging patterns may be the most difficult problem for us to overcome. The power of this master key can be found in following the steps listed here very carefully, to make these otherwise invisible patterns clearly seen so that you can install the changes required. To complete this process you must be also certain that the new patterns satisfy your principal needs even better than the old programs.

Principal Skills for Replacing Patterns:

▸ **How do you *analyze* your automatic patterns?** You must first raise your awareness to the higher self and gain a more objective perspective. From the higher self you can direct your attention to observe and analyze your patterns and programs. Watch what you do; listen to what you say; pay attention to what goes through your mind or the feelings you experience.

▸   **How do you *identify* patterns that should be replaced?**   As you review the various programs you repeat, evaluate them against the following set of criteria:

1. Why did this routine start? Do I do this deliberately or is it a habitual pattern? Is this pattern good for me and others? Does it promote good things?

2.   When you repeat this behavior, does it offend, disturb, annoy, or frustrate others?

3.   What are the results of this routine? Does it generate gratitude and appreciation?

4. Do the mental programs motivate, inspire, energize, build confidence, joy, or instead do they increase stress, anxiety, fears, anger, frustration, and steal hope away?

5. Are these thoughts, feelings, or activities positive, helpful, creative, adding to the wisdom and knowledge you can utilize, or are they rather negative, destructive, critical, and cause tension in your environment?

6. Would you want your child to repeat this program or statement to him or herself?

If any patterns are more negative or destructive to you or others, then consider how you can still meet your needs with a different set of patterns. Make a note of these unwanted patterns; write down what you are doing. If they are negative statements, then write them down exactly as you repeat them. (On the website under Resources you can find a form – "Replacing Patterns" that you can use for this exercise, which makes this process easier. These forms are also available in the *Achievement Workbook*.)

▸ **How do you create *opposite* behavioral patterns that can replace the old ones?**   After you have clearly identified unwanted patterns, you must seek and establish a healthy and positive way to meet your needs. The key to this is usually getting advice from an objective observer. The task is to determine how to satisfy your needs in a constructive and positive manner. This may take a few trials and errors, checking yourself with the criteria above until you succeed.

▸ **How do you create *opposite* mental patterns that can replace the old ones?** Once you have identified the negative statements and written them down, you must write the positive affirmations to replace them. The key to creating the opposite message or program is to formulate a very strong, yet simple statement. There are seven rules to writing affirmations; if you use the following, you should be able to construct your own replacement programs.

The seven rules of writing an affirmation

1. It must be simple.

2. The statement must be clear, not ambiguous.

3. The affirmation should express gratitude for your achievements.

4. You must imply success – that you already possess what you wish for.

5. An affirmation must be positive, not a negative statement.

6. It must be written in the active, present tense.

7. The affirmation must be opposite to the negative statement it is replacing.

▸ **How do you *replace* the negative pattern with a positive program?** The key to this process is to do it deliberately from the higher self so that you are directing this effort from a very conscious perspective. Read the negative statement out loud to evoke a sense of discomfort inside you. Then read the positive statement out loud at least three times. Repeat this exercise several times a day until the negative pattern fades away, being replaced by your positive affirmations. You should not work on more than three to six patterns at a time because it may get confusing.

▸ **How do you *stabilize* the new patterns?** Your automatic mind will now work for you. Every time you repeat the positive program, your mind will continue to create new wiring to direct mental traffic down the new path. To make the patterns more permanent, it is also necessary to be certain that your affirmations satisfy the principal needs that previously rewarded the bad programs. The key is to describe several good ways that the new patterns satisfy your needs. Then you can be certain that your desired changes will become permanent.

In summary, changing patterns is a very tricky business because the old patterns tend to be automatic and out of our awareness. This master key describes the specific steps you must follow to identify the negative patterns and replace them with positive programs you desire. Writing affirmations can be a difficult skill to master. The instructions here provide the rules to follow, but if you need help you may wish to check my website (**JohnRyderPhD.com**) for a list of positive affirmations, under resources. In addition, be alert that when you begin changing these old patterns, your automatic mind will surely protest by perhaps even creating new bad programs. It is your task to review what is going on and constantly clean up any negativity. In the chapter on Patterns, you will find examples of how this works.

Chapter 15

Master Key 8 The Power of Transforming

Do unto others, as you would want others to do unto you.

Jesus Christ

The concept of transformation refers to any possible change; combined with polarity shifting it means reversing direction into the opposite one. This is the fundamental concept of this book, to become aware of the direction you are going in. If it is wrong, unwanted, stupid, etc., then turn around and head in a better direction. The power of transforming lies in application of the rules described here to shift polarities from negative to positive. The more time you spend in the happy, healthy, and rewarding direction, the more fulfilling your life becomes.

As quoted in the Bible, Jesus offered a profound axiom for people to live by. The problem is that we find it difficult to act "spiritually" because our physical nature has a very powerful influence over us. Perhaps Jesus could be understood as an early advocate of polarity shifting because there truly is much to be gained from this process whether you are religious or not.

The master key of transforming is simple and universal. The reason it is so simple is because change is a basic building block of nature, so for us to live we must be able to change, adapt, keep the energy flowing, and direct our will power to achieve our dreams. Transformation is a set of rules to help us change whenever change is desirable. The reason it is universal is because the very nature of our universe is full of natural polarities. Nearly every category of life you can name has a spectrum that goes from the lowest to the highest, or from smallest to biggest, or most negative to totally positive. This represents the "Yin and Yang" of the Eastern philosophy. Since we live among polarities, then shifting polarities means transforming or changing our place from one spot on the spectrum to a better one. This makes transformation a universal aspect of change.

The key to successful and meaningful change is not about a small correction of direction or speed, but rather requires a significant reversal of direction - a polarity shift! As I have been explaining, your mind does not work to your benefit all the time. Our predisposition is to be pulled downward into fear, anger, pain, or disgust, to act impulsively, subjectively without concern for others, or even get stuck in self-destructive patterns. Our nature is biased, slanted, prone to, and more susceptible to the negative, much more than to the positive. To escape this stressful imbalance, you must shift polarities. By accessing your higher self, you can direct your attention, be more objective, and command your will power to achieve desired intentions. When you realize you are not where you want to be, make a polarity shift, reverse directions, and transform your situation for the better.

Naturally, when we are going in a relatively good direction, then transforming does not require a major reversal of direction, but rather just an adjustment. There are specific questions you must raise to determine if you are going in the best direction or not. This is a matter of superior judgment that was described previously.

What exactly do you want to transform?

Anything can be transformed. The most important thing to transform is your lower nature into your higher nature. If you recall, I described how reflexive emotions cause stress and how you must think "up" (to the deliberate mind) and learn to use your positive emotions. If you can accomplish this task, it will become easier to transform many other negative polarities. For example, it would be great to transform all of these: poverty into wealth, illness into health, weakness into strength, apathy into ambition, confusion into clarity, destructive forces into creative, segregation into integration, ugliness into beauty, pessimism into optimism, or even failure into success.

The organization of the Triplex Mind is changing the basic understanding of psychology. The reflexive part has its positive and negative aspects, those with which we are all born. While this system can guide us with intuitions, or just help us survive, the reflexive emotions usually cause stress, suffering, and chaos. The lower nature is not just the reflexive emotions, but also the dark, vile, mean, ugly, primitive, and generally unpleasant aspects of being a human. In contrast, the higher nature is more than just the deliberate positive emotions we learn to express; it represents our noble virtues, altruistic actions, idealism, and the lighter, good side of humanity; in essence, it is our spirituality. The key is to escape the reflexive mind and go up to the deliberate mind, the source of our higher emotions.

How to transform our primitive nature into our spiritual one?

The ultimate power of polarity shifting is to become more spiritual beings through our feelings and actions – to evolve away from the animal nature we were born with and develop our higher spiritual nature. This requires shifting polarities and transforming emotions. This is actually an easy process. It must occur one experience at a time to work. If you make an effort to recognize any of the negative emotions that you experience, then it is simple to think of the opposite feeling and transform one into the other.

The first step is to understand the **three purposes for all negative emotions** (refer to table 17 on page 297).

1. Every emotion triggers an alarm of some sort to alert us to what is happening.

2. You have a response to this emotion, acting in some way to deal with the feelings.

3. The third purpose is to think of the opposite emotion; if it is a better choice, then you should switch and transform the negative emotion to the polar opposite feeling. Obviously, this is not about changing positive feelings for negative ones.

The psychology of emotions is divided up into two separate polarities, the positive, higher nature virtues and the negative, lower nature vices. We were all born with those lower emotions dominated by the four categories of fear, anger, pain, and disgust. At the opposite polarity for each negative emotion is a positive one. The key is to identify which specific emotion is the exact opposite feeling from the four basic categories of positive emotions: courage, acceptance, happiness, and love. This knowledge will always allow you to decide whether to embrace your lower, animal nature or to transform those emotions into their opposite positive, spiritual experience.

This system gives spirituality a new definition, as the actions we take, rather than some abstract thought, feeling, or state of mind. The universe has many opposing forces. When we are challenged by conflicts or chaos on a personal, social, economic, or whatever level, it becomes our choice to remain in that negative energy or transform it into the polar opposite, positive energy.

If you intend to be a spiritual person, then you will need to study the emotions of our higher nature and exercise using them. When you learn to transform emotions, you will experience more fulfillment and less stress. For example, if you react with anger, you can transform it into acceptance, or if you get fearful, you can change it into courage. My explanation of the psychology of our emotions is easy to understand as a pendulum swinging back and forth. At one end you have the negative; at the other you have the positive emotions. The key is to recognize where you are at the moment and swing over to the positive side whenever you are being pulled in the negative direction. This is the main concept of polarity shifting, and you can see Figure 3 *Transforming Natures in the Triplex Mind* for a visual description of this process. You can also see Table 17, *The Higher and Lower Natures*. (See page 297 or look at the Matrix on page 244.)

One of the main ideas here is that you should always consider the polar opposite feelings. Even if you are very happy or courageous, for at least a brief moment you may sometimes think about the opposite emotions in order to be more aware of your own state. Sometimes you may receive an important intuition or increase your awareness of the situation for your benefit. However, the main activity will usually be transforming the negative, lower nature into the higher, positive nature. There will rarely be any reason to transform good feelings into negative ones. If you feel good, the best advice is to enjoy it and express your gratitude for being there.

Principal Skills of Transforming:

▸ **How do you *recognize* the nature of your emotional experience?**
In order to be clearly aware of the type of emotions you are experiencing, you must first think "up," accessing your higher self. From this more objective perspective, you can become aware of the feelings and compare them to the list in Table 17 (page 297) *The Higher and Lower Natures*. You must acknowledge what the alarming emotion is and what your response to it is. (Also refer to the Transformation Matrix on page 244.)

Figure 3. Transforming Natures in the Triplex Mind

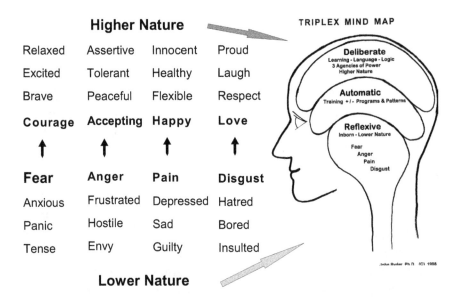

Higher Nature				TRIPLEX MIND MAP
Relaxed	Assertive	Innocent	Proud	
Excited	Tolerant	Healthy	Laugh	
Brave	Peaceful	Flexible	Respect	
Courage	**Accepting**	**Happy**	**Love**	
↑	↑	↑	↑	
Fear	**Anger**	**Pain**	**Disgust**	
Anxious	Frustrated	Depressed	Hatred	
Panic	Hostile	Sad	Bored	
Tense	Envy	Guilty	Insulted	
Lower Nature				

▶ **How to regain *control* of a stressful experience?** Whenever we are dragged down into the lower, negative emotions, the reflexive mind is usually in control. First, you must turn off the alarm and stop the normal response to the stressful feelings. Do this by relaxing your body and "letting go" of negative focus. Make it your intention to gain control and calm down. The main instrument to do this is your breath; slow down your breathing, making it deep, smooth, and easy. As you take a moment to relax, refocus your attention on the experience of gaining control of the stress. In the Appendix, you can find the relaxation exercise that describes this process in greater detail. You can also obtain a recorded CD or download the exercises recorded by my self or others that teach these techniques. (See the Appendix for details about Relaxation programs.)

▶ **How to redirect your attention to become more *deliberate*?** This process is aided by your narration, describing to yourself what you are experiencing and analyzing your situation. By forcing yourself to observe what is happening, this makes you more objective.

▶ **How to *identify* the polar opposite emotions?** The first step is to recognize and describe the emotion you are having. Then go to the opposite category of emotions in the higher nature and select the feeling that is the best polar opposite.   Table 17 offers a brief list of the main categories of emotions from both the lower and higher natures. Which one is most opposite for you is a personal choice, but it is one from the same category.

▸   **How to *activate* the positive emotion?**   When you decide on the correct polar opposite emotion, you must imagine it vividly. That means that you should recall an experience where this was a strong feeling. Recreate this emotional experience as clearly and vividly as possible, engage your passion and will power to activate this emotion. Change your body state to reflect the positive feeling.

▸   **How to *transform* the negative emotion into the positive emotion?** This requires you to stop and reflect for a moment about the negative emotions and the type of energy you are experiencing. You must make a deliberate effort to make a ***polarity shift***, going from the lower feeling up to the higher emotion that you have activated. This takes only a brief moment, but it is important to experience a purposeful shift of emotions. This is where you act on your intention to reverse directions from the negative emotions to the positive. Acknowledge the change in emotion verbally to yourself.

▸   **How to *anchor* the positive transformation?**   The success of shifting polarities is based on the positive experience that should reward you. When you escape the stress of your lower nature and embrace a positive emotion, it is usually a very good experience. An anchor represents a physical or mental gesture that "cements" the change into place. Anchoring also means that you recognize this transformation and acknowledge your satisfaction or pleasure and express some gratitude that you are in your higher nature. Now you can begin to appreciate the skill of reversing directions and acting spiritually to cultivate your virtues.

In summary, the master key of transforming refers to your skills to take any negative experience and switch directions and reach the polar opposite emotion or behavior. This is a simple exercise that allows you to escape the stress of fear, anger, pain, or disgust and embrace one the four positive emotions of your higher nature: courage, acceptance, happiness, or love. All of the feelings in your higher nature are part of what we commonly define as spiritual virtues. These higher emotions are universally accepted in all religions as noble virtues and have been advocated for thousands of years; however, it has been difficult for people to act on them for the reasons explained here. Now, you have a simple formula to follow and reach these aspired traits. The more time you spend in your higher nature, the more spiritual you will become and the more fulfilling life should be.

Transformation creates freedom.

Janusz Kapusta

Chapter 16

Master Key 9   Achieving Peak Potential

The biggest temptation is to settle for too little.   Thomas Merton

Everyone wants to be an achiever. It should be a legitimate claim for all. We all achieve the "normal" potentials we are born with, like walking, talking, feeding ourselves, or anything that comes naturally. There are thousands of things that every person can achieve because they are simple activities that anyone can learn easily. Beyond these normal achievements, we all can reach for higher potentials. These potentials take a progressively bigger effort to achieve, such as learning skills or developing talents that can take weeks, months, or many years to master. This master key describes the required steps to discover your true potentials, to reach your peak performance, and to achieve goals toward personal fulfillment.

Achievement is defined as success in reaching goals. This begins on the personal level, with being able to accomplish a task in any way possible. ***Peak performance*** is when you achieve a task without errors. This can be any activity, simple or complex, that you perform at your best, in that moment. The next level involves comparing your performance to everyone else's. When you can successfully perform a task better than 90% of the people, you have reached ***superior achievement***. This does not necessarily imply peak performance; it just means, that compared to others, you were excellent.

The highest level is ***outstanding achievement***, that is, when a task was performed superbly well compared to all others and unquestionably is in the top one percentile. This level of performance is extremely difficult and rare. It is usually the combination of exceptional talents, hard work, and constant striving for peak performance that is socially recognized.

In general, whenever we set our intentions on goals we can achieve and do so successfully, the basic sense of ***fulfillment*** should come easily. It is not wise to limit the experience of fulfillment to outstanding achievements because they are rare. Instead, the more frequently you feel successful, the more you are likely to achieve. Fulfillment is the opportunity to celebrate any progress you have made towards achieving your goals.

The concept of peak potentials refers to finding what you can do best. These can be your natural talents, skills you develop, or knowledge you learn. Usually our potentials lie hidden within us and require careful exploration to discover and then, years of practice to master. Once you are recognized as an expert in, or master of, some activity, you are tapping your peak potentials.

Achievement of higher potentials is possible for any person who makes a serious effort to overcome all the challenges. Curiously, most people report that upon achieving their peak potential, that activity becomes effortless, simple, graceful, exciting, fun, and very rewarding. Certainly, you have enjoyed watching others reach their peak abilities many times, because it is something we universally admire and appreciate. Peak performances are memorable, like your child reciting a poem, scoring a winning point in some sport, your friend catching a crystal vase just before it hits the floor after it was knocked off a shelf, or watching the Olympic athletes perform amazing feats of agility, speed, and precision.

The term "potential" refers to any behavior or knowledge that does not occur spontaneously, that requires us to make an effort to learn, practice, and develop. Very often, our potentials are based on some inborn *talents*. The idea of talents, or special gifts, means being born with the biological predisposition to learn to do something well. Like the quality of a person's voice and hearing can make it possible for him or her to become a great singer. We are all born with many potentials. Unfortunately, most people never develop many of these special talents. We all, however, can still reach our peak performance, which is anything that is done as perfectly as possible at the time.

Potentials in general refer to what exists inside of us, but have not yet been fully developed, such as an acorn that has a potential forest inside of it. The concept of potential in us describes what we can learn, either as knowledge or in actualizing our natural abilities. When we are born, we inherit a large variety of talents and skills from our ancestors. Some of these gifts can be extraordinary; others can be quite common. For example, every person can learn to sing, but only those with a natural talent will excel at this skill. This is true of every skill and aspect of knowledge.

Psychology has promoted the false concept that ***intelligence*** is mostly inherited and that some people have it and others just don't. This is absolutely wrong. Every person has a different type of intelligence that includes unique and uncommon skills.(25)   In reality, if one can identify his or her natural talents and makes an effort to develop them, every individual has the opportunity to excel and achieve great goals. These can be intellectual skills in the form of knowledge, like mathematics, linguistics, engineering, philosophy, and so on. These skills can also be behaviors seen in sports, art, music, cooking, and so on. Usually, there is a combination of both intellectual and physical skills that helps us excel. The question to ask yourself is what are your special talents? Don't assume that you already know; there are many potential skills that you would never explore unless given a special opportunity to do so.

Achievement in general refers to completing a task, reaching a goal, or obtaining knowledge for a task. All our behaviors are on a continuum from extremely poor to outstanding with the largest section being average in the middle. As described earlier, excellence in performance is being in the top ten percent.   Achievement can fall anywhere along that spectrum of performance from terrible to fantastic.   The more distinguished, exceptional, and successful the activity is, the higher it climbs the scale of achievement.

What can you do to reach your peak potential?

Most of us learn to do a job or a task well enough. It then gets coded into the automatic mind and becomes a routine pattern. This applies to anything we do repeatedly. To reach peak ability requires that you continue to direct your efforts *deliberately*, improving your work until your competence approaches perfection. This depends on utilizing your deliberate mind to control your actions, entering your higher self, and directing your will power to complete your intentions.   When your deliberate mind and automatic mind are performing in unison, you are at your peak ability. This basically takes training, practice, and effort. This is actually how anyone achieves a sense of superior performance or excellence.

The keys to superior performance are knowing what your natural talents are. This gives you a competitive edge over others trying to learn the same material. This is the key to your progress. When you are able to identify your strengths, you will have a tremendous advantage because two things happen. First, you learn faster and easier; secondly, you enjoy the process much more. *Do What You Love, the Money Will Follow*, a book by Marsha Sinetar, has a simple and true message: when we engage in things we love and are good at, we learn quickly and feel good about ourselves. The question is, how do we discover our best strengths and talents?(26)

In Chapter 2, I described the three spheres of consciousness and the general content of these fields (physical, emotional, and analytical). Your achievement begins with reviewing these three fields and determining which traits you are naturally gifted in – those are your talents. The ultimate test is how well you do in reality. If you think you are a talented singer, do enough people agree with you to make it a legitimate career for you? Whatever talents you have, as you explore them and make an effort to develop these skills, you must measure them among all the other people with similar talents. Society is not always fair, but in general, exceptional talents are recognized and encouraged to flourish. The possibilities for any individual to achieve recognition are vast, although it does take tremendous will power, time, and effort. These factors were described in the other master keys.

What is the difference between achievement and peak performance?

The desire to achieve goals is universal, and there are many goals we all share in common. When we achieve uncommon, difficult goals that began as our personal intention and desires, then we experience a greater sense of personal fulfillment. Achieving goals does not require superior or peak performance; rather, it is reaching a certain level of performance and simply attaining your goals. Peak performance is an internal experience of feeling you have done your best (your deliberate intentions are in sync with your automatic programs). These moments are examples of *energized awareness,* where you are more alert, focused, deliberate, and passionate about your actions. In reality, this is not very hard to attain; it simply takes desire, intention, and practice. We can all learn to do our normal activities at our best, or at peak performance at least occasionally.

There are many levels to peak performance. These levels depend on your experience. The more experience you accumulate, the higher your peak performance can be. It is like the difference between athletic competition in your local community and international Olympics. Because peak performance is relative to each situation, there is an infinite amount of opportunities to reach that special level of activity every day. Sometimes people even describe an experience of being guided, or other worldly, where they do not seem to be in control of their actions, but are doing it exceptionally well. These moments are being in *"The Flow"* as described by Csikszentmihalyi, where the individual moves into the background and the experience becomes everything.   These experiences are often transcendental or spiritual crossing of our regular boundaries to achieving a special status.

The following points describe the specific skills you can practice to become aware of your talents, develop your strengths, achieve your goals, and more often, reach your peak performance.   This search for achievement is completely voluntary; it all depends on you accessing your higher self and directing your will power and passion to achieve your goals.

Principal Skills for Achieving Peak Potential:

▸   **How do you *identify* your talents and potential?**   The first step is to acknowledge that everyone has talents and plenty of potential to discover and develop.   Utilize the three spheres of consciousness (Figure 1 and Table 4 page 63) to determine which traits are your strongest. Go through the list several times and prioritize the traits you believe are your best. Consider how these traits, talents, and skills can become your actualized potential and help you achieve larger, long-term goals.

▸   **How to raise *energy* levels to achieve goals?**   When you think "up," accessing your higher self, you enter a more objective perspective, gain control of your deliberate mind, and can exercise your will power. Your success depends on your ability to cultivate and harness the passionate energy you store inside. Think of previous experiences when you felt energized, focused, and extremely motivated. Make it your intention to maximize your energy levels and direct your will power to achieve the goals you have set for yourself.

▸   **What to do to *achieve* your desired goals?**   Your success depends on applying all the keys described here. Achievement becomes easier and more fulfilling when you 1) know what you want, 2) have a specific plan to reach those goals, 3) have the motivation, determination, and will power to strive for success, 4) you are prepared to deal with all the obstacles, challenges, and delay gratification until you get what you want, and 5) you remain clearly aware of the consequences of not completing your goals as well as the rewards awaiting you when you succeed. This is the summary of the most important factors. Fulfillment is a lifelong commitment to this process.

▸ **How to reach *peak* performance?**   The key to being at your best - peak ability - is to develop your natural talents and practice, practice, and more practice.   The other key is to be in the flow of the experience, spontaneous, alert, yet relaxed and being clear about your intentions. The moment you become aware of your energized consciousness focused on completing a task deliberately and knowing you are doing it just right, errorlessly, you are at peak performance.

▸ **How to become *outstanding*, achieving peak potential?**   We all have unique talents that if developed can propel us to fantastic goals. You can reach excellence when you make an effort at tasks that you enjoy and in which you have natural talent. Performing at the excellent level is defined as the top 10% of achievers.   Outstanding performance is when you distinguish yourself within this group and reach the upper one percent. To achieve extraordinary success requires talent, will power, clear intentions, tremendous effort, a great attitude (never giving up), and outside assistance in the form of a coach, mentor, trainer, producer, etc., that helps on every level. When you combine all the advantages together, then you have the best chance to achieve outstanding peak potential, along with the recognition that it often brings.

In summary, achievement can be separated into four categories. We are all achievers when we complete simple tasks. Most of us go on to achieve higher potentials, those that require greater effort and time. Very few of us go on to achieve outstanding results, but all of us can easily achieve superior performance in whatever we are naturally talented. Which ever path of success you are on, each can bring a sense of fulfillment or satisfaction with every small goal accomplished. Being deliberate and energized are important factors to perform at your best. In the Appendix you can find more information about the achievement.

Got to be in it, to win it!

Chapter 17

Conclusion: The Psychology of the Master Keys

This section presents the essential skills required to master your mind and your environment. The skills describe what to do to overcome many of the normal limitations, the mind's shortcomings, and challenges we all face in the world. There are ultimately only two things that happen; you either succeed or you do not meet all your goals. This means that you will either celebrate success or you must deal with some degree of failure. Those individuals who have a very positive attitude, never concede to failure, but learn from the experience and plan to succeed the next time.

When is adaptation required?

With every action, you embark on a quest for mastery or adaptation. When you achieve your goals, everything becomes simple; that is mastery. When anything else happens, life gets complicated. If you do not get the results you want, you must adapt to the situation and consider all the alternatives before you. This is the skill of adaptation. This is different from coping, feeling defeated, sad, or frustrated, and having to deal with the unwanted consequences. Adaptation is the ability to use the master keys to constantly "reframe" the "failure" as just a good learning experience and to continue to search for better ways to approach the challenge in a new way. Success often hinges upon seeking new routes to your goals when old ones have proven to be blocked. The idea of reframing is to "rename" something in a new context. An individual with a positive attitude will always see every difficulty, challenge, mistake, or even failure as an opportunity to prove he or she is worthy of success. These events at worst are called setbacks, but never failures. When you develop an invincible attitude to reach your goals no matter, eventually you will in some way.

Below is a summary list of the master keys described earlier. The next chapters describe the four JEEP factors and give examples about how to use the keys to deal most effectively with life.

Summary of Master Keys: Master Key = MK

MK 81 Attention

Everything can be seen on a spectrum from negative to positive. The skill of polarity shifting is to recognize alternatives that are opposite to the normal reactions we all have and to change our behavior or feelings for the better.

MK 82

Identify your preferred modality (visual, auditory, physical, or cerebral) and become aware of your weakest one as well. Be alert that you are more likely to make mistakes in that "weakest" modality. Use your preferred modality to improve your overall perception.

MK 83

The more modalities you utilize, the faster you can learn and better you will remember the information. Experiential learning is one of the best ways to develop new skills.

MK 84

Announce to yourself a clear plan of what you intend to achieve in the present moment.

MK 85

Vividly imagine following your plan, succeeding in reaching your goals.

MK 86

Engage the power of narrating your deliberate actions to monitor your progress.

MK 87

Establish specific rules about what you will and will not be distracted by while working on a planned task.

MK 88

Practice focusing your attention on a specific task by cycling through a small group of key elements while maintaining the right level of energy and deliberate action.

MK 89

Make clear predictions about the outcome of each progressive step, which includes the rewards you obtain upon completion or the consequences of not achieving your goals.

MK 90

Pace yourself carefully to make sure you have the stamina you need and to know when to take breaks.

MK 91

Practice relaxing and letting go so that you are easily able to release tension in your body and shift attention to the next item.

MK 92

Exercise the power of open awareness, remaining alert without focusing on any element before you, constantly shifting your attention.

MK 93

Establish clear criteria of what should get your attention and ignore all the other elements.

MK 94

Shifting your attention is based on constantly moving your focus very quickly to new elements in your internal or external perceptions.

MK 95 Perception

Increase your awareness of how each sensory experience contributes to your understanding of what you perceive.

MK 96

Seek to expand your perspective to make it as objective as possible; ask what others would think.

MK 97

Practice reviewing the many different dimensions and analyze where along the spectrum your perceptions rest. Be mindful not to be caught by illusions or distortions your mind is prone to.

MK 98 Higher Self

Access your Higher Self by thinking "up" and focus on your experience of being present in the here and now. This represents your inner, core essence of experiencing your life.

MK 99

The Higher Self is able to be more objective by considering how others feel, think, or would react to your thoughts, feelings, or actions.

MK 100

Make decisions, after considering and analyzing all the information, from the Higher Self.

MK 101

The Higher Self is your inner voice that creates intentions and directs your will power to be deliberate in your actions.

MK 102 **Energy**

Be aware of the energy or vibration you feel inside yourself or coming from others. How well does your energy resonate with others?

MK 103

Measure the energy levels carefully to determine how much energy you should be contributing.

MK 104

Verify that you are exchanging energy in a fair and just manner with each individual.

MK 105

Keep the energy flowing; release blockages; repair leakages; be generous with your passion.

MK 106 **Will Power**

Raise the level of passionate energy above what is required to complete your task.

MK 107

Exercise your will power every day; establish clear intentions, and then direct your deliberate actions until you achieve your goals.

MK 108

To maximize your will power, be prepared for any challenge, raise your energy and motivation levels and then deliberately narrate your progress until you reach every goal.

MK 109 **Judgment**

Analyze every situation to determine if you have the resources to overcome the challenges before you, and if confronted by overwhelming difficulties, consider reorganizing your strategies, changing directions or find alternative goals.

MK 110

Exercise the power of your judgment: analyze, compare, and make careful decisions.

MK 111

The rational approach requires you to consider all the facts, details, objective information, and to calculate the probabilities of the different outcomes to prepare a logical decision.

MK 112

The intuitive approach requires you to reflect on what your internal "radar" is telling you; listen to all your subjective feelings and any other information before making a judgment.

MK 113

Be mindful to collect all the information that may be relevant to the situation. As you analyze it, consider what the consequences will be for different alternatives before making a decision.

MK 114

Determine what is the simplest explanation to resolve a problem.

MK 115

Are you certain that this (explanation) is the only possible cause for some event.

MK 116

While analyzing all the subjective and objective information, compare alternatives, and then carefully prioritize your choices before making a final decision.

MK 117

Make accurate predictions based on your previous experience and knowledge of the probable consequences, and determine your level of confidence with each decision.

MK 118

Clarify if you can afford the consequences or troubles of your decision if it is wrong?

MK 119

Clarify if you can risk not taking action. What will the consequences be if you do nothing?

MK 120 **Patterns**

Most of your behaviors become automatic patterns or programs that require conscious monitoring to verify that you are going in a positive direction.

MK 121

Determine if a pattern or program creates any distress, negativity, tension, blockages, or limits progress to you or others. Ask: 'Would you want your child to say, do, or think this pattern?'

MK 122

Replace unwanted patterns or programs by following the seven steps described with the opposite thoughts, feelings, actions, attitudes, and so on.

MK 123

Repeat the positive programs until you have replaced the (opposite) negative patterns completely and establish new healthier patterns.

MK 124 **Transforming**

Transforming is polarity shifting; whenever you encounter something negative, seek the polar opposite, reverse directions, and move towards the positive side.

MK 125

Think UP. Go to your higher self; become more objectively aware of your situation, and determine what negative emotions you are experiencing; identify the polar opposite feelings in your higher nature; and then shift your focus to these positive emotions.

MK 126

Practice relaxing and letting go. Be able to quickly and easily release tension and shift focus in your mind.

MK 127

Exercise your ability to identify the polar opposite feelings between the lower and higher nature in your mind. (See Table 17 on page 297 or the transformation matrix on page 244.)

MK 128

When you identify the positive emotion, recreate a vivid experience of this feeling and focus your attention on transforming the negative into the polar opposite positive feelings.

MK 129

Remember to acknowledge any degree of success by shifting away from stressful emotions to healthy good feelings. Become aware of the rewards and benefits.

MK 130 **Achievement**

Identify your talents and potential by reviewing your strengths from the three spheres of consciousness.

MK 131

Maximize your energy levels by thinking up and entering your higher self; now reflect on your intentions. Direct your will power to create the motivation and determination to succeed reaching your goals.

MK 132

Reaching peak performance requires you to practice your talents and skills until they are easy for you to do just right, especially when your deliberate action is in sync with your automatic patterns.

MK 133

Achieve more desired goals by reaching your energized level of consciousness. When your intentions are clear, your actions deliberate, you are prepared for any challenge, and you have accessed all the resources you need to succeed.

MK 134

In your quest for mastering every challenge, those results that do not meet with complete success, require you to adapt, learn from this experience, seek new and better approaches, and maintain a positive attitude about your plans.

Chapter 18

The Locking J E E P Factors

> Everything happens for a reason and a purpose, and it serves us.
> Anthony Robbins

The four JEEP factors are the simplest way to group most of the things that our minds give us trouble with. Each factor is described here in a little more detail so that you can understand how it causes problems and what to do to resolve them. I begin with patterns and proceed to energy, emotions and judgment because I want to explain the simple factors first and end on the complex ones. There are a number of specific steps listed to demonstrate how to create a polarity shift for each factor, steps you should follow to make the most use of this system.

You will find ten examples for each factor. These are common problems or locks that most people experience in everyday life. These are not the only problems found in these factors. However, they illustrate how to deal with many different issues. In some cases there is an obvious direction to move in, while in other cases, it might be a matter of seeking greater balance between two extremes. The optimal direction to take is described in each case.

In general, the locks may appear in any part of the Triplex mind: Reflexive, Automatic, or Deliberate. Some locks are a combination of two parts, or even all three parts. The examples given describe how we get caught by our brains negative tendencies and what we can do about it. As you review the materials, you will begin to realize how easily you can shift polarities, and reverse the direction you are being pulled in, to go where you intend to.

What is the reciprocity of action?

Reciprocity of action is about the mind-body connection. It is not a hard concept to follow; obviously information travels both ways between the body and mind. What most people don't realize is that your thoughts will affect your body, just as much as changes in your body will affect your thoughts. There is a real reciprocity of activity between the body and mind. Some of the suggestions offered here serve to change your thinking to make you feel better; others serve to change your body to make you think differently. In either case, you are initiating a change in your state of being that will liberate you.

What is a reality check?

To use this system most effectively, you may want to begin with a brief **reality check.** After each example, ask yourself whether your life resembles the example in any way. Begin by changing your perspective, trying to be more objective, and then consider what your reality looks like. Review the evaluation questions to determine how much these issues affect you. Follow the suggested keys to open the locks and resolve potential problems. If the example is not you, perhaps you will realize that it reflects somebody you know. Then it is possible for you to try to solve these problems with the other person.

How to help others?

Helping others is a worthwhile activity; however, your approach must be diplomatic, compassionate, and reasonable in order to be well received. The key is to use questions. Ask the other person if he or she would like to learn some new tools. Would they be interested in doing things differently if you could show them a better way to accomplish their goals? A gentle approach will tend to generate better results. Although, in some cases it is necessary to be confrontational, set strict boundaries, and assert yourself very clearly.

Usually, you will have a specific issue (like anger) to confront the other person about. Ask them: "How much do you enjoy getting angry?" "Are you aware how your behavior appears to others?" "Do you think you could accomplish more acting in a different way?" These questions should lead to a discussion about alternatives. Offer the person the basic concept about shifting polarities and reversing directions. Get him or her to acknowledge that they understand what the issue is you are complaining about. Explain the key instructions so that he or she can try to act in a different manner. Encourage any small shift in behavior with compliments, praise, and positive feedback. Continue to support the person and help them explore new, better ways of acting. After all, it will improve your relationship with him or her as well.

Basic rules of dealing with difficult people:

1. Stop and perform a reality check; what is really going on and what does it mean?

2. Identify what the other person is trying to achieve – what is important to them.

3. Ask this person if he or she would like to accomplish the goals in an easier way?

4. If they are willing to listen, then verify the goal he or she wants to achieve.

5. Propose how he or she can shift polarities and achieve the desired goal in a different way.

6. Ask if this new approach works better than the old one, and would he or she be willing to use it in the future?

7. If he or she is not willing to listen, then you must assert yourself, set very clear boundaries (that will stop the unacceptable behavior). Request that he or she respect these new boundaries. This may result in some degree of conflict; your will power can help assert yourself. If necessary, you may want to distance yourself from such people, avoiding or limiting contact if possible.

Freedom is not a right, it is something we are born to exercise.

Chapter 19

Patterns

We are not creatures of circumstance; we are creators of circumstance.

Benjamin Disraeli

What are Patterns?

Patterns are everything. When you think about the universe, everything is part of some sort of pattern. That is why our brains are "pattern-mongers;" we are designed to detect patterns around us and turn anything into a new pattern. Consequently, our lives are made of patterns, routines, and programs that we repeat over and over.

I began this section with *patterns* because they are the most general, common factor, and relatively easy to deal with. Whatever part of the world you observe, you will notice patterns in it. Some are very easy to see, like the shape and manner in which grass grows. Other patterns are hidden and difficult to notice, like the electromagnetic waves that bring us radio and television signals. You cannot see these waves, but you know they are there when you tune the radio to your favorite station. The same is true of your life. The problem for us is how to notice all the patterns that we are in.

To make this story simple, let's just focus on patterns that really influence your life. Any behavior that becomes an automatic routine, program, or habit can be considered a pattern. These can be behaviors you actually do, feelings you experience or express, or even thoughts that just cycle through your mind repeatedly. If you can do something without paying much attention to the activity, then it certainly can qualify as an automatic pattern. These programs come from the Automatic part of the Triplex mind. In psychology, they are often referred to as conditioned behaviors; however, anyone can develop the ability to deliberately control any of these automatic patterns.

What is their purpose?

Patterns are meant to simplify our life, making things that require effort easier. This is one way the brain conserves energy, by making anything we repeat over and over a routine so that it becomes less of a burden to the brain and body to perform.

How do patterns work?

The Automatic mind is a special part of the brain designed to store any repeated activity in memory. That means that your automatic mind participates in every activity: mental, emotional, or physical and memorizes the steps required to perform any activity. Some intense experiences only require one trial, and they can be permanently stored (usually these are very dramatic or traumatic events). Other times we must repeat a behavior many times before we can do it subconsciously or not deliberately. The automatic mind allows our attention to be focused on something else while we repeat the routine, habit, or internal program. There are many advantages to this system. However, there equally many serious problems or errors that the automatic mind creates for us.

What are the polarities?

On the positive side, the automatic mind does simplify the burdens that we must carry by making even very complex tasks simple routines. If it were not for the automatic mind and patterns, we would not be able to drive a car and carry on a conversation. Consider typing on a keyboard a good example of a routine that can be done very automatically. I only have thoughts in my mind and my fingers will bang out the letters effortlessly. However, there are serious problems caused by the automatic mind when we engage in any kind of destructive habit or routine. When a routine has a negative polarity, it limits freedom and imprisons us in some way – bad habits like smoking, overeating, or drinking too much; or can be seen in obsessive behaviors like control freaks or neat freaks. Sabotaging routines like people who are constantly critical and never supportive. Any person that frequently repeats very negative things about themselves like "I hate myself, or I can't do it," are caught in very self destructive patterns.

There are very clear polarities about most routines ranging from very positive to extremely negative and damaging. The biggest problem is that once something becomes a pattern it is difficult to change it. In general, everything we repeatedly do over and over becomes another pattern in our automatic mind. This creates layer upon layer of routine. The older a pattern is, the harder it can be to change it or eliminate it. Keep in mind that although the automatic mind operates outside of normal awareness, it is possible to make a deliberate effort to make changes in these routines.

What are the psychological lessons?

The first step to raising your awareness about the automatic mind is to ask whether you can tell when you or someone else is acting like an automaton or robot. There are many people who indulge in bad habits or stupid routines without any regret. This is often considered acting without thinking. When we ignore the consequences of our actions, trouble tends to follow. This is more frequently the case with automatic patterns because we do not monitor these activities well, which results in stress to ourselves or others. The first question about your automatic patterns is to determine whether the routine is sustainable, good for you and others?

What are the locks?

Most of the locks originate on the biological level of the brain. The automatic mind is designed to take any behavior and repeat it regardless of whether it is desirable or toxic. The psychological locks arise from our brain's lack of awareness. That is, the deliberate mind may or may not pay attention to what the automatic mind is doing. Since our automatic patterns do not require monitoring, bad things can occur very easily. Most of the problems caused by our patterns are indirect and accumulate over time.

What are the Key Instructions to Correct Patterns?

Let's assume that you have discovered a bad pattern that you want to stop and replace with a better one. Below are the Master Keys to replace patterns and an additional list of the general steps to follow to change patterns in your life. Depending on each specific pattern, there may be slight variations; the steps outlined here are the most common.

The questions to ask to identify and evaluate problems with patterns.

1. Are you engaged in this activity on purpose, because you want to do it, or is it just a routine you are repeating that might be done better differently?

2. If you were to change this activity, would that bother you, make you anxious, frustrated or sad?

3. When did you first start this routine and why do you keep repeating it?

4. Is this pattern good for myself and others? Does it promote good things?

5. When you repeat this behavior, does it offend, disturb, annoy, or frustrate others?

6. What are the results of this routine; does it generate gratitude and appreciation?

7. Do the mental programs motivate, inspire, energize, build confidence, joy, or instead do they increase stress, anxiety, fears, anger, frustration, and steal hope away?

8. Are these thoughts, feelings, or activities positive, helpful, creative, adding to the wisdom and knowledge you can utilize or are they rather negative, destructive, critical and cause tension in your environment?

9. Would you want your child to repeat this program or statement to himself or herself?

These are the Master Keys described earlier to deal with patterns.

MK 120

Most of your behaviors become automatic patterns or programs that require conscious monitoring to verify that you are going in a positive direction.

MK 121

Determine if a pattern or program creates any distress, negativity, tension, blockages, or limits progress to you or others.

MK 122

Replace unwanted patterns or programs by following the seven steps described with the opposite thoughts, feelings, actions, attitudes, and so on.

MK 123

Repeat the positive programs until you have replaced the (opposite) negative patterns completely and establish new healthier patterns.

Become aware of what to do and what to say to fix patterns

What to do:

1. Raise your awareness; return to the deliberate mind; focus your attention on the pattern that you have been in and continue to evaluate the consequences.

2. Access your higher self to seek a better, more objective perspective. You are no longer a prisoner of the pattern; you are free to make changes in your behaviors.

3. From your higher mind identify several alternatives, analyze the situation, and make a decision to try a new pattern. Engage your will power to create the intentions to act on this decision.

4. Acknowledge any discomfort; identify what is the cause of these feelings. Prepare yourself to transcend the unwanted patterns.

5. Transform any negative destructive patterns into their polar opposite positive programs. Confirm that you are in a positive state of physical energy and visualize yourself performing a different pattern in a state of feeling good.

6. Assert that you have made the decision with the intention to transcend or deliberately let go of the old patterns and shift your attention to the new pattern.

7. Being deliberate, consciously try the new pattern while you monitor yourself to remain in a positive state of mind and body.

8. Practice the new pattern while you acknowledge the changes and evaluate how sustainable the new routine is compared to the old one. If you have found a new pattern that is acceptable, you have increased your freedom; if not, start over and try again until you succeed.

What to say:

1a. I am glad to be increasing my awareness about my life so that I can think clearly about my patterns.

2a. Now within my higher self I must be objective about my situation because I am free to change my life.

3a. As I become aware of the best alternatives, I recognize the right choice and create new intentions.

4a. I am aware of the negative patterns holding me back, and I am glad to be ready to change.

5a. Polarity shifting now puts me on a new positive pattern that feels good and does good.

6a. I am glad to raise my confidence to let go of the old patterns and start better ones.

7a. This is my opportunity to prove my strength and determination to change and improve my life.

8a. It feels good to practice a new pattern that is better, smarter, and more rewarding to me.

What are the Top Ten Problems with Patterns?

Automatisms

These are any of the thousands of little routine patterns that get used at the wrong time in the wrong place. These are the simple habits we rely on in one situation, but accidentally intrude in a different one.

The psychology of automatisms: These are a very normal part of life that we all experience occasionally. These are essentially mistakes of your brain's output. Usually they are harmless, although they can be very annoying.

Examples:

▸   Writing the previous year on checks or notes long after the new year has passed.

▸   Turning the key in your front door in the direction to lock it when you are trying to open it.

▸   Pulling up to a gasoline pump on the wrong side of a new car you got because the old car had the gas cap on the opposite side.

The lock is the lack of awareness combined with an automatic routine. There are hundreds of automatisms that tend to be a good pattern in the wrong place.

The keys are to become alert, raise your awareness to the deliberate mind, and make a conscious effort to correct the error. As you perform the action deliberately the right way, establish new cues to remind yourself in the future what is correct - which way to turn the key or which side the gas cap is on and so forth.

The ideal is to be more alert, deliberate, and avoid these little mistakes; when they occur, take note and do not get disturbed.

Addictions

Anytime a person develops a craving or urge for something and gets very disturbed if he or she cannot have it, then it probably qualifies as an addiction. That means that they have a strong psychological and physiological dependence on a substance or activity that is habitual.

The psychology of addictions: there are many common ways that we become addicted; they can be healthy or they can be very unhealthy. If relying on something causes problems, then it is advisable to escape this pattern.

Examples:

▸ Normal indulgences, like caffeine, sugar, chocolate, etc., can be addictions.

▸ Some individuals are easily addicted to chemicals like cigarettes, alcohol, and drugs whether they are prescribed or recreational.

▸ Other individuals get addicted to activities like gambling or horse racing.

The lock is that the body creates a strong physical and mental craving that must be satisfied or the person experiences a great deal of stress, discomfort, and withdrawal symptoms.

The key is to first recognize that it is an addiction. Then, raise your awareness to your deliberate mind and make it your clear intention to escape these behaviors and replace them with healthy habits. Your success depends on being able to create new patterns that are truly desirable and satisfy your needs in a positive manner. Then the key is to develop your will power and assert your true intention to do what you have decided is the correct action.

The ideal is to develop your will power in order to have the discipline to overcome any urge or craving, eliminating unhealthy addictions from your life.

Assumptions

This is a pattern when we jump to conclusions and decide that we already know everything we need to. There are many reasons the mind wants to ignore important information; the consequence is that we never really know what the truth is.

The psychology of assumptions is that they can be valuable because they may speed up the process of making decisions. However, if they are wrong, then they create a cascade of problems.

Examples:

▸ You wake up to find it is raining outside; you assume it is a bad day for outdoor activities, so you cancel all your plans; then the rain ends and the sun comes out an hour later.

▸   Your child comes home with a bad grade; you may assume that he or she did not study, but there could easily be many other good reasons for a poor mark.

The lock is from the mind's desire to be quick. Rather than evaluate the matter carefully, the mind imagines what might be true and then assumes that is a matter of fact.

The key is to become more alert and raise your awareness to the deliberate mind to evaluate the situation more objectively. The truth is often not apparent or may take time to discover. If your assumptions cannot be verified, then you are obligated to learn more and/or analyze the information more carefully. Sometimes it requires time to observe how things resolve naturally.

The ideal is to avoid making assumptions that cannot be verified; instead, use your insights to ask the questions that may help resolve the issues.

Rationalization or Denial

These are the most common way we all cope with difficult circumstances. Either people try to explain why it is not their fault; they find external reasons for why something happened - they rationalize. Or, they may simply deny that it is their fault or even that nothing really happened - they are in denial.

The psychology of explaining why events happen is an important part of our every day life. Taking responsibility or at least responding to a situation in a realistic manner is the positive polarity; the negative side is when people either deny or rationalize that whatever happened has nothing to do with them. The brain wants to avoid being blamed for problems.

Examples:

▸   Returning from a supermarket you rationalize why you forgot the eggs, "The store was very crowded and noisy so I just got what I could."

▸   Same scenario if you deny forgetting the eggs, "Nobody told me to get eggs. I did not know I was supposed to get eggs, so I didn't."

The lock is the mind's need to be right or fear to be wrong. Rationalization and denial are means to remove blame or accountability from some action. Once we have used these tools a few times successfully, they become an automatic routine.

The key is to become alert, raise your awareness to the deliberate mind, and make a conscious effort to evaluate the situation. What are the negative consequences of taking responsibility for whatever happened? Recognize the ease with which you can accept at least some of the responsibility and what you can do to resolve the problem. The main key is to acknowledge the need to deal with the problem rather than protect your image or reputation.

The ideal is to constantly perform a reality check, to what degree are you responsible and what can you do to resolve the problem rather than relying on these coping mechanisms.

Responsibility

The act of taking responsibility is exceedingly important in life; it means that you are aware of the causes and consequences of your actions, especially when they are not apparent.

The psychology of responsibility is a complex set of skills that takes time to learn. As people learn to be responsible, some actually overdo it, but many fail to be responsible. The mind may learn to carry all the world's problems on its shoulders, experiencing excessive guilt and burdens. Or, the mind may learn to remain apathetic, lazy and escape any sense of responsibility. Over time, either one of these patterns become an automatic routine.

Examples:
▸ Some people believe they cannot do enough to stop hunger around the world. They carry a burden of guilt and suffering on their shoulders.
▸ Other people constantly complain that life is unfair and that never get what they want. However, often these people fail to develop the discipline to take action to achieve their goals.

The lock develops over time as a person continues to repeat one pattern of activity or inactivity. This also requires knowledge of the laws of cause and effect as well as the skills of how to get things accomplished. If an individual does not learn these factors, he or she will create limitations on his or her potentials. For those who become overly responsible, it can be due to the mind's failure to accurately evaluate the causes and consequences of events.

The key is to recognize the need to be accurate when looking at the causes and consequences of events in your life. Raise your awareness to the deliberate mind and make a conscious effort to analyze the situation and consider how minimizing or exaggerating your responsibility can affect the ultimate goals you have. The main key is to shift polarities away from any extreme position that blocks you and seek the correct balance of responsibility that is accurate. Take action.

The ideal sense of responsibility is dynamic, constantly evaluating your actions to be aware of what has happened or what may happen. It is balanced, prepared to take responsibility for events you are involved with and yet, remains accurate regarding the degree of responsibility you and others may need to carry.

Sensitivity

This is a matter of two systems, how well your radar works and how flexible and strong you are. Sensitivity can refer to our awareness of others or lack of it, and it can also refer to our internal strength to deal with adversity or crumble under pressure. The two positive polarities of sensitivity are important and valuable. One system is your intuitive radar and rational mind that can quickly inform you of all the subtle events going on around you. The other system demonstrates strength, resilience, and the stamina to tolerate great hardship.

The psychology of sensitivity refers to two separate systems. The sensitivity to external events gives us the ability to empathize, sympathize, be kind, understand, and relate to others in a caring manner. The polar opposite is a person who is cold, callous, disconnected from others, calculating, manipulative, self-serving, and does not care how others feel. The internal system refers to how sensitive one is to the difficulties of life. The positive end is a person who is incredibly flexible, adaptive, and hardened to deal with anything without complaining. The opposite polarity is a person who is too sensitive, so that any adversity (physical, mental or emotional) crushes him or her; they are wimps.

Examples:

► You notice a friend at a party who is unusually quiet; you make an effort to pull him or her aside and ask him or her to confide in you if there is something that you could help them with. Conversely, someone asks you for help, but you shun him off because you have no patience for his complaints.

► At a high-pressure job, your replacement for the next shift never makes it, so you take no breaks and start your second shift. Conversely, someone may ask you to mind their tasks so they can go to a bathroom and you complain that it is too much to do.

The locks are found in the reflexive mind, which is more likely to push you in the negative direction. The fears and need for self preservation lead to patterns that create an illusion that the negative polarities are more desirable.

There are two keys, the first is to become more aware of your intuition and learn to listen to your inner radar, as well as the rational ability to pick up subtle cues that help you be more sensitive. This requires asking questions and investigating what may not be obvious. This also means that a sensitive person develops the criteria to analyze how others feel or how well they are doing. The other key is build up your resilience, develop a self image that is tough, ready for any challenge, prepared to tolerate pain or hardship without complaining. This requires a very strong will power and a clear set of intentions in your deliberate mind. When you practice dealing with adversity, your stamina improves.

The ideal is when you are very sensitive to other people's needs you are able to predict and respond to what should be done. In addition, it is a great advantage to develop a tough protective shield for yourself to enable you to tolerate all the burdens you must confront.

Attitudes

There is a vast variety of attitudes that make life easier or more complicated. The most basic polarity is between positive, optimistic, and adaptive attitudes versus the negative, pessimistic, and stressful ones.

The psychology of attitudes refers to many separate systems; whatever they are, each can be divided along the same polarities - positive or negative. In general, attitudes are positions or approaches we have about life. They must be learned over many years; then they become a simple pattern. The positive polarity is open, receptive, flexible, filled with hope, faith, and is based on the anticipation of happy events. The opposite direction predicts negative events, lacks hope, is not adaptive and arouses fear, anger and pain. One side is optimistic, the other pessimistic; it is easy to go in the negative direction, but certainly possible to reverse polarities.

Examples:

▸   The optimist is constantly telling you everything will work out, have faith; believe in yourself; with a positive attitude, you are bound to succeed.

▸   T he pessimist is focused on all the problems: what did not work; what is likely to fail; and questions the merit of everything, raising the levels of anxiety and stress.

The locks are the result of the complex interaction of events and emotional reactions. The greater the number of negative emotional events in life, the harder it is to be an optimist. One could argue that either being an optimist or a pessimist is just distortions of reality because you cannot count on either attitude. However, the optimistic approach is unquestionably better and healthier, despite reality.

The key to escape hopelessness and not be stuck in a pessimistic perspective requires constant polarity shifting. Every time a negative thought arises, it must be countered by a realistic positive one. This is accomplished by being alert, focused on the higher mind, and establishing clear intentions of an optimistic attitude. That means adopting a positive, flexible, open, happy mindset that enables you to gather the energy to reach your goals.

The ideal attitude is truthfully total optimism, believing in yourself and your goals, remaining flexible and doing your best to adapt in good ways to difficult events. Whenever doubt raises its ugly face, you must quickly reverse polarities and return to faith in yourself.

Obsessiveness

This is a pattern that most people have to deal with on some level. To obsess means to focus on something and be unable to release it from attention: a person just cannot let go of whatever it is. If we were not obsessive, we would never have been able to put a man on the moon or accomplish any other feat that requires prolonged concentration. Obsession can be good and bad. When you cannot forget something bad that happened, you may drive yourself and others crazy about it.

The psychology of obsessiveness begins with simply directing attention; with time and repetition, what might have been an important activity may become an unwanted obsessive pattern. This may occur on the level of activities, feelings, or just thinking. Whatever form the obsession is in, if it fails to produce valuable and desirable effects, it should be stopped. There are countless patterns of obsessive behaviors; when they begin to create stress, then it is time to switch polarities.

Examples:

▸ You realize an important exam is approaching, so you suspend all other activities for a couple of weeks to just obsessively study and prepare for the test.

▸ A close relationship turns sour; all the plans fall apart, and it ends up that neither person wants to remain friends with the other, but despite the bad feelings both people cannot stop thinking and complaining about each other.

The locks for obsessiveness are complex. In general, the mind makes something that was important the unnecessary focus of attention. The reflexive mind makes you unwilling to stop because it causes anxiety or anger to keep the obsession going. The true test for an obsession is very simply to see what really happens when you stop; usually nothing.

The keys are first to recognize that you are in an unproductive pattern. The question to ask is, "What am I gaining from obsessing about this now?" One solution might be just to allow time to intervene. The main key is to learn how to *Let Go*, to release the matter from attention and shift your focus onto something useful. This may require a few steps because the anxiety or anger the obsession creates may be paralyzing and must be transformed as well. In short, reverse directions, relax, gain control, accept the past and move forward. This process also requires a very strong will and clear intentions of what will move you away from wasting time and help you become more productive.

The ideal process begins with quickly identifying a behavior as an unwanted obsession, deciding on a better direction, letting go of everything associated with the old pattern, and shifting focus to the new goals.

Sabotage

This is a common pattern of destructiveness to yourself or others. Sabotage can take one of two negative directions: increased attention with excessive criticism or ignoring and not caring about someone. The result is that the individual's potentials, performance and achievement are crippled by persistent sabotage.

The psychology of sabotage can be described as two separate systems. The sabotage can be the result of focusing attention on a person's performance with intense, unrelenting criticism. This can come from another person or it can be internalized and self-directed. The other cause is from a lack of attention, total disregard for a person's performance, and an absence of any feedback. This usually is externally directed, but it can be internalized as well. When such sabotage continues repeatedly, it becomes a powerful pattern. The consequence either way is the inevitable fall of performance and failure to achieve the intended potentials.

Examples:

▸ The critical comments you listened to for a long time finally became your own automatic patterns, sabotaging yourself with negative thoughts like, "it is not worth it; you will never succeed."

▸ You feel isolated, unwelcome, an outsider that nobody wants to talk to or interact with. You have no idea whether your work is acceptable or not; no one cares about what you do.

The locks are the result of negative events repeated for so long that they create an internal pattern. These are typical problems for the automatic mind because it is very easy to repeat the pattern, but it is very difficult to become aware of how destructive it is.

The keys to solve this problem begin with becoming more aware of your patterns and accessing your higher self. Then you must confront the negative patterns and create opposite positive programs that can replace the unwanted ideas. Now switch polarities, instead of critical sabotage, repeat encouraging affirmations. Do not let yourself be intimidated by your own thoughts or listen to negative stories from others. Sometimes this requires you to assert yourself and demand more respect with honest and constructive feedback.

The ideal is when you immediately realize that any criticism or lack of recognition cannot throw you off the path to success. You are able to stop any of the negativity and replace it with absolutely positive statements like,

"I am confident to succeed; every effort I make will reward me; I am glad my intentions are to achieve every goal; I intend to exceed everyone's expectations including my own!" These are the polarity shifts you must make to keep a positive attitude and reach your goals.

Neurotic behaviors

Ultimately we all live in patterns because that is what makes us feel comfortable. We may start doing things in various ways until we find our own way to do it and develop a routine. This routine creates a comfort zone for us. Now we become locked into this comfortable routine. We lose freedom because we refuse to be flexible; instead, we always go to our routine pattern. This is where we all get stuck, repeating a pattern that may give us comfort, but that steals away our freedom. Curiously, these routines do not bother us, but they do tend to annoy others because they are quick to see the other possibilities being ignored. This is the most common human problem: inflexibility or "neurotic behavior." We all develop comfortable routines. When these patterns limit our own or other people's freedom, then they become neurotic.

Every person becomes neurotic to some degree, developing routines that he or she does not want to give up. In reality, most of us are flexible enough to break away with little discomfort from many of these routines if motivated to do so. Others suffer anxiety or general stress when forced to alter their patterns. Being a little neurotic is completely normal. However, the more routines a person has that he or she cannot change, the less flexible his or her life becomes. When an individual is dominated by patterns that must be followed, he or she enters a self-imposed prison. Not only does this person lose freedom, he or she becomes extremely anxious or angry at even the suggestion of changing the routines.

Any behavior can be "neurotic" if despite having many possible choices, you always choose just one pattern, usually because it is comfortable. We are quick to give up our freedom to enjoy a comfortable routine. It is paradoxical that we also desire to feel free, able to do whatever we want to do, which goes directly against this natural tendency to get stuck in routines. Curiously, we only experience discomfort from another person's neurotic behavior, never our own. That is because it is stressful, frustrating, or just unpleasant to have our freedom limited by someone else.

The psychology of patterns that we get stuck in represents our basic lack of flexibility. This is the result of the interaction of the automatic mind and our desire for simple, familiar routines that are easy for us to repeat. Despite the fact that these routines tend to limit our freedom, they simplify our lives. We universally enjoy repeating patterns that are pleasant to us. Once we create a comfort zone about a behavior routine, it becomes very difficult to change. These neurotic patterns are linked to obsessions and compulsions which imply the internal pressure to do something despite any actual requirement. Any effort to change one of these patterns usually evokes intense emotions of anxiety or anger to keep things the same. The basic question to determine if some routine is neurotic or not is to ask, "if there are many other choices to pick from, do you still feel compelled to follow your routine, or are you eager to try other possibilities?" If you can be flexible and try new things you are ok; if the answer is to follow a routine, then you are stuck in a neurotic pattern.

Examples

▸   Some people must arrange all their bills facing the same way; however, if you are behind them in line, it becomes annoying waiting for them to put away their money.

▸   Do you know people who cannot leave dirty dishes in the sink even when they are late to a special social event, and obviously the dishes can wait harmlessly till the next day.

▸   Many people have a set routine about getting intimate; their mate often becomes frustrated by his or her partner's inflexibility to try anything new or different.

▸   There are people who must go to the exact same place for their one vacation a year and no amount of pleading from their family could motivate them to try a different place.

▸   Ever drive with someone instructing the driver about everything they do behind the wheel?

▸   Some people are meticulously neat and organized;, everything must be in its place; then there are others who are the opposite, messy, and don't care where they place anything. When these people are near each other there is an instant conflict.

The locks are due to a lack or awareness of the effect some behavior has on you or others. Nearly everyone gets stuck in a routine because it is either very rewarding to repeat it or extremely stressful if it is not repeated. We do not like change. Once a pattern is learned, the comfort zone keeps us locked to that behavior.

The keys are to increase self-awareness by going to your higher self and become sensitive to other people's feelings. If your action is causing irritation to someone, then it is time to reflect about your behavior to see if your pattern could change. If your routine limits your or other's options, then acknowledge that behavior might be neurotic. Consider all the possible alternatives available to you; make it your intention to be more flexible, and decide to try a good alternative. Do not expect the new pattern to feel as comfortable as your old routine, but with time every new pattern can reach a new comfort zone. It may be necessary for you to transform any negative feelings about changing behaviors into positive emotions. Shift away from the neurotic patterns. Decide to gain freedom and flexibility to try something new or different. Realize that the new routine can actually be better than the old one and certainly create more harmony with others around you. The polarity shift for these patterns is focused on the inflexibility and reversing directions toward greater flexibility. That has always been touted as a valuable capacity among people. Successful change does require a strong will power to explore and initiate new alternatives to your previous patterns.

The Ideal is to always be sensitive to your own habitual routines and see how they affect others. Usually our own neurotic behaviors do not bother us, but they annoy others. Consequently, if we can be more flexible, adventurous, creative, constantly exploring new possibilities, it is less likely we will get stuck in undesirable patterns. Being eager and ready to seek change, variety, or doing old things in different ways can help keep us and others more sane. Otherwise we all know how the neurotic things people do drive us crazy.

Conclusion: This chapter introduced you to the techniques of shifting polarities from unwanted to the desired direction. Each of the JEEP factors will be described in a similar manner. On page 284 you have a summary table that describes the negative and positive differences for each of the four aspects. Apply these tools in your life and go in positive directions!

Chapter 20

Energy

If you try sometimes, you may find that you get what you need.

Mick Jagger

What is Energy?

Energy is the currency of life. Everything you do involves some amount of energy. The best term to describe this energy is passion. The more passion you produce and exchange, the more energy flows around you. This is what makes people feel prosperous, important, and happy - attracting more energy into their lives. The energetic level is the specialization of the Eastern approach to life; this is the intuitive information we perceive, the subtle signals that we do not always notice.

On a simple level, energy can be seen in any movement; the faster and more powerful, the greater the level of energy, much like a karate champion breaking several boards with his hand. It can also be felt in a handshake, a hug, or a massage. Passion can be expressed in the tone of your voice, the excitement on your face, the sparkle in your eyes, or the gestures you make. A speech can be boring, lifeless and monotone, or the same speech can be presented in a very dynamic way, with lots of passion and enthusiasm that makes it come alive. The key is in how things are done – either with or without energy. You are born with an automatic energy radar that tells you exactly how much you are getting or spending.

What is the purpose of energy?

The main purpose of energy is to make things happen. The nature of energy is such that the more energy or passion one puts into something, the more will happen. The question then is how do you increase the amount of energy in your life? As you discover the ways to increase passion in your actions, you will enjoy more of the benefits of a passionate life. We all awake with a set amount of energy every day. How you use your energy is your choice; you can waste it, conserve it, or you can maximize it.

How does energy work?

Each part of the Triplex mind contributes its share to the overall amount of energy you express. Vibration is the mechanism by which energy moves. Passion is experienced as various levels of vibration. The internal radar instantly tells us how much energy is there and which direction it is moving in. Emotional energy is the most obvious form of passion; people can scream with excitement or whisper with satisfaction. You can see energy at work watching athletes performing amazing feats of agility in the air. Similarly, you can observe two chess champions concentrating over a board game. In every situation, the amount of energy being generated or exchanged, and the direction it is moving in is easy to notice. The problems begin when the flow of energy is blocked or interfered with in some way.

What are the polarities?

On the positive side, you are free to express passion by acting in fun and dynamic ways. This passion usually generates attention, confidence, power, motivation, stamina, assertiveness, health, and vitality. On the negative side, you can feel weak, fatigued, lazy, apathetic, isolated, lonely, unwanted, rejected, jealous, envious, lacking vigor, or just being ill. There is a very wide spread between the positive and negative aspects of energy. There are countless varieties of vibration that can appear at many different levels of energy

What are the psychological lessons?

The most important discovery about energy is to keep it flowing. There are only two things that energy can do; be stored for later use or be utilized. Some of your physical energy is dependent on your nutrition, but most of your energy is psychological. That means that regardless of how much food or physical energy you may have available, your passion depends mostly on your state of mind and how well you can express that energy in good ways. Many things influence your state of mind, which affects how much energy you feel. The key is to build awareness of what level of passion you are feeling, how to keep it flowing, and being in a good mood.

What are the locks?

Most of the locks originate in all three levels of the Triplex mind, but are often triggered on the social level. You may feel uncomfortable, awkward, shy, or insecure, or have some sort of sabotaging programs, illusions, or distortions that can rob you of strength. Frequently, the social situation you find yourself in can cause these negative polarities to take over your life. Unless you react to this problem, reverse directions, and generate more passion, you will remain stuck.

The locks are often manifested as blockages, slowing the flow of energy, leakages that drain strength, or cause difficulty in connecting with the available energy. The greatest loss of energy usually is caused by individuals with an over inflated ego and an exaggerated sense of entitlement. These people make unreasonable demands and always expect more than they receive; he or she may constantly want to be the center of attention at everyone else's expense.

What are the Key Instructions to Correct Energy Imbalances?

Let's assume that you have discovered an imbalance of energy that you want to correct. Below are the Master Keys to correct the imbalance of energy or to increase its flow when there are blockages. First is a set of questions to evaluate the energy condition. This is followed by the Master Keys and a list of general steps to change the level of passion in your life. Depending on each specific lock of energy, there may be slight variations; the steps outlined here are the most common. After reviewing these instructions, you will find ten typical examples of energy locks and be given the keys to deal with them.

The questions to ask to identify and evaluate problems with energy:

1. What type of energy or passion are you dealing with, and what is its source?

2. Measure the current level of energy, and consider how much more flow is possible.

3. When you reflect about your situation and the level of energy, can you determine how much the circumstances around have affected your energy?

4. What can you change about the internal or external conditions to promote a greater flow of passionate energy at this moment?

5. Do your behaviors inhibit or interfere with the flow of energy in others?

6. Are you able to connect with and generate more of the energy in others around you?

7. What can you do to express more passion in your life?

8. Can you express more positive energy like smiling, happy, enthusiastic, eager, humorous, fun, and playful behaviors?

These are the Master Keys described earlier to deal with energy:

MK 102

Be aware of the energy or vibration you feel inside yourself or coming from others; how well does your energy resonate with others?

MK 103

Measure the energy levels carefully to determine how much energy you should be contributing.

MK 104

Verify that you are exchanging energy in a fair and just manner with each individual.

MK 105

Keep the energy flowing; release blockages; repair leakages; be generous with your passion.

MK 106

Raise the level of passionate energy above what is required to complete your task.

Now become aware of what to do and what to say:

What to do:

1. Raise your awareness; return to the deliberate mind; focus your attention on your radar to measure the energy levels and direction it is moving in.

2. Access your higher self to seek a better, more objective perspective. Determine the quantity and quality of the energy in you and around you.

3. From your higher mind identify any blockages, leaks, or poor connections to the energy around you. Engage your will power to create the intentions to correct the problem.

4. Acknowledge any discomfort; identify what is the cause of these feelings. Prepare yourself to transform unwanted emotions.

5. Transform any negative destructive vibrations into their polar opposite positive emotions. Confirm that you are in a positive state of physical energy, and visualize yourself performing your tasks with passion and enthusiasm.

6. Assert that you have made it your intention to increase the amount of positive passionate energy flowing through you.

7. Being deliberate, try to connect with positive sources of energy to have an abundance to exchange with others at the right time, building your patience and tolerance.

8. Practice exchanging positive energy with others, verifying that your vibration is beneficial to you and others. As you confront unwanted forms of energy or unpleasant individuals, build your compassion and boundaries to protect yourself until you experience a healthy balance of energy.

What to say:

1a. I am glad to be increasing awareness of my life so that I can be very sensitive to the energy flowing around me.

2a. Now within my higher self, I must be objective about my situation because I am free to improve my life.

3a. As I become aware of any limitations to the flow of energy, I recognize the best way to increase the exchange.

4a. I am aware of the negative emotions holding me back, and I am glad to be ready to change.

5a. Polarity shifting now puts me on a new positive vibration that feels good and does good.

6a. I am glad to raise my confidence to generously exchange positive energy with others.

7a. This is my opportunity to exercise my strength and control over the energy in my life.

8a. It feels good to maintain a healthy balance of energy, building my patience and tolerance for challenges in life.

What are the Top Ten Problems with Energy?

Attention

The act of paying attention gives energy; similarly, ignoring someone takes energy away. These are the two polarities of attention, spending it or acquiring it. This includes your will power and the intentions you decide to focus on or ignore.

The psychology of attention begins with an automatic mechanism attracting your focus on important events around you; the system continues to develop the ability to direct attention wherever you decide you want to. This requires tools described earlier about attention. This includes your ability to feel motivated, ambitious, determined, and focused on reaching certain goals. With practice, you improve your ability to express more enthusiasm, patience, excitement, tolerance, passion, and self-control to act more effectively. The more control you develop over your attention, the easier it is for you to decide what to focus on or what to ignore.

Examples:
- When someone monopolizes a conversation and insists that you listen to every word, especially if the content is only about them and not really important after a few minutes, you may want to ignore him or her.
- Perhaps you take some children to see a magic show that does not interest you; however, when the magician takes a hundred dollar bill from you and makes it disappear, you certainly will pay attention to the show and your money.

The lock can be either the result of the unequal exchange of energy or just the unfair demand for more attention than necessary.

The keys are to become alert; if your radar sends an alarm because there is an imbalance of energy, redirect your attention to regain a comfortable balance. Raise the awareness of the other people who may not be exchanging energy in a fair manner. Help others find a balanced way to pay attention. You may need to shift your attention elsewhere or decide to ignore something. Any unfair demand of attention is very draining; do not allow such situations to continue for long.

The ideal is to be more aware of your radar's signals and quickly respond to inequalities. Be mindful of what you are paying attention to and what you are ignoring. Seek an objective perspective to verify that your attention is being used effectively and fairly.

Lack of Will Power

The subject of will power has been addressed in the master keys. When there is a lack of this vital energy, things just do not get done. Once we establish a plan or intentions, we engage our will power to achieve goals. "Will" refers to a clear intent, and "power" means the physical, emotional, and mental strength to complete a task. In order for this system to do the job correctly, it requires a good plan, resources, and opportunity. Naturally, if any of these basic aspects are missing you will lack the energy to accomplish your goals.

The psychology of will power: the main skills required are knowing how to be motivated, determined, enthusiastic, energetic, and having the resilience, stamina, vitality, and the knowledge to utilize these tools. On a mental level, a good imagination is required to keep clear images of what you want to accomplish in your mind. This also includes good judgment in order to make the right decisions about what your intentions are. The intentions must be realistic, well planned, and built upon the resources available.

The common problems concern something that may be missing. The lack of physical will power results in weakness, fatigue, and laziness. On the mental level, the inability to imagine the future impairs intentions and actions. And on the emotional level, passion either delivers the "electricity," or it does not have enough "voltage" to drive anything.

Examples:

▸ You give a great talk, but don't do the walk. You tell people how ambitious you are, how much you want to accomplish, yet you spend most of your time sprawled out on a couch watching television. This is a lack of energy.

▸ You have the energy to make things happen, but you remain uncertain or confused about where to start and what to do; this leaves you paralyzed. This is a lack of imagination.

▸ Some individuals have a vision, get excited and start working intensely on their goals, but soon they lose their passion, become disillusioned, and eventually just give up. This is a lack of will power.

The locks arise from three sources. Most commonly, people just do not have the physical energy or passion to reach their goals. Others lack the imagination to visualize their plans or intentions clearly enough to develop a viable strategy to accomplish their goals. There are some people who have the vision and energy, but lack the passion to build up their drive, ambition, desire and determination for reaching their goals. Together or separately, these locks result in a lack of will power.

The key is to first recognize which aspect is missing or not functioning well. This requires you to increase awareness objectively and maximize the physical strength, emotional passion, and the mental imagination. Acknowledge any weakness you may be experiencing and determine what you can add to boost that aspect. Physically, build up your endurance and stamina by exercising the body and practicing your activities. To increase the passion, you must recall a previous peak experience that you are certain was extremely energetic and emotionally powerful. Recreate that feeling while directing your attention on your new goals. Anchor this energy with a power move to your body with specific intentions. Creating superior visions of the future requires practice and continual enhancement. Start with a general plan. Then develop more specific strategies writing all the details down. (These are exercises that are offered in the live workshop format; see the Appendix for details.)

The ideal is to develop your will power with a superior amount of physical energy, passion, and absolute clarity of intentions. When you know what you want, have a precise plan to get there, and feel inspired and determined – nothing should stop you.

Excessive Will Power or Stubbornness

The more successfully one leads his or her life, the more such a journey demands that each aspect be well developed. Those individuals who create a very strong will power without clear perceptions and good judgment are setting themselves or others up for a great deal of frustration. The problem is that when you have set your intention on an unrealistic goal or fail to notice important factors then regardless of how much drive and energy you have, the goal remains unattainable. Stubbornness or unfair demands are often something that you have to deal with because it is imposed on you by others. This again is an imbalance of energy going in one direction rather than moving back and forth.

The psychology of excessive will power: This is a condition where the greatest strength is found in an individual's will to have things his or her way. There is a disproportionate investment of energy in satisfying the person's needs in the absence of what is most appropriate or fair. We use the term stubborn to refer to a person who will not change his or her personal desires regardless of the reasons to do so. There may be many explanations for a person to behave in such a way. If you are dealing with a stubborn person you will experience difficulties and imbalances in energy. The challenge is to deal with excessive will power in a constructive way promoting a balanced exchange of energy.

Examples:

▸ It is common to hear someone ask the same question over and over because he or she is not satisfied with the answer given.

▸ A typical argument couples often have is who decides what they will do. Usually the man is the stubborn one who insists on what both will do, while the spouse agrees after some amount of ineffective protest.

The locks arise from two sources. Most people fail to develop all three sources of power evenly. Among these people, some develop will power much more than the power of perception and/or judgment. This creates a lock by impairing access to at least one of the other necessary powers. The other lock appears from an over inflated ego or sense of self-importance. The ego issue will be addressed in the last example. The problem for people with a very strong will is that when they try to reach an unrealistic goal, it becomes very frustrating. These activities are seen as pure stubbornness, they will not lead to any achievements.

The keys begin with recognizing what is an objective evaluation of the energy being exchanged; is it balanced or not? As you increase the sensitivity of your radar, you can begin to adjust your behavior to match the right amount of will power for the situation. Those who deal with stubborn people must attempt to point out, in a very concrete way, what a balanced exchange of energy is. The rules of reciprocity here are obvious, but there are people who will not accept these rules. The only thing that can be done in some situations is to escape and then avoid contact with these people. For those of you who are being told by others that you are stubborn, it is simple to raise your awareness and surrender to do things someone else wants to do.

The ideal is to have a very sensitive radar to immediately know when others feel that the energy exchange is not balanced and ask them how to reciprocate. A superior person will constantly work to develop all three sources of power in order to avoid the problems listed above. Will power shall always remain a vital skill to achieve realistic goals with good strategies.

Connecting with Energy

This is a matter of all the various ways that we find to connect to others, events, places, feelings, thoughts, just about any source of energy at all. This requires a sensitive radar that we all have, but do not always rely on. This radar is an internal system by which we can instantly measure the quantity, quality, and nature of energy first inside of us and then from any external source. There are situations in which you immediately feel comfortable and others that remain just awkward no matter what. To connect to anything we must "read" the type of vibration or energy coming from that source and then decide whether we resonate with it or not. This is a very natural and vital part of life.

The psychology of connecting with energy is based on what we relate to and how close we feel to those things or people. There are no limits to what you can connect to. When you resonate with another person or place, that means there is a rewarding connection that feels positive and happy. You most likely also have good associations with that source. Connecting requires little skill, just an effort to engage, receive, and give energy on some level.

Examples:
▸ The classic is, boy meets girl. Do you remember that moment when you met that special person? You both looked at each other and knew there was a real connection.
▸ Perhaps you remember being invited to a party where you did not know anyone except the one person who invited you. As you walk around greeting a few more friendly people, you still wait to find the close friend who you hope will introduce you to others.

The lock is experienced when you turn off your radar, or when you really fail to find anyone that you can connect to. The problem is how to turn up the sensitivity of your radar. There is always a possibility to connect with somebody on some level, if you are searching for some mutual vibe. There is also the problem of connecting to sources of energy; when the mind inhibits you from receiving good energy, then you may miss out on important opportunities. This lock may work on many levels that can block a person from connecting and absorbing valuable energy.

The key is to become more alert and raise your awareness of the situation you are in. As you look around, search for any aspects that you might be able to relate to. Then try to tune your radar to those aspects and focus your attention there to increase your intuitive sensitivity. Become aware of whatever you notice – images, thoughts, feelings, etc. Start searching for meaningful associations that feel good. Then make an effort to express whatever you experience to others and wait for a response. If you generate a connection, you will know; if not, you can try again. In essence, the more we connect with the abundance of energy around us, the better life gets.

The ideal is to have excellent control over your radar's sensitivity and be able to tune it to every situation easily to facilitate connecting to all the interesting sources of energy around you. For those more adventurous, you can attempt to transcend many of the conventional levels of energy and try to connect to the more mystical sources or esoteric vibrations.

The Flow

This is a matter of learning to appreciate the various forms in which energy flows. I remember watching the Hudson River at high tide when the downstream movement became swirling patterns. The river became a battle ground between the upstream water fighting against a wall of seawater being pushed by the tide. The waves were choppy and erratic. Sometimes it appeared chaotic; eventually the water would begin to move in one direction. That is the nature of flow; it is alive, moving, changing, struggling, or just flowing peacefully.

The psychology of flow refers to the movement and direction of energy. There exists an endless assortment of energetic movements. We all have our own favorites. The sound of your car or motorcycle as you accelerate around a nice country road. The smell and sound of food cooking. Listening to music that perfectly fits the moment. Energy is about movement. The essential skill we all possess is to sense that movement; and then we can relate to it. Psychologically we respond to the energy on many levels. We can act generously, promoting the flow, or act with greed and block the flow. We can appreciate the vibration, express gratitude, or we can ignore the energy and complain that there is not enough. This can be compared to basic ideas of Eastern philosophy – being in the moment and embracing the activity near you.

Examples:

▸   Perhaps you recall enjoying some event. What if you are sitting next to someone who is constantly answering business calls on his cell phone. It is likely that would be disturbing, blocking you from fully appreciating the event.

▸   Have you ever seen somebody make a big fuss at a nice restaurant, complaining about everything that he or she is served? If they are sitting near you, it can easily interfere with your meal.

The locks are from the mind's tendency to be negative. We easily get caught up in our own routines and forget to notice the bigger perspective. This may lead us to do something that interferes with the flow of events around us. Sometimes we cause the energy to leak; that means to be drained too quickly because the demands we make are too big or there is a lack of reciprocity. Other times people will block the flow of energy completely.

The key is to raise your awareness up to the deliberate mind and evaluate your situation more objectively. Make it your intention not to block the flow of energy, interfere with it, or make others feel that you are draining them unfairly. Review the movement of energy around you and eliminate any negative impact you might have had. Promote the optimal flow, be generous, enthusiastic, eager, optimistic, and generate strong positive energy yourself. If you are confronted by other people who are blocking or disturbing the flow of energy, alert them to the problem with a suggestion about how to correct it. Encourage others to think up, shifting negative polarities into positive ones.

The ideal is to be a role model of an energetic, positive, enthusiastic person who is sensitive to the flow of energy, does not interfere with that flow, and instead keeps increasing the amount of energy flowing.

Patience and Rewards

Energy can be utilized immediately or it can be stored for later. Learning how to effectively store energy for another time is a vital skill. The problem is that we are born impatient, and immediate rewards are usually more attractive than distant ones. The most successful utilization of energy arises from knowing how and when to invest your energy. This is a matter of developing patience and learning to delay your rewards.

The psychology of storing energy is based on knowing how to connect to good sources of energy, finding efficient ways to store it, and then being able to utilize it when ready. While this is a very natural process, it is difficult to be patient and not impulsive, especially when something tempting is right in front of you. This in part is, the will power, to control your intentions. This is also the ability to deal with the movement of energy. When you get an impulse to jump, there is a surge of energy that you may need to redirect if your intention is not to jump. The fact is that resisting any kind of urge, temptation, impulse, or desire is difficult; after all, it is what your body wants. Suppressing this energy takes skills and practice. Increasing your patience or delaying your rewards are valuable skills that the mind constantly fights. The reason for the battle is that we are born hungry for energy, which makes us impulsive. We must learn to be patient and control these impulses; these skills in part rely on our ability to store energy.

Examples:

▸ A couple is in a hurry to go to some social event; one is not ready, and the other must wait patiently without getting anxious, angry, or frustrated. Why is it so difficult?

▸ Some good friends invite you to take a vacation trip with them. You have an important examination that you must study to pass. Your impulse is to go, but your intention is to study instead. What would most people do?

The lock is from the mind's desire to gain energy as quickly as possible. The mind does not enjoy waiting for rewards; it always wants instant gratification. You have been "wired" to be impulsive, and any interference causes the reflexive mind to raise the alarm.

The key is to recognize your weakness and work at overcoming it. Begin by accessing your higher self and make it your intention to develop patience and to put off some rewards for the long term. Learn to bank the efforts you make and act patiently; that means, to identify yourself as a patient person and appreciate the skills you demonstrate waiting. Adopt a healthy attitude. By exercising your patience you build your virtues and show others how to be tolerant. Transform any negative feelings into their polar opposite emotions. Exercise good judgment by evaluating situations and making decisions that will generate the best rewards in the long run. Visualize the benefits of being patient – the appreciation you may get or the ultimate rewards you may earn – by delaying gratification until later. Usually the longer you wait for the rewards, the better they are.

The ideal is to have superior patience, allowing you to wait, when necessary without becoming stressed. This leads to an overall ability to easily resist quick rewards and establish very clear long term rewards that have a much greater value. This enables you to store energy until you are ready to use it.

Money

This is the simplest energy to understand, but a difficult one to master. Money is the principal way we exchange the invested energy we own. Although a dollar is always worth the same amount, everyone makes a different effort to earn it. What is the relationship between effort and money? Doesn't every person value money in a different way? One of the biggest challenges is to have a healthy relationship to money – earning it and spending it. Regardless of how much money is flowing into your life, it often is not enough. That is why arguments about finances are among the most common in families. This is about energy, not money. Depending on how each person translates the value of a sum of money, it represents either an abundance or scarcity. This leads to comfort or stress.

The psychology of money has been a primary topic of modern life. The issue here is not the money, but rather the energy associated with it. Our lives are dominated by the circulation of money; consequently, every person desires to have his or her fair share. The question of energy is a matter of what is that "fair share" in relation to all the other factors. That means that every person feels that the effort he or she makes, along with his or her knowledge, age, experience, and any other factor, determines how much he or she thinks he or she should earn. This is also true going in the opposite direction; whatever you spend, you automatically make a judgment whether it was a fair exchange or not. The psychology of money is separated in those two directions. Did you earn enough money for the energy you put in and did you get enough energy for the money you spent? The polarities are obvious: if positive, we are pleased; if negative, we feel cheated or short changed.

Examples:

▸   What happens when you find out that another person with less experience, knowledge, and similar effort to you is actually earning much more money than you? The job and your income may have been acceptable until you learn of this apparent inequity. How would you feel?

▸   While on a long distance trip, you stop at the only gas station for miles. The price is double what you normally pay. How does it feel to fill up the tank?

The lock is found in the complex relationship we develop between money and ourselves. There are many factors that play into how we think and feel about money and the energy surrounding it. The mind is always quick to slip toward the negative side, feeling that there is not enough money; something costs too much, or the exchange is just not fair for some reason.

The key is to raise awareness to your deliberate mind to evaluate the situation more objectively. What is the basis of the exchange of money? Is it advantageous, reasonable, or unfair? Based on all the previous tools you have learned, seek to establish a better balance. When someone else is unfair with you, it is time to assert yourself and set boundaries that will protect your sense of worth and respect. Problems with money often evoke strong negative reactions from your reflexive mind; if this occurs, shift polarities and transform any negative emotions into positive ones. If you realize that you were causing an imbalance in the energy, then reverse directions and become more generous, create more, share more, and make an effort to promote a fair exchange of money.

The ideal balance is to be very successful at generating large amounts of money and then find ways to generously share the energy. The key is to be aware of how others feel about the exchange of energy and money; usually there are many ways to regain a good balance. Some are based on money; others may rely more on other sources of energy besides the dollar.

The Energy of Sex

This subject will continue to be a central issue in our society. In general, sex has always been a major form of energy that we value very highly. The polarities of sex spread from the deepest and truest love with passionate intimacy, all the way to prostitution with sex for sale, and everything in between. The energetic aspect is reflected in what we do for that intimate pleasure. Both men and women have been known to go to extremes to obtain what they want. The focus here is the energy, not the sex. Although, obviously when the sex is easily available, it requires less investment of energy, and when it is not available, men and women often are ready to invest a great deal of energy to get it when the situation is right.

Psychology has always included the study of sex because it is one of the most important aspects of life. American culture is extremely focused on sexuality, attractiveness, and the power associated with it. Sex, the potential promise of it, even the hint of its availability are all very strong rewards, motivating people to struggle for some of that energy. However, most of the time sexual energy does not lead to actual sex; that is because this energy can be very casual, friendly, flirtatious behavior, formal compliments, or even just personal fantasies about someone. We think about sex far more than we act on it. Consequently, the energy we exchange often gets contaminated by the mind and other factors that distort this sexual energy.

The subject of love is separate from sexual energy. Love is a very special, deep experience that connects two people. If the physical chemistry is good, then intimate encounters are rewarding and love triumphs. If the sexual energy between is poor, then intimacy is not fulfilling. Despite that, it may be passively satisfying. In these cases, the love part of the relationship struggles. There are many possible combinations of love and chemistry that result in either a positive flow of energy, a blockage, or some distortion of reality.

We invest a significant effort every day to experience some of that powerful sexual energy on some level. The major polarities are to feel it flow or experience difficulties that interfere with the movement of this energy.

Examples:
▸   Men, notorious for leaving their wives of many years, give up large fortunes to enter relationships with younger ladies. Consider all the intense emotions people live through during these changes.
▸   Many relationships would not survive all the stresses and difficulties they are forced to endure if sex did not help rebuild the balance of energy. Consider what happens if that energy is blocked.

The locks in this case are the interactions of our lower natures (lust and desire to procreate) with our deliberate minds searching for clever ways to obtain what we want. When our motives become corrupted by our desires, all sorts of strange activities begin. On one hand, ulterior motives create manipulative games in order to get the prize – sex. The deliberate mind is responsible for twisting reality, creating illusions, all in the hope of gaining that special energy only sex can offer. The other lock is a lack of this vital energy. The libido (sex drive) can be shut down or lowered very easily by stress or problems in life. In reality, the energy we get from sex can be very healing and liberating. If this energy is blocked for the wrong reasons, the problems only multiply.

The keys are to become more aware of objective reality. Which problem are you dealing with? Are there blockages to the flow of energy or has the sexual energy been diverted or distorted? If the energy has been blocked, where, by whom, and why? Usually, tension between a couple causes blockages of this energy. This requires a polarity shift; make a deliberate effort to transform any negative feelings into the opposite emotions. The stronger person should apologize and ask how to rebuild a good connection. This is a process and may take time; perseverance leads to rewards. Try to make other forms of energy flow between you until big flood gates open.

The more complicated distortions of energy flow require a great deal more analysis and reflection. You can easily be misled or fooled by your mind or another person who is manipulative. To begin, test the authenticity of the feelings and determine whether actions are being motivated by true feelings. Is it possible that your mind or the other person's has been creating illusions or distorting reality? This requires good judgment and constant verification. If you suspect being led on a detour, then reconsider what your true intentions are and how to return to them. Make your intentions well known and redirect your will power to achieve your wishes.

The ideal is to find true love with a beautiful person with whom you connect naturally and very deeply. The extra special prize is when you both enjoy great chemistry and life becomes very rewarding. Then the sexual energy is constantly flowing, stimulating other aspects in a positive manner.

Intuitions

Intuitions are modes of instant awareness. The experience of intuition can be on a physical, mental, emotional, or a combination of all three levels. In contrast to factual information, intuition is usually just a feeling or sense about something that cannot be explained. We all have had an intuition about people or events in our lives that may have helped us or not. This is another form of energy available to us to make life easier if we know how to use it.

The psychology of intuition is not well understood. There are various theories that try to explain it, however; regardless of how it works, we all recognize its value. That "gut" feeling we get about something, or some inner vision that suddenly comes to us, or a voice advising us, are all examples of intuition. More often, intuition or instincts give us a warning about some form of danger, deception, or distrust. Although intuition has proven to be accurate and very helpful in many instances, there have been equally as many times that it has misled people. When we get a premonition that warns us or encourages us about something, it must be coming from somewhere; even if wrong, it is a reflection of what is going on inside the mind. The information generated by our intuition should always be respected and considered, even if not followed.

Examples:

‣   You meet an outwardly cheerful person, but your intuition warns you that he or she has a dark side which you ignore. As the relationship continues, you realize that your instincts were right.

‣   Did you ever get an intuition that a rational decision you made was wrong? Perhaps you changed your mind or stuck to your original choice only to regret it later.

The lock is found in your struggle to predict events in your world. Although you can make rational choices and reasonable predictions about the future, intuition is your radar to bypass logic and facts. The intuition often goes against the other information you have collected that is objective. The instinctual reactions or feelings you get are very subjective, so that creates a conflict for you to decide which part to listen to – logic or intuition.

The key is to be alert and listen to your internal radar. If you get a strong intuition about something, it is best to take it into consideration. The information is there to help you make a prediction – approach or avoid. If your radar is a warning, best to heed the advice unless you cannot afford to avoid it. Ask yourself what will be the cost if you do it or not. If there is a conflict between your logic and intuition, it should dissolve when you can demonstrate that the risk or cost are not worth ignoring. When you can afford the mistake, at least keep track of your gut feelings for the next time. The idea is to take advantage of this internal energy and make life easier.

When your intuition is urging you to do something against your rational judgment, calculate the cost factors of doing it or not. If you feel comfortable with taking the chance, follow the intuition, you will either succeed at something or get a valuable lesson in life.

The ideal is to develop a very sensitive intuition that consistently steers you away from trouble and guides you toward greater success and prosperity. The internal radar is designed to help you sense the world better; when you learn to trust it, the conflict with the logical and rational process vanishes.

The Ego and Self Worth

This subject is about our personality and self esteem. The ego is commonly used to describe a person's sense of importance or self worth. It actually is much more complicated. The ego refers to a dynamic part of the personality that contributes to maintaining a stable identity. This internal identity or self-image we have is constantly used to deal with events in our everyday life. There are two obvious polarities: those people with a big ego have an exaggerated sense of importance and entitlement, while those with a small ego have poor self-esteem, are insecure, cannot defend themselves, and are easily dominated. The issue here is not the ego, rather the energy that a person controls by the force of his or her <u>character</u>. A healthy sense of self worth is essential to be a successful person. The purpose of a strong ego is to defend the self-image or identity, rather than attack or control others. All individuals express a different amount of energy when they interact with others; some are more meek, while others are extremely demanding and intimidating. This is matter of understanding these differences and dealing with people's energies effectively.

The psychology of the ego and personality traits has filled many books. The main point here is to identify the characteristics of a strong, yet healthy ego that manages an individual's energy resources very well. Those people who have big egos tend to be bossy, controlling, demanding, and feel very important. These individuals use their power to take energy away from others. Conversely, people with small egos tend to be accommodating, insecure, not assertive, not controlling, and usually feel very modest. These individuals easily surrender their energy to others and fail to exercise their power to achieve goals.

The qualities of a strong and healthy ego are available to all, but many get dragged by the mind into one of the two extreme directions. The purpose of the ego is to construct and support a diverse sense of identity. That means that as we grow up we discover all the different things we can do or be and integrate them all together. As our sense of individuality grows we become increasingly confident of who we are and what we can do. The ego helps us in this process and is supposed to protect us if anyone puts us down, criticizes us, or tries to minimize us. In this way, a healthy ego gives us power to defend our identity, feel more confident, and have the energy to achieve our goals.

Examples:

▸   Do you recall meeting a person who thinks he or she is entitled to special privileges, is vain, treats others like servants, makes unreasonable demands and is critical of everything, but can never be wrong? This inflated sense of importance is a common part of a big ego.

▸   Have you watched a competition where the most talented person is the most insecure, shy and self-conscious person among all the people? This individual has not developed his or her ego fully and still lacks confidence.

The locks arise from the failure of the ego to develop a healthy sense of identity or from an ego that is over developed, creating unwarranted expectations from life. The big ego demands energy from others without any reciprocity. The small ego lacks power to assert him or herself and gives away energy without expecting any in return. Both of these directions range from mild to extreme; they always cause a significant imbalance in the energy exchanged between people and are responsible for major problems in life.

The key is to raise your awareness to the higher self and begin to imagine how others see you in order to evaluate yourself more <u>objectively</u>. Shift any negative polarities to positive ones. In the case of a big ego, transform the anger, criticism, arrogance, self-importance, self-love into the opposite emotions or attitudes. This requires individuals with inflated egos to surrender their sense of entitlement, move toward modesty, express more acceptance, tolerance, and caring. In contrast, those who have a small ego must build up their confidence and verify what is an accurate or realistic sense of what he or she deserves. Respect is the central concept for matters of the ego; it is equally important to have respect for yourself and others. Beyond these points, transform any negative feelings into the opposite emotions. As you observe the situation you are in, determine if the energy being exchanged is fair. Make it your intention to correct any imbalance and inquire with others to verify everyone feels comfortable.

The ideal is to develop a stable sense of identity with a strong ego that is programmed to defend the self-image without attacking others. A healthy ego is one that builds and supports characteristics that create a diverse identity with universally admirable traits. It also provides a resilience that handles criticism well, failures easily, and is generous with his or her energy resources. One of the most important attitudes such a person is known for is an incredibly optimistic perspective anchored in an objective reality.

Conclusion

This chapter described the various ways energy is directed, shared or taken. When we exchange our energy there is an unwritten rule that it should be relatively fair. That means that every person anticipates getting approximately the same amount of energy back that he or she puts in; if this exchange is out of balance, it creates problems, anxiety, anger, pain or disgust. The main key is to increase awareness and shift polarities towards a positive healthy balance of energy. Those who learn to manage the flow of energy enjoy the rewards of a fulfilling life.

Sometimes the duality of life is perfectly balanced.

Chapter 21

Emotions

This chapter discusses an important part of my system – the integrated perspective of the Eastern and Western understanding of emotions and a new strategy of how to deal with them more effectively. As you discover the simplicity and new connections that have not been pointed out previously, you will gain a bigger sense of power and control over your life.

What are Emotions?

There is a vast number of emotions that range from the darkest, most negative to the brightest, most positive feelings we experience. We are all born with the negative emotions that arise from the lower nature of our Reflexive Mind. All the positive emotions must be learned and developed and arise from the higher nature of our deliberate mind. The nature of emotions is directly coded into our bodies and brains. The general experience of each feeling is very similar for everyone. However, the specific meaning or intensity of each feeling is more subjective because our personal experiences shape all the details.

What is the purpose of emotions?

Above all, emotions are the substance of the meaning that we get from life. Without feelings, our experience of life would be empty, with no preferences, no likes or dislikes. The actual purpose of each emotion has been divided into three specific parts.

1. Each emotion functions as an alarm to make us aware of a state of being that focuses our attention on specific events.

2. Every person then has a psychological response to feeling; we get scared and run, or we become happy, laugh, and have fun. These are the normal ways feelings make us behave.

3. Each emotion is supposed to stimulate us to at least think of the polar opposite feeling, if where we are feels good, then stay, if not shift. If you feel happy, you need not reverse your emotions and get sad, but being aware of how far above negative you are can enhance your positive feelings. If the emotions are negative, certainly you can reverse them.

The concept of shifting polarities refers to the natural opposites and the process of going from one extreme to the other. Emotions range across two polarities; if we are experiencing the negative group of feelings, we must go to the opposite emotions to turn stress off.

This can be compared to an empty stomach that has not eaten in twelve hours; how does it feel? What does the stomach do? It cannot speak, but it certainly sends us a clear message of what it wants. Similarly, the strong feelings in our bodies are a way for some part of us to "tell" us we need the opposite emotion; for example, if you feel scared, it is a way to create a hunger to call up your courage. The message that comes with any emotion is to seek the polar opposite for balance and to broaden your perspective. If you feel depressed, it is because a part of you wants to search for happiness; if you are lonely, you should seek company, and so on. Even if you are feeling brave, thinking about the fear factor may, in fact, save your life from taking too big a risk of some sort.

How do emotions work?

Every emotion works different parts of the mind and body. That means that when we experience negative feelings like fear, anger, or pain, we are using the reflexive mind, turning on parts of the nervous system that result in stress, and we feel the physical sensations of those feelings. In addition, we may attract similar negative energy and even resonate with others feeling similar emotions. When we experience positive feelings like courage, tolerance, and happiness we use the deliberate mind, turn on the part of the nervous system that brings balance and harmony, and generate the physical sensations of these higher emotions. You also attract that type of energy and resonate with others who enjoy similar emotions. All emotions represent a set amount of energy as well. The more passion we put into the emotion, the more intense it becomes.

What are the polarities?

Emotional polarities are very clearly grouped and completely separated from each other. The main four groups of negative feelings (fear, anger, pain, and disgust) that arise in the lower nature of our reflexive mind have a direct counterpart in the higher nature of the deliberate mind (courage, acceptance, happiness, and love). See the Matrix on page 244.

What are the psychological lessons?

The most important lesson is transformation – changing the negative emotions into positive ones. The key is to know which group of emotions is directly opposite the ones you are experiencing. When you identify the specific feelings you must transform, then you become ready to shift polarities. Reversing directions and then experiencing the positive emotions, relieves stress and allows you to think more clearly and deal with your situation more effectively.

What are the locks?

Most of these locks originate on the biological level of the brain. The negative emotions cause stress: are automatic, instantaneous, go all over your body, have no off-switch, and are at least twenty times larger and faster than the opposite system. They are usually not pleasant, interfere with thinking, and cause other problems.

What are the Key Instructions to Transform Emotions?

The following questions and instructions are the general approach I suggest to transform negative emotions into positive ones. Naturally, specific problems may require slight variations; the steps outlined here are the most common. See the Appendix about various forms of *anchoring*.

The questions to ask to identify and evaluate problems with emotions:

1. What are the exact feelings you are experiencing?

2. What is the alarm and response to these feelings?

3. What are the polar opposite emotions to the experience you are having?

4. Can you recall an experience with these positive emotions?

5. Do you realize how much stress the negative emotions are causing?

6. Can you imagine how the situation will change when you shift polarities?

These are the Master Keys described earlier to deal with emotions.

MK 124

Transforming is shifting polarities; whenever you encounter something negative you seek the polar opposite, reverse directions, and move towards the positive side.

MK 125

Think UP. Go to your higher self, become more objectively aware of your situation and determine what negative emotions you are experiencing. Identify the polar opposite feelings in your higher nature, and then shift your focus to these positive emotions.

MK 126

Practice relaxing and letting go. Be able to quickly and easily release tension and shift focus in your mind.

MK 127

Exercise your ability to identify the polar opposite feelings between the lower and higher nature in your mind. (See the Transformation Matrix page 244.)

MK 128

When you identify the positive emotion, recreate a vivid experience of this feeling and focus your attention on transforming the negative into the polar opposite positive feelings.

MK 129

Remember to acknowledge any degree of success shifting away from stressful emotions to healthy good feelings; become aware of the rewards and benefits.

Now become aware of what to do and what to say:

What to do:

1. Recognize the problem that started the emotions you are experiencing. Raise your awareness to the deliberate mind and identify your feelings.

2. Access your higher self to find a more objective perspective. Notice what is the <u>alarm</u> and your normal <u>response</u> to the challenge you are confronting.

3. Become aware of the stress, pressure, and difficulty thinking at this moment. First, make a decision to stop the stress, relax, and let go. Refocus your attention to slow down your breathing and begin calming your body.

4. From your deliberate mind search the higher nature to identify the specific polar opposite emotions to your negative feelings. Refocus your attention on these positive emotions and recreate their experience.

5. Deliberately transform any negative feelings into the opposite positive emotions you are focused on. Shift polarities! Assert your intention to reverse directions and now express those positive feelings; continue relaxing.

6. Confirm that you are now in a positive state of physical energy and anchor yourself to this new more calm state. Embrace the new emotions, experience the shift, and reconsider the situation you are in.

7. Realize that now you have regained control, decreased stress so that you can more clearly analyze the original problem, and find the best resolution for the situation.

8. Acknowledge the transformation and be certain that you are now feeling good, doing good, and promoting good energy.

What to say:

1a. I am glad to be alert to analyze my situation and know what I am feeling.

2a. It is easy to understand the reason for the alarm and what used to be my normal response.

3a. I am prepared to stop stressing and relax my body now. My intention is to gain control.

4a. I am refocusing my attention on the positive emotions I vividly recall.

5a. I am taking control by shifting polarities now to new positive feelings.

6a. I am glad to experience the positive emotions, releasing tension, and relieving stress.

7a. This proves my ability to shift polarities to gain control of my life.

8a. It feels good to express my positive emotions and promote good energy.

Transformation Matrix

Changing Emotions from Negative to Positive

These are examples of which negative emotions changes into their opposite positive ones. There is no right or wrong answer, any of the feelings in the positive category opposite the negative may be appropriate. The main point is to **shift in the positive direction**.

Negative Lower Nature	Transform these emotions into the polar opposite positive	Pick which one of these emotions is most opposite the negative feelings	Positive Higher Nature
Fear	Anxiety → Doubt → Scared → Tension → Distrust →	Confidence Secure Courageous Relaxed Trustful	**Courage**
Anger	Angry → Frustrated → Jealous → Rage → Greedy →	Accepting Resilient Tolerant Compassionate Generous	**Accepting**
Pain	Sad → Depressed → Guilty → Miserable →	Happy Hopeful Innocent Balanced	**Happy**
Disgust	Disrespect → Pessimistic → Apathetic → Hatred →	Respectful Optimistic Caring Love	**Love**

What are the Top Ten Problems with Emotions?

Fear and Anxiety

This category of feelings – fear and anxiety – protects us from danger. It starts with a simple startle reflex and goes all the way to terror. In general, fear has a paralyzing effect on us; it stops us from acting. It is supposed to motivate us to escape danger. These feelings can cause a tremendous amount of stress physically, emotionally, and mentally. Although anxiety is the most universal feeling, each individual experiences it in a slightly different way.

The psychology of fear starts at the lowest levels of doubts, worries, insecurity, tension, and nervousness. These are feelings that every person has experienced because we are born with them. Anxiety continues to increase from mild to extreme intensity. Most people have had an anxiety attack for some reason. Fear can escalate to panic attacks or even a state of terror. <u>Remember that there is no "off-switch" for anxiety (see page 73) so that the only way to stop the stress and reactions of fear are by "turning on" relaxation</u>. This requires shifting polarities to courage, confidence, security, ambition, and so on. The positive aspect of fear is that it does protect us from dangers. Our anxiety is a very sensitive radar that quickly notices potential dangers that we actually observe, or it can detect even hidden threats through our intuition. In short, anxiety is a way to get information of what to expect. Unfortunately, the mind can easily distort these messages and make us very frightened for no good reason.

Examples:

▸ You are driving on a very slippery road when suddenly your car begins to skid out of control. You quickly try to determine if you will hit another car or something on the road – you are having an anxiety attack.

▸ After a medical exam, a person is told he or she requires surgery to remove a tumor, but only after the operation will it be known how bad the problem really is. This causes lots of fear.

The locks are in the reflexive mind and all the biological systems that contribute to the experience of fear. It causes us to speed up breathing and make it shallow or even to hold our breath. Fear is often experienced as tension, stomach pains, sweating, among many other symptoms. If the anxiety is chronic, it may cause many serious health problems. The main problem is that fear is self-generating; it grows by itself, and the brain can easily distort images or thoughts to create anxiety.

The keys are to become more alert and raise your awareness to the deliberate mind. Recognize the causes for your fear or anxiety, and analyze if you are really in any danger. Then make it your intention to stop the stress by relaxing and letting go. (See page 307 for details.) Become aware of the fear or anxiety and identify the polar opposite feelings in your higher nature – courage, confidence, and security. Recall these emotions so you can recreate a vivid, positive experience. Now shift polarities, and transform the negative into the positive; think about the fear and then shift to courage. Focus your attention on this positive feeling and continue relaxing, regaining control of the situation. Realize that you are either calm or excited in a positive way, thinking clearly, and ready to resolve any problems successfully. Even if you discovered that you really were in some danger, it is better to approach the problem with a calm body, confidence, and a clear mind. You can always think more effectively with less stress.

The ideal is to be prepared to shift from any level of anxiety to a positive sense of confidence quickly and easily. Learn to be able to relax and regain control over tension almost instantly. Then proceed to resolve the problems that caused the stress with full awareness of your mind.

Worry, Doubt, and Tension

These are emotions that every one of us experiences. They exist to alert us to potential, future trouble. Very often these feelings are generated by our own negative thoughts. These low levels of anxiety can be legitimate or they can be the result of distortions of reality. Ultimately, the purpose of worry is to force us to pay more attention to something potentially threatening.

The psychology of low levels of anxiety begins with the same symptoms, but with less intensity. It is common for us to experience some degree of tension or worry because we are uncertain of what will happen next or we are expecting something unpleasant. The purpose of these feelings is to prepare us for confronting challenges; however, doubts will actually often interfere with achieving our goals and dreams more than they will protect us. The positive aspect of worry is that it builds up just enough tension to help us concentrate better or perform at our best, but if this tension goes over a certain level, it does more harm than good. At the opposite polarity, you will find confidence, excitement, strength, faith, hope, and a relaxed, calm state of being.

Examples:

▸   How often do you worry about money? Will you have enough to pay all the bills, college tuition, the dentist, car repairs, tax increases, and so on?

▸   Remember the last challenge you had at your job, a presentation or special project; did you experience any doubts or tension getting it done?

The lock is from the mind's radar for noticing any potential trouble approaching you. Tension literally builds up in the muscles in preparation for the challenge we will face. Doubt is our way to rehearse failure; what if we cannot do it? Doubt is our internalized sabotage; first, through negative thoughts, and then accompanied by an increasing sense of anxiety. Worry is the mental and emotional stressing over future events. Like fear, worry and tension are self-generating, starting at low levels and continue to grow in intensity. The distortions our minds make lock us into worry.

The keys begin with recognizing the alarm and analyzing the situation carefully. This is time for a reality check. Is there any real problem? What is the worst case? Are you able to prepare for the situation and deal with it effectively? Shift your polarities, connect with your sense of confidence, strength, excitement and replace the worry, tension, or doubts by returning to a relaxed state of mind. From your deliberate mind establish very clear intentions to pull together any resources you require and make a plan to resolve problems with a clear head and plenty of confidence.

The ideal is to never spend or waste much time or energy in worry, tension, or doubt; instead transform these into positive emotions. Regain a relaxed, confident perspective, one that is prepared to deal with any situation intelligently.

Panic Attack

This is a sudden, overwhelming experience of massive anxiety. The common symptoms are emotional panic, extremely high anxiety, difficulty breathing, heart palpitations, sweating, shaking, mental confusion, and the fear of dying. This is not a pleasant feeling. Very often people experiencing a panic attack will end up in an emergency room because they believe they are having a heart attack. Any event (that is personally difficult) can trigger an anxiety attack of some sort. This is simply a very loud alarm in your body to be cautious, to protect yourself from possible danger, even if there is none.

The psychology of anxiety attacks is just a special case of fear in general. What is unique about panic is the sudden, intense impact it has on the individual. This is a good example of how vulnerable we are and how powerful the reflexive system is; even a small trigger can generate a massive anxiety attack. The opposite polarity is a deep state of peaceful relaxation, the mind clear and tranquil.

Example:

▸ Driving along, you enter a long, dark tunnel, and suddenly you become overwhelmed with fear. The walls seem to be caving in on you; you barely make it out to the open road and must pull over because, shaking with anxiety, you cannot drive any more.

The lock is from the reflexive mind taking complete control of the whole body and mind. Most often a panic attack is the result of a distortion of reality. The symptoms of stress can be extreme, and usually this requires professional assistance to manage this problem effectively through psychotherapy or with medication.

The keys are to acknowledge the alarm of an anxiety attack, raise your awareness to the deliberate mind, and evaluate the situation more objectively. Notice what started the problem. Verify that you are safe; even if you think you are having a heart attack you should relax, slow down your breathing and refocus your mind on pleasant thoughts. (See the relaxation exercise in the Appendix) Think of a beautiful, tranquil place where you would feel safe and comfortable. Visualize yourself there and take a few long, slow, deep breaths. Take a few minutes to calm down. Focus on the experience of relaxing very deeply and embrace the image of being there. Begin to notice the changes in your body; the heart rate should be slowing down; the breath flowing easily, your muscles relaxing. Realize that you are all right, and there is no danger. Affirm that this was just an anxiety attack, and there is no reason to panic.

The ideal is practice relaxing and letting go enough so that no event in your life throws you into a panic; instead you remain calm, focused, and able to deal with the situation. Anxiety should be reserved for your intuition that can help identify hidden troubles before you get entangled.

Pain and Depression

The fact is that we are all vulnerable to pain, whether it is physical, emotional, or mental. There are many reasons for our suffering, and the intensity of it depends on our personal experience. Pain is different for every individual. The meaning, significance, duration, and depth of misery ranges from one extreme to another. In general, we all feel depressed occasionally; some people spend more time there than necessary. Depression can be minimal or excruciating. Depression is a state of mind and body where energy is depleted; the mind is filled with negative thoughts, feelings, and images. As noted before, the third purpose of each emotion is to force us to search for the opposite feeling. Certainly the purpose of life is not to suffer.

The psychology of pain is a complex story. The main point here is that it reflects a loss of energy and requires us to seek ways to recharge ourselves, to fill up with positive energy, and to find happiness. Pain is another alarm, warning us that we are in danger. Depression is an internal alarm that we are unfortunate, life is unjust, we are losing, failing, and unable to be where we want to be. Curiously, this may be an entirely subjective experience, because an onlooker may see a very successful individual who is apparently depressed. This is because depression reflects the internal measure of our sense of fulfillment. Others may not notice anything missing, but the depressed person is extremely aware of what is lacking. The positive side of suffering is that it makes us more empathic and able to understand what it must be for others to be unhappy. The opposite polarity is to search for that sense of fulfillment, happiness, feeling energized, and healthy.

Examples:
▸ Perhaps you know of a family whose child has a serious illness and was taken to the hospital. The family is understandably in pain because they don't want the child to go through such an ordeal.

▸ The most profound depression comes from the loss of a loved one. It could be a breakup, or even death, that leaves those behind lonely, sad, and depressed.

The lock is from physical intensity of suffering and the unrelenting nature of changes. Pain can be a very powerful experience, as depression can be.

The loss and lack of energy can be profound, leaving the person in a state of helplessness.

The key is to respond to the alarm of pain. Raise your awareness to the deliberate mind to evaluate the situation more objectively. Remember the mind is likely to distort reality and make things look worse than they really are. Verify the situation you are in, and discuss it with others who can be objective and whom you trust. Note the causes of the pain or depression. Identify the opposite feelings and recreate the experience of the positive emotions. Recharge the mind and body with positive energy, in the least with peace, faith, hope, comfort, and if possible even happiness. The key is to regain balance and harmony; release the negative thoughts and replace them with positive images. Acknowledge the difficulties and assert your intention to shift polarities; embrace the positive perspective and express these emotions. Now, affirm your desire to continue to enjoy life full of positive energy.

The ideal is to respond quickly to events in your life that are painful or depressing. It is important to acknowledge what is happening, to be aware of the causes and consequences of events around you and inside of you. Then utilize your deliberate power to escape the suffering, shift polarities, and return to what you consider the positive energy of a happy life.

Guilt

This emotion is misunderstood very often. What is the reason our mind created the experience of guilt? It is not to feel bad. Rather, the first moment of guilt is an alarm to warn us that we might have done something wrong. The purpose of guilt is to ask whether we have done any harm, damage, anything disturbing, offensive, or unpleasant. This inquiry is the most important step; if indeed we did something wrong, well then, we can apologize and try to redeem ourselves. On the other hand, if we discover that we did not do anything wrong, or at least not intentionally, then we should respond differently to the situation. What is the feeling opposite guilt?

The psychology of guilt begins with the reflexive mind's radar realizing that you might have done something wrong. Most people immediately experience a great deal of discomfort feeling very guilty about a situation that may not warrant it. This is a common distortion or illusion of the mind evaluating events. It is easy to assume that bad events were caused by your actions. It is equally wrong to take responsibility for events that you, in fact, are not responsible for. The question is, are you accountable for some observed problem and was it intentional or accidental? The next issue is determining how to correct the situation. This includes forgiveness, or shifting polarities to feel innocent, the opposite of guilty. There are also people who refuse to accept responsibility; even when they are in fact the cause of some problem.

Examples:

▸   Do you recall turning off a computer without saving the material there only to find out that someone else had been working on some project for hours? Oops, that was an unintentional mistake.

▸   Perhaps a friend told you a secret, making you promise not to tell anyone, and yet, you reveal the secret to the wrong person resulting in an embarrassing situation; that was an intentional error.

The lock is from the mind's radar to notice mistakes you have made; the reflexive mind generates feelings of guilt. Curiously, most guilt is evoked by unintentional errors you make, while the bad things you do intentionally do not usually cause the same sense of guilt. Most people get caught in the experience of guilt and do not analyze the situation to ascertain the degree of responsibility. Feelings of guilt can linger a lifetime, even if they are illusions.

The key starts with recognizing the "guilt" alarm and analyzing the situation carefully, asking if in fact something wrong happened that you are responsible for.   The next question is to determine if you did it intentionally, through careless negligence, or completely accidentally. The greater the degree of responsibility, the larger the response should be; such as an apology followed by an attempt to correct the problem. If, on the other hand, there really is no responsibility, then you may still want to help repair a problem you observe without any sense of guilt. In either case, the first step is to shift polarities and seek the experience of innocence to transform guilt. The next step is to take action to correct the problem if one exists and then to redeem yourself in a manner that brings balance back to the situation. When you can walk away feeling good knowing you have done everything you can, the guilt should not return.

The ideal is to respond to each situation with a sincere effort to correct any problems and regain your sense of innocence. Never deny responsibility if you are the cause of some problem. Take action to establish a sense of justice among all concerned.

Jealousy, Envy, and Greed

These are troubling emotions that create many social problems. These feelings reflect our territoriality, what we want to be ours. They have nothing to do with reality. These attitudes actually disturb the balance of energy among people. Jealousy, envy, and greed are part of a warning system to protect our possessions. However, they are usually the result of illusions and distortions of reality. The world would be better if they did not exist.

The psychology of possessiveness is hard wired into your body to help you survive, but these feelings rarely are used for any worthy purpose. The experience of jealousy, envy, or greed reflect your radar overreacting to events around you. These feelings are part of a distortion of fears that you will lose your possessions or not get what you want. Greed can also be expressed as stinginess, being very materialistic. The opposite polarities are very clear virtues, like compassion, acceptance, generosity, and happiness.

Examples:

▸   You are arriving home from repairing your car; the neighbors just bought two new cars and one is your favorite. Pulling up in your driveway, you are forced to compare cars, and you wish the new car were yours; a feeling of envy grips you.

▸   The wealthy parents of a young bride and her new husband collect all the envelopes with money and tell the young couple that they need the money more than the newlyweds.

The lock is from the reflexive mind's fear of not having enough. This scarcity thinking is very common among people, but is a distortion of reality. These feelings of jealousy or greed do not assure anyone of greater possessions; rather, these feelings create conflicts between people.

The key is to raise your awareness to the deliberate mind to evaluate the situation more objectively. This requires some reality testing and good judgment that helps identify what exactly you have earned based on your efforts and talents. The first step is to relax and let go of the negative feelings and to refocus on the polar opposite emotions. Recall the experience of appreciation, compassion, generosity, and similar feelings. Shift polarities, release the initial sensations, and embrace your higher nature. Acknowledge that you possess many valuable things and personal qualities. Realize that you can also obtain more by investing your energy wisely and achieving goals. Affirm that you reject scarcity thinking and that you believe in abundance.

The ideal is to develop a very profound sense of abundance on all the different levels. Prevent yourself from experiencing negative feelings like jealousy or greed by practicing being generous and expressing appreciation for the good things in life.

Anger

This is a powerful emotion that is often misused because our brain is wired for it. The purpose of anger – aggressive behavior, hostility, rage, and violence – is to gain control of a situation or of others through dominance. This engages a major portion of our nervous system to raise the energy levels to defend our own territory or take over others' possessions. We all get angry, and it can be a valuable feeling to protect ourselves or to demand fair treatment in an unjust world. Anger is not a problem in itself, only that it quickly impairs logical thinking, makes us more impulsive, and leads to all forms of aggressive behavior, which include screaming, violence, and even murder.

The psychology of anger is that we are all born with nervous systems biased towards these negative emotions. Given any situation that triggers our need to fight to defend ourselves, anger generates the energy to fight in whatever way may work for us. There are many ways that anger is manifested, from a nearly invisible level to blood boiling intensity. Because the reflexive system can gain command of attention easily, it separates us from the deliberate mind and impairs rational thinking. That is why so many acts of violence seem so senseless. At the opposite polarity inside the higher nature one can call up feelings of acceptance, tolerance, compassion, peacefulness, and so on. That does not mean that we should not assert ourselves; when we are challenged, it may be necessary to elicit some anger to fight an injustice. However, it is unwise to remain in the state of anger a long time. It is also socially inappropriate to use anger to manipulate or intimidate others, which happens all the time. Anger and fear are the two emotions most responsible for stress in our lives, especially when they are continuous.

Examples:

▸ Searching for a parking space in town, you pull up to back into an open spot when some car behind you pulls in. That was not fair of the other driver. What would you do? Some people will honk their horns. Others get out of their cars and begin an argument; some may just drive off.

▸   A couple is going over their bills. One accuses the other of spending too much money. They raise their voices, calling each other names, and both start yelling. How far does it go?

The locks are multiple. Starting with the physical intensity and how that impairs our rational thinking, makes anger a very difficult emotion to manage. Anger is a self-escalating experience; if a small amount does not work, we automatically generate more intensity. When the reflexive mind takes control, it dominates attention. When anger reaches rage levels, it becomes almost impossible to think logically. Worst of all, the mind distorts reality so that the individual does not believe he/she or his or her actions can be wrong. Anger blocks our ability to be objective.

The keys are to begin listening to the "anger" alarm, recognizing what in this situation is triggering anger. Raise your awareness to the deliberate mind, and make it your priority to stop the anger first. Analyze your situation objectively; is there any real danger; is there any injustice; what are the alternatives to resolve the problems? Regain conscious control of your body and mind, relax, and turn off the stress alarm. Be prepared to ignore illusions or distortions. From your deliberate mind determine the best course of action. If you must assert yourself, then do so by relying on the facts and maintain self-control. That means not to be overrun with anger; instead, relax your body and breathe deeply and slowly. Refocus your mind on your goals and what others must understand to achieve justice.

If you realize your anger was an unnecessary reaction, which usually is the case, then you must regain self-control. In either case, shift polarities and focus on tolerance, acceptance, peacefulness, and similar emotions. As you create these positive emotions, your anger will quickly fade away. With practice, even highly aggressive individuals can learn to regain control, stop their anger, and act in a rational and reasonable way. The main point is to reverse directions quickly when we react with anger to problems in life. Then you can return to the deliberate mind and use all the power of your knowledge, experience, and intelligence to resolve problems effectively with the least stress possible.

The ideal is to be able to assert yourself very effectively, with passion, but without anger. This requires a superior sense of self-control, developing the skill to release tension and to ignore the impulse to become angry.

Instead, remain confident that you can resolve the problem with all your resources.

Disgust

This is a less frequent problem, but one we all experience. Whenever we are confronted by something that makes us go "yuk!" that is disgust. Everyone develops boundaries or codes of behavior that we approve of or not. If we observe anything that crosses our boundaries of acceptability then we react with a feeling of disgust; it becomes repulsive, offensive, or at least tasteless. In a more general sense, this category of disgust includes apathy, boredom, hatred, inhibition, and similar feelings. There will be events, places, and people that disgust us; the purpose of this feeling is for us to avoid them in the future.

The psychology of disgust starts on the neurological level that makes us physically shudder, grimace, or even feel nauseous upon encountering something unpleasant. Through experience, we develop expectations that range from very wonderful to totally horrible. When something crosses that line of acceptability, it becomes disgusting. Other boundaries may refer to a certain level of excitement we expect, otherwise we feel bored or apathetic. The worst case is when we feel hatred because we are convinced that some event, object, or person is terrible. These are usually prejudiced thoughts, and yet very common. This again is simply the way the brain is wired which causes very strong emotions based on a distorted reality. The truth is that our world has plenty of room for all the diversity we find in it; what may disgust one group may attract another. There is nothing that is universally disgusting.

Examples:
- There are many forms of nudity in art; some may be widely appreciated, while other images of nudity are considered offensive because they cross some personal boundaries. The notion of disgust is entirely subjective; for some it may be art, but for others it may be pornographic.
- Perhaps you are disgusted with yourself because you ate too much or got very drunk.
- Do you recall going to a movie that you expected to be very exciting but wasn't at all? Instead, you felt very bored and could not wait for it to end.

The lock is from the internal scale of what is considered disgusting. We can all be disgusted by different experiences that make us want to avoid future contact with them. The problem is that it is easy for our minds to distort reality and create a prejudice against something for poor reasons. This can quickly become a fixed pattern in our lives that causes us much trouble. Disgust itself is also a very strong sensation that is hard to overcome.

The key is not to respond to the alarm of disgust immediately; rather, raise your awareness to the deliberate mind and analyze the situation objectively. Depending on what you observe, it may be possible for you to perform a reality check, verifying what is important, acceptable, and if not, how far beyond any boundaries has something crossed? Based on this information, you may decide to shift polarities and find the beauty or humor in something; perhaps you are able to admire it or even express your love for it. In the least you can show respect for it. The purpose is to eliminate the sense of disgust and return to a neutral position, if not a positive one. Similarly, with apathy or boredom, you can seek curiosity or excitement about it.

The ideal is to reach a level of flexibility in your boundaries where you can accept most of the events, people, or experiences you encounter without evoking disgust. If there are events that arouse negative feelings, you should be able to reverse directions and embrace the opposite polarities easily.

Pessimism and Gloom

Is the glass half full or half empty? Pessimism refers to a gloomy sense of the future. This may reflect a set of complex emotions that we all encounter very often. Because we all have an imagination, we anticipate the future. Depending on our personal experience, we expect good things or bad ones. Gloom refers to the apprehensive feeling that something unpleasant is going to happen. This often is a distortion of the way our minds work, but it actually feels very real to us, and so we adapt a pessimistic perspective preparing for troubles, failure, pain, and so on.

The psychology of gloom begins with the deliberate mind's assuming the future is not good; rather, it's filled with trouble. This can be the result of distortions, illusions, very unreasonable expectations, or just anxiety about the future. When we develop automatic patterns that reflect that negative perspective back to us, we become pessimistic and gloomy. This is a consequence of the internal sabotage that started as bad assumptions in thinking. Although the purpose of these emotions is to prepare us for challenges, they actually weaken us and make it more likely that we fail. Pessimism and gloom are also contagious; these feelings easily spread to others, draining them of energy as well. At the opposite polarity you have optimism, hope, enthusiasm, joyfulness, and similar positive attitudes.

Examples:

‣   Upon preparing for a picnic, have you heard someone complain that it is pointless, the weather will be bad, you won't have fun, it will take too long to get there, and so on? That's pessimism.

‣   Have you heard someone approaching his or her fortieth birthday with only apprehensive gloom? He or she will be so old; life will be over; they are useless; they don't want to celebrate, and so on.

The lock starts with the deliberate mind not observing the world accurately, so it assumes you cannot avoid unwanted events; this causes gloom. The apprehension we experience limits our freedom and creates a strong resistance to change our thinking. Consequently, it is difficult to get people out of pessimistic thinking unless they truly want to escape it.

The key starts with the willingness to question your conclusions. Most of the time, gloom and pessimism can be identified as just temporary; by gathering more information, you can disqualify the apprehension and shift polarities to optimistic thinking, hope, and joyful enthusiasm. This requires you to be in the deliberate mind and to create the intentions to eliminate the negativity. You must review the situation objectively and perhaps seek verification of the information. The worst case should be neutral, or a fifty-fifty chance of good results. Optimism suggests we always expect the best results. The idea is to be prepared for problems, but not to limit yourself or the potentials with negative thoughts or feelings. Hence, you count on your resources to deal with any difficulties with a positive mind set to succeed.

The ideal is never to surrender to gloom; instead, maintain a positive and optimistic perspective on life and your potential.

Frustration

This emotion has become one of the most frequent experiences in modern society. The more things we are supposed to accomplish, the more opportunities are there for us to feel frustrated. Any event that does not meet with complete success as planned can cause frustration. Frustration is the physical, mental, and emotional stress of any form of disappointment. This is a feeling that emerges from anger and can even lead to rage in the worst cases.   Usually, frustration just makes us feel uncomfortable, awkward, incompetent, and a bit stressed. It is supposed to motivate us to work harder to reach our goals, but in reality, often hampers our success.

The psychology of frustration is very individualized.   Every person develops different levels of tolerance for frustration and various responses to it. In general, it ranges from minimal, mildly unpleasant feelings to moderate frustration that may motivate us to quit, and it can become overwhelming with a violent reaction in the end.   Unfortunately, our society has done a lot to eliminate frustration for people growing up, making life artificially easier. Consequently, most people never develop the ability to cope with frustration very well. Those people who aspire for perfection must endure enormous amounts of stress because their lives are naturally very frustrating. The major issue here is to recognize frustration as a product of the effort we make to succeed in life. Minimizing the stress and negative aspects of frustration (anger, confusion, wish to give up) is necessary to continue to reach success in life.

Examples:
- Do you remember the last time you were trying to follow poorly written instructions to put something together or make some new machine work? The longer it takes, the more frustrated you feel, wondering if it is worth the trouble.
- Perhaps you wanted to listen to a particular song; after searching everywhere for the record and wasting an hour, you may not care to hear the song anymore.

The lock is from the deliberate mind that determines that a task should be easy. If it takes longer than expected, feelings of frustration pile up. The lock arises from the energy you put into achieving the goal that is taking more time than necessary. For example, it may be about finding a parking spot in town, which is a matter of chance. It could also be a computer engineer unable to make a simple computer work, which may be more a matter of competency. Either case can be very frustrating which can lead to anger, desire to quit, and a loss of self worth. The locks of frustration can be quite complex, stealing energy away from those who struggle to achieve.

The key starts with recognizing the feeling of frustration as part of the journey toward success. Raise your awareness to the deliberate mind; analyze the situation carefully to determine how much energy achieving this task is worth investing or what the alternatives are. Make it your intention to complete the task or perhaps take a break and go back to it later. If the task is not important, then giving up may be appropriate as well. The main point is to decrease the stress. Relieve the frustration first by relaxing and releasing the necessity of completing the task immediately. Then, raise the level of motivation to gain more energy to return to the task without the stress. This requires you to shift polarities and embrace the feelings of acceptance, tolerance, resilience, flexibility, confidence, and most of all, patience. All this renews the individual's strength to overcome the obstacles and achieve his or her goals. Frustration is not meant to stop your progress or make you suffer to reach your goals.

The ideal is to develop the will power and determination to see every project through regardless of the difficulties and to simultaneously, build up patience to not get frustrated while struggling to achieve goals.

Conclusion

This chapter described common emotional problems we all experience. When any of the negative emotions grip our life, it limits our freedom, power, and well being. The primary cause of stress in life is due to negative feelings we live with that affect our thinking and physical body. The major point here is that we are not supposed to suffer negative feelings. To the contrary, the stress we experience is meant to motivate us to reverse directions and return to balance and harmony. That is the principle concept of shifting polarities. Do not get caught in negativity; it is there just to indicate what is the opposite emotion you need. The process begins with raising awareness, relaxing to turn off the stress, and then refocusing your mind on the positive emotions that can liberate you to resolve the problems and then achieve your goals.

It's not the will to win that matters, everyone has that. It is the will to prepare to win that matters.   Paul Bear Bryant

Chapter 22

Judgment

What is Judgment?

Every person learns to make judgments. Judgments are decisions to take one alternative over another. Earlier, I described the master keys for making better judgments; here I explain the most common reasons that block us from good judgment. We have all made very bad judgments and a few very good ones. Because life imposes countless decisions for us to make, we all have to make a tremendous number of decisions each day, week, month, and year. Some of our choices will be excellent; others will be catastrophic, and most will be somewhere in the middle. The question is what stops us from making better judgments?

To be clear, judgment is the act of making a decision, making an evaluation, usually prioritizing, comparing alternatives, and selecting what you think is the best choice. What makes this process so difficult? Several factors are obvious: no one is born with the skills to make good judgments; we must develop these skills. Secondly, the brain has a number of inherent problems that makes it more likely for us to make bad decisions. Third, sometimes the complexity of the problem we are facing makes it extremely difficult to decide what is best.

Making judgments can be a quick and simple process, or it can be very lengthy and complex. We can make decisions impulsively from the reflexive mind, or we can get into a bad habit of making decisions based on flipping a coin, that would be the Automatic Mind working. When we actually analyze a situation, evaluate our options, or think about what will be the best choice before making our final judgment, then we are using our Deliberate Mind. Good judgment promotes progress and positive results. This matter is different from being "judgmental," voicing your opinion about someone's behavior or being critical.

What is the purpose of judgment?

Life is all about decisions. The right choice can catapult you to great success, just as the wrong one can send you spiraling downward. Judgment is our ultimate tool to outsmart reality and utilize the hidden possibilities. The purpose of judgment is to enable us to continually adapt in better ways to an ever-changing world. Sometimes it can even invent or create improvements in our life.

How does judgment work?

Many things in life do not require complicated analysis to make a good judgment. Usually, we are able to instantly decide our preference without a problem. However, there are circumstances that do require careful consideration before making a judgment; otherwise we may incur some terrible consequence. So, one principle action of our judgment is to predict the future and decide what will be the best choice. Judgment can also play an important role deciding what we believe, what career we choose, where we live, who we marry, and so on. When we do not use judgment, we are basically relying on others to make our decisions. This may work sometimes, but why would we have the power of judgment if we were not meant to use it?

What are the polarities?

On the positive side, the deliberate mind gives us the tools to analyze, compare, and select the alternative we think is best. Good judgment is a very important power that we all use, but few take time to develop. The power of judgment is found in a variety of skills and knowledge described below. On the negative side, if we make bad decisions and do not consider the consequences or care what happens, then certainly our lives will be filled with troubles, perhaps even injuries or death. History is full of poor judgments that have led to terrible consequences including social tragedies and economic disasters.

What are the psychological lessons?

The first point is that good judgment does not require intelligence. In fact, average intelligence is plenty for making excellent decisions. There are many very intelligent people who are unsuccessful, unhappy, or even sitting in jail because of their poor judgments. If it is not intelligence, then what is it that enables us to develop superior judgment? The answer is <u>thinking</u>. As we develop the ability to think, we automatically improve the various skills required for making judgments.

What are the locks?

The locks originate at every level of the mind. Problems can result from negative emotions of the reflexive mind or from destructive patterns of the automatic mind. Equally, there are many locks on the deliberate mind level as well. Judgment is the most complicated of the JEEP factors. However, just as with all the other locks, there are always keys to open the locks of judgment.

What are the Key Instructions for the Best Judgments?

Realize the importance of improving your skills and knowledge about judgment. First, there is a list of questions for evaluating judgments. Below are the Master Keys previously described about making better judgments. Then I summarize the key instructions for removing the eleven common locks that impair judgment. Depending on each specific problem you encounter, there may be slight variations in the steps outlined here.

Master questions to ask to increase awareness of problems in making decisions:

1. Do I see all the choices and understand exactly what the problem is?

2. Have I identified all the possible causes of the problems?

3. Is my perspective wide enough to observe the situation objectively?

4. What are all the potential alternatives to resolving the problem including any hidden solutions or last moment ideas? Is your decision reversible?

5. As I compare different possibilities, how clearly do I see the consequences and how confident am I of the results?

6. Have I considered the rational side with all the fact, and consequences?

7. Have I considered the intuitive side with all the feelings or energies pulling me in one direction or the other?

8. Am I ready to compare the alternatives and my predictions so I can analyze the best choice?

9. Can I afford the decision I am making even if it proves to be the wrong one? Can I afford not to make a decision swiftly?

10. Once I have made my decision, am I determined to initiate the will power to achieve my goals?

11. As I proceed with my plans, have I created contingency plans to change directions if my goals are not reached?

These are the Master Keys described earlier to deal with Judgment:

MK 109

Analyze every situation to determine if you have the resources to overcome the challenges before you, and if confronted by overwhelming difficulties consider reorganizing your strategies, changing directions, or finding alternative goals.

MK 110

Exercise the power of your judgment making decisions carefully.

MK 111

The rational approach requires you consider all the facts, details, and objective information, calculating the probabilities of different outcomes, to form a logical decision.

MK 112

The intuitive approach requires you to reflect on what your internal "radar" is telling you. Listen to all your subjective feelings and any other information before making a judgment.

MK 113

Be mindful to collect all information that may be relevant to the situation. As you analyze it, consider what the consequences will be for different alternatives before making a decision.

MK 114

Determine what is the simplest explanation to resolve a problem.

MK 115

Are you certain that this _____ is the only possible cause for some event?

MK 116

Analyze all the subjective and objective information, compare alternatives, carefully prioritize your choices, then make a final decision.

MK 117

Make accurate predictions, based on your previous experience and knowledge of the probable consequences and determine your level of confidence with each decision.

MK 118

Clarify if you can afford the consequences or troubles of your decision if it is wrong.

MK 119

Clarify if you can risk not taking action; what will the consequences be if you do nothing?

What to do:

1. Expand your awareness, access the higher self, and observe the situation as objectively as possible; describe the problem in detail with all the causes and potential solutions. Can you subtract yourself from the situation and consider what others would think in your place?

2. Determine if you know enough to make a good decision, or how you can gain more information, correct any distortions, or expand your perspective. Do you have experience with this matter or should you consult someone who has?

3. Now review all the rational facts and details. Then consider any intuitions you have about the situation. Establish a clear list of alternatives to analyze and compare.

4. Make your predictions; evaluate the possible results critically; compare alternatives and prioritize them. Review the best choices both rationally and intuitively. Can you afford this choice?

5. From your higher self, make a clear decision based on the best alternative, and then initiate your will power to act with determination on your new intentions.

6. Verify that you have made the best decision and are making progress towards your desired goals. If problems persist, then review and consider other available options.

7. Being aware of your judgment and the results you have achieved, store this information for later use.

What to say:

1a. I am glad to be expanding my objective awareness so that I can think clearly about the problems and solutions.

2a. The power to change my life comes through my higher self that observes objectively and gives me freedom to improve.

3a. I appreciate my mind's ability to consider all the alternatives and trust it to make the right choices and create new intentions.

4a. I am glad to use all my resources to determine the best choice to take.

5a. I am confident my choice is the best direction to take at this time.

6a. As I verify my progress, it raises my confidence in my decisions.

7a. I am glad to acknowledge the power of my judgment to make good decisions now and in th future.

What are the Top Eleven Problems with Judgment?

Lack of Attention

The ability to concentrate and not be distracted is a vital skill. Judgment depends on unrestricted access to all information relevant to making a decision. If you cannot pay attention or are easily distracted, then important information that hinders judgment is likely to be missed. There are many reasons that we lack attention; we may be tired, sleepy, stressed, bored, lazy, or impaired by alcohol or drugs.

The psychology of attention has been described earlier. Difficulties in focusing our attention is a universal problem. As explained, there are three levels of conscious awareness: passive, active, and energized. The time we spend in passive awareness is not likely to be very attentive. Even during active awareness, we may easily be distracted. When making important decisions, it is essential to gain command of your attention. This can help you avoid impulsive decisions that were not well thought out.

Examples:
▸ Your spouse sends you to the market to pick up a special ingredient; you return home to discover that you bought the wrong thing because you were not paying attention to the details.

The lock is failure to develop skills of concentration or to let go of distractions that make it hard to pay attention. The mind is automatically attracted by any new stimulation. Even if the new stimulation is not important, it can take your mind off what it should be focused on. Your attention is also easily impaired by drugs and alcohol.

The keys are to become alert, raise your awareness to the deliberate mind, and focus on the subject before you. Set rules of what to ignore and what to pay attention to. Gain as large a perspective as necessary to be objective and collect all the information you need to make your judgments. Ask yourself if you have missed any hidden details or if you have verified what you have learned with others. The first step in making a good judgment is knowing exactly what the problem is, what caused it, and what the circumstances are. With the right information, it gets easier to make the right choice.

The ideal is to be alert, able to focus on the subject matter, and to clearly observe all the important information before making any decisions.

Lack of Knowledge

The more complex a problem or subject you are dealing with, the more information needs to be analyzed before making a judgment. There are many choices we make that do not require additional information (what do you prefer, vanilla or chocolate?). Then, there are situations in which you cannot collect enough information to make a good decision (which politician is better). Usually, not knowing the details, not understanding what really matters can lead to very bad judgments. Consequently, making an effort to gain knowledge before making decisions is highly advisable. Sometimes it is just an insight that can answer all your questions. Other times you may need to invest a lot of energy into learning about a problem. One must pose the right questions to make a good judgment. The knowledge you gather from the right questions will increase the power of your judgment. The problem with ignorance is very simple: you don't know what you don't know.

The psychology of collecting information is not a matter of intelligence. As long as a person develops the ability for rational thought and basic logic, this is plenty to acquire the knowledge for good judgment. It is also important that the information collected is not limited; rather the information should come from as wide a perspective as possible. This includes abstract and concrete information that may also include misperceptions. At first, get as much information as possible, and then begin to organize and prioritize it. The lack of knowledge is quickly replaced with valuable information when effort is made to collect it. Learning to ask the right questions is a vital part of eliminating ignorance.

Examples:
- Your friends are organizing a party and ask you to buy the snacks, but you do not ask how many people they are expecting. Your shopping will be very different for twenty or two hundred.
- Perhaps you went to vote and did not get enough information about the local politicians and felt awkward choosing one based on the name and nothing else.

The locks are ignorance and the mind's desire to believe that whatever it does know is enough when in fact it often is not. This is when our assumptions limit our desire for information and lead to poor judgment. A lack of knowledge locks us into ignorance; misunderstanding the information we do have or not learning from our mistakes, is plain old stupidity.

The keys are to raise your awareness to the higher self and make a conscious effort to collect as much information as possible. Determine that your perspective is open, not narrow; both abstract and concrete information are sought and analyzed. Be certain that you invest the right amount of energy gathering the knowledge you need and that you do not ignore any relevant sources even if they do not support your ideas. Do not restrict either subjective or objective data. Continue your search for as much information as you can find, then begin the process of comparing and analyzing it. Your judgment usually should be based on verifiable, objective information; actual knowledge, not assumptions.

The ideal is to constantly acquire more knowledge from as many sources as possible. The more information you have in your resources, the better decisions you can make.

Lack of Experience

Wisdom is the slow process of collecting life experiences, that we learn something new. Not all experience is so valuable, but those moments that actually give us some insight into what life is about are precious. Only those individuals whose life is filled with valuable experiences become wise; the rest, if lucky, just grow old. Wisdom is different from intelligence or knowledge. Certainly, most people can claim at least a bit of one or the other, and those who make an effort, even both. You may be smart, but without the right experience, intelligence alone does little. If you have learned a lot, collected a great amount of knowledge (information), still without the necessary experience, your knowledge may be useless. More than any other factor, it is experience that is most valuable in life. The richer the experience of life is, the more often it can be applied with great success to completely new situations. Consequently, the lack of valuable experience is a major impairment in making judgments.

The psychology of consciousness is the actual subject here. Recall the three levels of conscious energy: passive, active, and energized. The most valuable experience comes from the energized level of consciousness, where you are super charged, extremely alert, storing every event into permanent memory. The active level of consciousness also produces valuable experience because you are alert, on task, and making a deliberate effort to accomplish something that you can remember. The stuff from the passive level usually does not contribute to wisdom. Consequently, the more passionate energy you invest in your life, the more valuable it becomes. Ultimately, you may gain wisdom. The point here is that, the more experience you have in life, the more likely you will have the wisdom to make better judgments; that is, if you also get past all the other problems listed here.

Example:

▸   Perhaps you are interested in the game of billiards. You are very intelligent and buy books about playing pool, watch several videotapes about the game, and then you are invited to play a game. All your knowledge and intelligence is worthless without the experience of actually practicing pool; that is the only way you learn the skills and judgment of how to hit the balls.

The locks are the lack of ambition, passion, curiosity, creativity, imagination, or a poor memory. The mind's tendency to be rigid, fearful, and lazy certainly limits the amount of experience you can gather.

The keys are to be alert, raise your level of energy, and live in the moment. Access your higher self and expand your perspective as widely as possible. Notice any limitations on your experience, either internal or external, and try to eliminate them. Make it your intention to seek flexibility, express your passion, and exercise your curiosity, creativity, and imagination. Develop the power of your memory. Strive to act from the active or energized level of consciousness. Then you may actually be able to utilize your resources to make better judgments.

The ideal is to live with passion, enthusiasm, ambition, excitement, courage, compassion, empathy, confidence, in a healthy way, with plenty of prosperity, and love. This certainly makes for life filled with good experience.

Illusions and Distortions

The mind is paradoxical. Our minds are extremely vulnerable to illusions and distortions of reality. At the same time, the mind is the only instrument we have to actually discover true reality. The significance of this problem is simple; unless you are cautious, there will be many instances that your mind will distort reality or create an illusion of it. If we cannot tell reality from fantasy, we will have a difficult time making judgments. The brain is easily fooled by the way we interpret perceptions.

The psychology of perception is a complex science; what we do know is that our senses construct reality in our head. These perceptions are often false, misleading, distorted, mistaken, or just incomplete. The mind works very quickly. Consequently, it usually does not have enough time to accurately analyze what it sees, hears, feels, or thinks. Frequently, our perceptions are simply not complete, but our minds presume what we think they should be; hence, you have illusions and distortions of reality. The paradox is that the mind is also capable of eliminating distortions or illusions by verifying, testing, and examining whatever we observe more carefully.

Examples:
▸   In a crowd of people you recognize a friend. As you come closer, calling out her name she does not react, and then you realize that you were mistaken.

▸ A young couple meet and go out on a date; the actions of one convinces the other that this person really likes him, but then at the end of a nice night, the opposite turns out to be true.

The lock is the desire of the mind to be correct when it actually is wrong. Another lock is the ease with which the brain makes errors. Even our environment cooperates in this conspiracy because it is very natural for things to not appear as they are.

The keys are to become alert, raise your awareness to the deliberate mind, and learn to be more cautious and reluctant to immediately believe what you observe. This means becoming a bit skeptical, trying to verify whatever you think you observed by examining it more carefully, and asking others to validate your experiences. By questioning the information you perceive, it is more likely that you can avoid illusions or distortions that can twist your reality. When you have made an effort to verify your first impression, it can become a more valid, real impression.

The ideal is to be skeptical of your first impressions and to verify what you observe objectively; this can lead to a more realistic impression of the world and ultimately to better judgments.

Irrational

The problem with irrational thought is that it never seems unreasonable to the person having it; even if all others may think that it is illogical, mistaken, or strange. There is nothing abnormal about irrational thinking; it may sometimes even be creative, but usually it cannot happen. Language helps us learn to be logical; gaining knowledge and experience should further develop our rational thinking. This is also a matter of understanding the laws of cause and effect. If you are not able to evaluate the probable consequences of your actions, then they may be irrational. Judgment cannot be made based on irrational thoughts or what may be false beliefs.

The psychology of rational thinking is a matter of cognitive processes. We are not born thinking rationally; that is what we learn to do, to some degree dependent on our experiences. The mind is not designed to automatically detect irrational thoughts. Actually, it takes knowledge, experience, and judgment to determine if a thought is logical or not. It is easy to think irrationally, just that judgments based on such thoughts are most often doomed to fail. This can also refer to false beliefs that people embrace to belong to a group or superstitions that some follow out of tradition.

Examples:

▶ Flying aboard a large jet, someone begins to have a panic attack. He wants to get out now; he wants the plane to land immediately. These are irrational thoughts because you cannot exit a plane in the sky, nor can it land just anywhere.

▶ A person suffers a death in the family and becomes very depressed. She begins taking aspirins in large quantities everyday hoping that it will eliminate the sadness, but all that happens is a stomach ache. Aspirin is not the treatment for depression.

The lock is lack of awareness of the difference between what exactly we are thinking as compared to reality. The problems are due to wrong assumptions that the mind defends and does not want to question.

The keys are to raise your awareness to the deliberate mind and make your intention to question thoughts. How realistic, logical, or possible is your thought? How easily can this idea be criticized, discounted, or ruled out by careful examination of the situation? What objective evidence is there that can support the thought? Can you identify several other alternatives and determine which one may lead to better results?

Questioning the irrational thought removes an obvious error in thinking. Now, find good alternatives to improve your judgment.

The ideal is to be aware of any thoughts that seem unreasonable. Such thoughts require careful testing; if the ideas are irrational, the thoughts should be abandoned. Seek what logical ideas are likely to achieve positive results.

Ignoring Intuition

This refers to the energetic level of human experience – our gut feelings, premonitions, images, and impressions. We are all born with this internal radar that sends us information about the world not through the normal five senses. This information may be right or wrong, but it is usually valuable to consider and compare with all the other details collected. If you ignore your intuition completely, you disregard a valuable source of information. Intuition is the radar that may help us in a variety of ways if we at least think about it.

The psychology of intuition is incomplete. There is no doubt that we all experience gut feelings that urge us to avoid or approach something. The mechanisms of our intuitive impressions are not well understood. Whatever form intuition takes, the information does seem to appear spontaneously bypassing our normal sensory pathways. Most often these messages are positive or negative feelings, although they can be complete "stories" as well. This information is different from the rational objective, fact-based detail. Instead, intuition is very subjective and personal. The purpose of intuition is to offer another subjective radar resource to use; unfortunately, it is also vulnerable to errors. Despite the fact that intuition can be wrong, it is advisable to consider this information and at least determine what the rational mind thinks it means. The truth is that if we were given an internal radar, it must be useful sometimes.

Examples:

▸ Two people meet, and one has a hidden agenda; the other person gets a strong intuition to avoid that person. What would you do?

▸ You are being offered two new job positions; both are appealing and promise higher income. One position may be less money, but you get a better feeling about it; or you could take the better paying job which feels less comfortable. Which one would you take?

The lock is the lack of awareness about the value of intuitive information. It is possible your deliberate mind blocks you from considering subjective feelings in making decisions. You may also believe that intuition cannot be valuable, or in contrast, that it must be right.

The keys are to raise your awareness to receive any form of information; consider it carefully, and then determine what to do with it. The questions to ask are: how strong do these intuitions feel; how likely are they real; what does your rational mind tell you about this information? Intuition comes from the internal radar system. If you have time, go up to your deliberate mind and analyze this information. If there is no time, the best advice is usually to go with the intuition, especially if it is some kind of warning. In either case, never ignore your radar. Intuition is not superstition or supernatural. This is about the energy you can sense around you; perhaps it is good and attracting, or bad and telling you to avoid this. A clarifying question is if you go with the intuition, can you afford the cost if it was wrong? Conversely, can you afford to go against intuition if it turns out to be correct? Sometimes it is possible to find a compromise between the rational part and intuitive feelings; this is a matter of good judgment.

The ideal is to always be very sensitive to your intuition and develop its power to serve you. The more you use the intuition, the better it will help you in making judgments.

Lack of being Analytical

Several practical skills are required to make good judgments; this is the secret behind being analytical. Up to this point, I have focused on the information and approach you need to take to avoid the limitations on your judgment. Three essential skills are needed to make an accurate discrimination between different alternatives: analysis, prediction, and comparison. No judgment can be made reliably without these three basic steps. The concept of being analytical refers to thinking, not feeling. Everyone can think. The more skills you develop with respect to thinking, the greater grows the power of your judgment.

Analysis represents a review of all available information, that is identifying what is important. The next step is to make predictions and to generate ideas about what you think will happen. Predictions refer to guessing what is likely to happen, not what you want to happen. The final step is to make comparisons between alternatives. This is an abstract game in your imagination, although it may be valuable to write down the options. Comparing ideas requires a mental operation of thinking about the predicted results of each alternative and then calculating which alternative generates the best outcome. This can be a very simple process, as in deciding which products to purchase at the supermarket; or a very complex and difficult process of elimination of what may be medically wrong with a patient in a hospital. The lack of analytical skills will impair your judgment.

The psychology of being analytical has filled volumes of books. Here, the main points are the three vital skills to make judgments. Thinking is the most natural process. To think analytically is a special, developed ability that nearly everyone can learn. It does not depend on intelligence. As long as a person can avoid the locks described here, he or she will be able to think analytically. To make judgments you must be able to analyze the situation, make predictions, and compare alternatives. This process does not guarantee the best judgment. Nothing can do that, but these analytical steps will prepare you to make well thought out judgments.

Examples:

▸ You are preparing to go to college. Based on grades, academic standing, and test scores you analyze which schools are affordable and likely to accept you.

▸ From a group of (ten) schools you make predictions as to which one will give you the best education and will be the right environment.

▸ Now comparing all the alternatives, you rank the three best schools and search for more information to make the final judgment or decision.

The locks in this case are numerous; the lack of these skills implies a failure to discover the power of these tools. If you do not know how to make predictions or comparisons, you will be limited in making judgments.

The keys are to raise awareness to the deliberate mind and to make it your intention to be analytical. Take the time to analyze the situation and consider all the information you can gather. Set out to make careful predictions with the alternatives you have found. Predictions are an exercise of imagining future outcomes for each possibility. Now compare these alternatives and determine which are most likely to give the best results. Consider how rewarding and how difficult the choices are. Debate whether you have the resources to achieve your goals. Be prepared to commit the time and energy to reach your goals. Make your decision with confidence.

The ideal is to be constantly developing your analytical skills and improving the speed with which you think and resolve complex problems. Recognize the unlimited power of your mind to analyze, predict, and compare alternatives to decide what is your best judgment.

Ambiguity

The result of every judgment is a decision. If we are unable to decide for any reason, then we suffer from ambiguity. This is not a lack of will power or perception. The final step in every judgment is selecting a course of action and making a commitment to follow it. There are two basic problems, one is fear – what if I pick the wrong choice; the other is confusion – I do not know what to choose! Either way the person remains locked in ambiguity. There are rare times when waiting longer to make a decision is an advantage; otherwise you are either wasting time, missing an opportunity, or failing to learn the lessons.

The psychology about making decisions belongs to the whole mind. It is up to you to take advantage of everything you can to make judgments. As you combine all the resources you have, a stream of information fills your mind. You then can go through the process to analyze, predict, and compare to eventually figure out what you decide to do. Those gripped by fear become paralyzed; each solution may be wrong and cause unknown trouble. Those who are confused by all the information cannot separate alternatives into clear independent choices. Both leave the individual in a state of indecision. One solution is found in eliminating the fear, shifting polarities to gain confidence to make your choice. The other solution is to collect more information, analyze it more critically, and determine, by a process of elimination what the best decision is. There are problems in life that truly do not have a good solution. However, ambiguity is not a solution. By making a final decision, you move forward, and even if wrong, you stand to learn and ultimately reach your desired goals. Indecision limits progress.

Examples:

- What do you prefer: vanilla or chocolate?
- It is time to buy a new car. The family needs something safe and

roomy, and your dream car is small, sporty, and expensive. If you can only get one car, what do you decide?

▸   You have consulted four doctors. Two are urging you to amputate a foot because of a serious illness, and the other two suggest treatment that may spare the foot, but if it fails you will need to amputate the entire leg. Decisions can be difficult, but not impossible.

The lock is the fear of making a mistake or being confused, unable to go through the decision process effectively. Ambiguity is self rewarding because the fear of making a mistake is worse than delaying the decision temporarily. This is why indecision is such a common problem.

The keys are to go to the deliberate mind and make it a clear intention to decide on the best option. If you are experiencing any anxiety about the decision, shift polarities, gain a sense of confidence. Review your choices and take a courageous step forward. If you are confused and unable to find a clear choice, repeat the decision process described earlier. Review the information, both intuitive and the rational, and then continue ranking the choices from best to worst. Eventually something must begin to stand out more than the other choices. Prepare yourself for the possible outcomes. Consider what you will do if the results are not what you want. Be certain that life continues and that taking action now is necessary. Act on your intention; whatever it takes, make your judgment.

The ideal is not to get stuck in ambiguity. Whenever decisions become difficult you are always able to call up the resources you need to make a final judgment quickly.

Bad Patterns, Energy, or Emotions

These are the other three JEEP factors that can cause difficulty in making decisions. There are obvious patterns that interfere with judgments. Individuals who are caught in a very draining situation may lack the energy to make a decision. Negative emotions can also easily block us from clear thinking. In the process of making a judgment, you must be aware of limitations imposed by other factors in your life, not just the difficulty of the decision itself.

The psychology of judgment has been described as an elaborate process that can be blocked by a variety of internal locks. The "judgment" locks are not the only problems we deal with when making decisions. The locks we experience from bad patterns, loss of energy, or negative emotions are also responsible for difficulties we have making decisions. In order to have the best conditions for making clear, intelligent judgments, we must be free of the burdens that the other JEEP factors can create. The previous chapters described what to do to eliminate the problems that these factors can produce.

Examples:

▸ You have a habit of being impulsive; your new spouse doesn't like this pattern, and it causes arguments between the two of you.

▸ You have decided to study for a major exam, but an old friend wants your attention. Although you think this matter can wait, this person insists on calling and draining you of energy.

▸ You want to plan a vacation, you learn that your spouse has invited the in-laws which makes you very angry and frustrated. Your ability to plan the vacation crumbles.

The locks have been described with respect to each factor. The main point is that each part of the mind fights for control of the other parts. Given an opportunity, each of the negative JEEP factors can disturb the balance and harmony of the system.

The keys are to raise your awareness to the deliberate mind and evaluate your situation in an objective manner. Identify any problems, especially from the JEEP factors. The best approach to each specific problem has been described earlier. Shift polarities and eliminate the disturbances. Return to your intentions; focus attention on making the right decision.

The ideal is to develop greater balance, order, and harmony in your life. Gain control of disturbing factors quickly and refocus your attention on resolving problems effectively. From a clear mind your judgments will be better.

The Ego Filter of Reality

Every person's ego creates a stable sense of identity, that which we all need to deal with the world. What is interesting is the way this ego or identity actually works to filter our world. Depending on the type of ego you have, it will interpret the world accordingly. This can become the source of enormous problems for everyone because it is difficult for any two people to agree on the meaning of events. The ego can block the flow of energy based on who feels more important. With respect to judgment, the locks that the ego creates are in how we understand reality. Depending on the type of ego a person has, the more it changes or filters the world to match what we expect or want it to be. The following describes the ego locks, the problems that can emerge from the ego; naturally many individuals learn to manage the ego to avoid these troubles.

The ego has two polarities: one is an over inflated ego and the other is an underdeveloped ego. The first one has an exaggerated sense of entitlement ("I deserve... I want to be given..."). These individuals tend to be very critical, demanding, controlling, and abrasive. Big ego people often believe themselves to be flawless; they see the world and people as their servants; whatever they do is great; what others do is never enough. The second case is the insecure, fearful, rather undeserving ego ("I shouldn't ask... I am not worthy..."), which also filters the way these individuals experience the world. These people usually see the world as unfriendly, dangerous, difficult, and so on. Most people fit somewhere in between these two polarities, but everyone has to deal with people who come from one extreme or the other. As you recognize what type of ego you have or others have, you begin to understand how it filters judgments and it should give you greater leverage to change things for the better.

The psychology of identity is a never-ending story. The ego serves as the glue that holds your personality together as a stable sense of identity and self-image. In the process of maintaining your identity, the ego decides what the world around you should look like. In order to keep the internal image stable, the ego will filter out anything that does not fit in with your personality. The problem of an ego being too over or too under-developed is common. Many people have an unreasonable sense of entitlement or lack of worthiness. That is why this "ego lock" is a serious issue, it distorts reality to help people believe that either - *they are entitled* or *they are unworthy*. Even if the ego is not bent in one direction or the other, it is designed to distort reality in favor of whatever it thinks is important. The ego can help us deny, repress, ignore, or not pay attention to something, or the opposite, it will obsess, become controlling, or focus on just one thing. The ego filters the world we experience; often it will not appear as the same world others observe. This is common and troubling to many relationships. However, the ego can also be both strong and healthy by following a set of objective rules to view the world as realistically as possible.

Examples:

‣ A contestant in a talent competition thinks he has a great voice, terrific personality, and is absolutely positive he will win until he begins to sing and is told to stop and gets disqualified. His protests are offensive, and he accuses the judge of having no clue about real talent.

‣ Another contestant is forced to sign up by her friend. She does not believe that she has any talent and believes she will lose. When she begins to sing, she impresses everyone, including the judges. She remains incredulous that she has been picked and feels undeserving.

The lock is the lack of awareness about how the ego changes what we observe. When the ego interprets reality, it must match the ego's expectations. If the real world is different from what ego wants it to be, the ego secretly distorts that reality and creates one that fits what it wants. This is an excellent defense; it makes us feel better and makes us believe the world is the way we predict it should be. Even if our expectations are wrong for us or others, the ego locks us into that fake reality.

The keys are to raise your awareness to the higher self and seek an objective perspective. Consider your situation from another person's perspective; how would he or she describe your position? Be curious about what others observe, feel, and think. Verify the impressions you have about the world with others. If the view you have is significantly different from other people's perspective, then consider accepting at least a compromise between the two views. Be aware of the reactions others have to your expectations. Are they surprised? Inquire whether what you expect is too much or not enough. Then adjust your expectations. The ego filters the world in a hidden or secret way. As you try to verify your view, it is always possible for you to become more flexible and enlarge your perspective. Shift polarities. For big egos seek respect, kindness, patience, compassion, love, and integrity. Transform small egos into a feeling of greater confidence, respect, ambition, assertiveness, love, and integrity. The ultimate questions to answer are: "Does this feel good to me, good for others, and serve the greater good?" The aim is to establish a healthy ego that is open and flexible, assertive and confident, and attentive to the needs of others or the situation. When the ego is really in sync with your condition, your judgments or decisions will be in harmony with the world.

The ideal is to be constantly monitoring your ego, not to let it shrink or overgrow. When a person embraces respect for him or herself as well as for all others, it is a demonstration of integrity. A healthy ego is always prepared to defend itself, but will not attack others. A strong ego is one that is filled with confidence, ambition, compassion, etc., but is ready to question what it observes and seek objective verification.

Wrong Will Power

The power of judgment is useless unless we are prepared to act on our decisions. Unfortunately, we are also prone to apply our will power in the wrong manner; this creates another lock that interferes with our judgment, relationships, or achievement. Will power is an important Master Key that gives us the energy to act on our intentions. Your accomplishments depend on the development of your will power: the skills to direct your attention and the energy to achieve your goals. Will power can also cause trouble when it is overdeveloped or applied to the wrong situation. It can equally be underdeveloped or not applied to the right situation. These are the two negative polarities of will power – too much or not enough. Wrong will power can cause a variety of locks. An overdeveloped will can make you rigid, prejudiced, selfish, critical, destructive, and obsessive. In the opposite direction, an underdeveloped will can make you weak, apathetic, insecure, lacking in stamina, impulsive, pessimistic, and lazy without ambition, motivation or drive.

The psychology of will power is a controversial subject. The main point here is to develop this resource and learn to apply it in the right way. Every person is born with will power; it is part of your nature to survive, eat, sleep, procreate, and so on. Developing these skills and learning how to use them effectively is a complex task. The vast majority of us develop enough will power to get by with average success. If the will is weak, then you lack the drive, ambition or determination to push for your goals. You give up easily and you feel like a slave or puppet. Lack of will makes you more vulnerable to unwanted urges, temptations, or desires.

If the will is overdeveloped, then you tend to become obsessive, demanding, impatient, and extremely rigid in your ways. You expect things to be done the way you want and become intolerant of others' input; these individuals tend to be very critical and controlling. Imposing their will on others; they are often described as stubborn. Another way to describe excessive will power is that the higher self is underdeveloped, lacks awareness, and is not capable of driving a strong will in a fair and reasonable manner. Strong will power is not a problem if it is properly managed. When strong will power is combined with an over inflated ego, you get tyrants who drive everyone around them crazy. The polarities of will power can go in two directions; too strong or never strong enough. The key is to develop strong will power with an equally evolved higher self and a very stable and flexible ego so that it can easily adapt personal intentions to the greater good.

Examples:

▸   The weak-willed person never refuses a temptation, urge, or craving even if he or she swore not to indulge in it for whatever reason.

▸   Probably there have been times in your life when you felt tired of life, unambitious, apathetic, and just lazy, and every goal seemed distant, not worth the effort. This describes weak will power.

▸   Perhaps you know of a perfectionist, who is very demanding and highly critical. Nothing is good enough. He or she is very controlling and rigid; everything must be done his or her way.

The lock is the lack of awareness of what the consequences of either too much or not enough will power are. Here, obviously, the will power locks are self-fulfilling. This makes you believe that your will power is correct, when in fact it is wrong. It impairs your judgment by limiting your intentions when weak or exaggerating them if strong. It disturbs relationships because there is a sense of injustice and imbalance of power. It also interferes with achieving your desired goals because you lack the drive to overcome obstacles.

The keys begin with realizing the importance of will power and raising your awareness to the higher self to be able to direct the will consciously. First, developing will power requires either a favorable childhood experience or an expanded, heightened higher self that can push to increase will power later in life. You can exercise will power on every level, building the energy and drive to force yourself to do something challenging or, equally to stop yourself from doing something that you intend not to do. This is accomplished by starting out on a simple and easy level and increasing the difficulty with each successful application of will power. (See the Master Key of Will Power on page 157.) Shift polarities and make it a clear intention to master your life with perseverance, persistence, patience, and determination. Reverse any weakness, and raise your energy levels. Seek inspiration, motivation, ambition, and passion to drive your intentions to completion. Transform uncertainty, pessimism, and negativity into their polar opposites by building an invincible will power, commitment, belief in yourself, and super optimistic attitude.

In the case of harnessing strong will power and directing it more effectively, you must also increase self-awareness. This is a matter of expanding consciousness, being more aware of what the right intentions are and the consequences of your actions. Determine if these actions feel good, are good for you, good for others, and serve the greater good. These goals do require greater objectivity and an earnest desire to know what others think and feel about your actions. Such curiosity informs you of what is really going on around you, which should liberate you to make better judgments and execute your intentions more effectively.

Instead of being critical, try to be analytical, help others understand where they went wrong, and advise them how to improve their performance. The purpose is to transform a controlling will into role modeling so others can follow. Shift polarities from rigid to flexible, and acknowledge all the ways your greater flexibility serves you and others. Transform any prejudice into respect and acceptance. Reverse selfish behaviors into acts of generosity. Transmute any destructive attitudes into creative ones; imagine future rewards after embracing the creative path. Determine if any obsessive behaviors can be better satisfied in other ways. The key is to develop greater flexibility to successfully adapt to the challenges around you. Now with these tools you can exercise superior judgment transforming potential loss into triumph.

The ideal is to develop every valuable aspect of your personality, especially that of an extremely strong will power commanded by a very highly evolved, stable identity that is flexible and keenly aware of what is important. A person with a strong ego is most resilient, adaptive, confident, and ambitious. These individuals can direct their will power from the higher self with clear well planned intentions that meet their own needs and serve the greater good. These people live with exceptional passion, energy, and determination, which empowers them to realize their visions and missions. The reason it works so well is that once you know what you really are supposed to achieve, then decisions become easier, liberating more energy to increase the motivation, ambition, and determination to reach your goals.

Conclusion

You make decisions every day of your life. Make each one count. Every judgment you make can either bring you closer to fulfilling your goals or take you on some crazy detour if it is wrong. I have just reviewed about eighteen major locks that often impair our judgment to some degree. Reviewing the keys on how to constructively deal with these problems should equip you with the skills and knowledge to make better decisions. This section is also designed to prepare you to deal with others who are dominated by some of these locks. Ask the right questions and perhaps you will be able to liberate some of these people from the problems that limit them or others.

The issue of judgment is complex and important. Making the right choice is sometimes extremely easy; other times it is impossible. There is no perfect system to make your decisions always correct. There are strategies that make the process of analysis and judgment more reliable than others. The weaknesses of the system have been described here briefly. The keys presented offer suggestions to minimize problems and facilitate making the best decisions available to you at the time. The following chapters further explain how to use the keys and achieve your goals. At least, right now, make it your intention to acknowledge your desire to not get caught in the "judgment locks." Rather, always seek flexibility and opportunity to use all your resources to exercise the best judgment you can.

Remember to maintain a balanced perspective because life often tips the scales in the wrong direction, only your careful judgment can lead to good decisions.

Shifting JEEP Polarities from Sabotage to Achievement

Factors	Negative Polarity	Shifting to the Positive Polarity
Judgment	Distortions or illusions irrational, mistaken, prejudiced, unaware, confused thinking, indecision and bad choices	Analytical and intuitive thinking, increased awareness, subjective and objective evaluation, good, clear decisions
Emotions	Fear, anger, pain and disgust - stress protection: fight - flight response	Courage, acceptance, happiness, and love - passion, ambition, confidence, etc...
Energy	Lacking, losing, using, stealing, leaking, abusing, blocking or limiting the flow - greedy, selfish, lazy	Abundant power flowing, sharing, exchanging, giving generously and receiving gratefully
Patterns	Sabotaging negative: mental, physical, and emotional programs, self destructive, limiting, blocking	Deliberate intentions: adaptive positive patterns, simplifying life, successful, positive, constructive

This is a summary of the dualities of the JEEP system describing the positive direction you can always take.

Chapter 23

The Gold Keys for
Escaping Stress and Increasing Happiness

The promise this book makes is that you will be given the keys to escape stress and increase happiness. The first section provided the *Vital Knowledge* to understand how your brain works and the basic natural laws. The Master Keys described in detail the *Required Skills* to deal most effectively with challenges in life. Together, these are the psychological tools everyone needs to turn stress off and to achieve goals.

The reason we have such a difficult time fending off stress and fulfilling our dreams is because our minds have a number of major handicaps. I have grouped these internal shortcomings into the four JEEP factors. Each of these factors represents the negative side of the respective Master Keys. These four factors describe over forty common problems we all experience. These are examples of what often goes wrong in our minds and how to correct these problems. Even with all this information you cannot eliminate all the stress or conflict in life. The truth is that problems are a normal part of everyday life. With the tools presented here you can become a master of escaping stress and finding fulfillment.

You have been presented with a lot of information. The next step is for you to begin to develop your own system and find ways to apply this material to your personal life. The best system must be simple and easy to use. Consequently, I have simplified all the details you have reviewed into seven *Gold Keys*. To make life easier, the vital knowledge and required skills are synthesized into seven basic rules to remember.

We will always experience some fear, anger, pain, and all the other negative emotions, conflicts, loss, and stress in general. The main point is that although you cannot eliminate stress from life, you can, with the right tools, always shift polarities and stop stress. This liberates time and energy to achieve your goals more easily. These Gold Keys are universal and are easy to apply in any situation.

The Gold keys are the most important strategies to gain better control of your own mind and to counterbalance any of the internal inadequacies that make it difficult for you to deal with life. If you at least apply these seven keys to your life, I guarantee it will improve. If you utilize all of the Master Keys, you will become a master locksmith and be able to open all of the locks that limited you previously. As you practice using these tools, you will get better and faster at changing the negative stress producing events into something positive. This represents the process of developing your own system to deal with the dualities of life.

What are the three instructions for shifting polarities?

The Gold keys offer a set of tools to change feelings or situations in life that are unwanted or unpleasant. This is accomplished by applying one of the following three strategies to triumph over a problem. Throughout this book I have described how to *Transform* situations – changing one thing into another. When it is not possible to transform something, then you may *Transcend* it by escaping the situation – letting it go, practicing non-attachment, and moving your focus. The third possibility, when the others do not work, is to use *Integration* to merge opposites together. This is done by combining various polarities, conflicts, or opposing views into a new synthesis, embracing the new situation and accepting it as a part of your life. This can also be called *creation*, making something new that resolves the situation.

Transformation, transcendence, and integration are the techniques we can use to escape conflicts, hardships, and pain, and to achieve more in life. As far as I know, we are never actually given specific instructions about how to best apply these tools in our lives. Consequently, I have provided you detailed explanations on how to become a master of these techniques. There are significant advantages to rely on specific instructions to achieve goals, rather than just criticizing or blaming yourself or others about the lack of progress. The key is to be clear about your desired outcome; then seek the most explicit instructions to help yourself and others change or improve performance to reach results aimed for. There is little to be gained from criticism, and much more can be achieved by instruction. As you apply these tools to your life, you will develop your own personal style, one that feels and works best for you.

Gold Keys for Escaping Stress and Increasing Happiness

Think Up!

Go up to your deliberate mind, become more aware. Establish a clear set of intentions. Gain control of yourself and act on your intentions.

Relax and Let Go!

Turn off stress by breathing slowly, deeply, and relaxing.

Shift your attention away from problems and refocus on your intentions.

Think with Flexibility!

Remain open, bendable, and curious about alternatives; do not get rigid. Be flexible, rely on both the subjective or intuitive and objective or rational information to make your decisions.

Shift Polarities!

Exercise reversing directions to escape stress and go to your higher nature. Identify the opposite emotions and transform the negative into positive.

Direct Your Will Power!

Build up your passion to act with deliberate intent and be prepared to work on your goals ambitiously, with confidence and determination.

Keep Energy Flowing!

Appreciate all the energy you receive and promote the free and generous exchange of energy in all forms. Respect yourself and others by striving to reciprocate any energy you receive.

Build Your Faith!

Everything depends on believing in yourself and the purpose of your life. Have faith in the positive possibilities of the universe and maintain meaning and confidence in your own life.

Naturally, we are all limited by our resources and other factors beyond our control. These techniques work very well in every situation, but there will be times when it can be extremely difficult to shift polarities. There will be challenges in life for which you cannot prepare for enough, and it will feel overwhelming, very distressing, and confusing or simply throw you off balance. This is a normal part of life.

> **Ryderize:** *Advise instead of criticize; achieve more when you seek the best instructions to improve performance.*

There is absolutely nothing you can do about the unpredictable nature of life. Remember that chaos is a normal, ever present part of life. Usually, chaos is insignificant, just inconvenient like spilling your drink, although chaos can reach horrific levels that cause total destruction and annihilation such as witnessed on 9-11. The stress that we experience everyday can be easily transformed into positive directions. When stress reaches extreme levels of crisis, we need additional techniques.

Basic Steps for Stress Relief

You will be confronted by stress producing situations countless times through your life. Since you cannot eliminate stress completely, you either must put up with it or do something about it. The key is to have a practical system that works; otherwise, you must constantly endure the stress. Learn to use the skills being described here. In the beginning, it may be somewhat difficult, but each time you go through this routine, it will become easier. To summarize the basic instructions of how to relieve regular stress in life, follow these steps:

1. Stress is just an alarm; be alert and aware of what is happening.
2. Refocus on your higher self; make it your intention to gain control.
3. Relax your body and let go of the problem – turn off the stress, breathing slowly, relaxing, and visualizing or imagining a pleasant scene.
4. Identify the polar opposite feelings, shift to positive emotions.
5. Think carefully and take deliberate action to resolve the situation.

This system is a great improvement over the one you were born with (reflexive mind) or the one that you use routinely (automatic mind).

Normally, problems cause us to react with some form of stress – "getting unglued," "freaked out," "pissed off," "driven crazy," or whatever is your personal style. There are also many ways that we have evolved to deal with the stress in life. The *first way* is to react emotionally; the *second way* is to react with some pattern; and the *third way* is to go to the deliberate mind and gain as much control as possible.

What to do when total chaos strikes?

There will be events in life that are catastrophic, extremely painful, horrific, and out of your control. These are divided into two types of extreme situations; either there is something that could be done to stop or decrease the danger, or the tragedy is over and nothing more can be done. The first case is the emergency situation like a serious illness or accident, a fire, flood, hurricane, an act of violence, or even psychological trauma like betrayal, abandonment, humiliation, and so on. These events require an immediate response to prevent greater loss. The second case is the aftermath of the first one, but it is too late to do anything. These situations are all the tragedies, such as death, your house burning down, the consequences of some natural disaster, and any other crisis that is actually over. We find it extremely difficult to deal with these problems because we are in fact helpless to change the results. Although it is unlikely that anyone could be prepared for these types of terrible stressors, you can learn to deal with total chaos constructively.

To deal with total chaos requires tremendous strength physically, emotionally, and mentally. When terrible things happen most people will panic with terror, cry with despair, or resort to aggressive behavior; these are the three reflexive ways we commonly react to a crisis. However, there are other ways, those that rely on extraordinary skills of self-control and excellent judgment of what to do next.

Emergencies and what is the Fourth Way?

During an emergency, actions based on fear, anger, or despair are not helpful. These reflexive emotions impair our judgment, steal our strength, and interfere with resolving the situation. There is what I refer to as the *fourth way* to deal with a crisis; it is a demonstration of courage, endurance, self-sacrifice, and extremely strong will power to act deliberately rather than be dragged into an emotional trauma.

Most people are not able to deal with a crisis very well. Usually you must be specially trained to deal with an emergency or catastrophe like firefighters, police officers, doctors, members of special forces in the military, and similar groups. When we observe regular people responding to a terrible situation in a positive way, we are surprised and impressed. What is the secret? What do these individuals have that others lack? Can you develop the same strengths?

How do you apply the Fourth Way?

The *fourth way* represents an internal perspective that absolutely nothing will throw you off balance, that you will think clearly, listen to your intuition, and maintain complete control with your will power. If you encounter an emergency, tragedy, terrible pain, or some sort of crisis, it is imperative to remain in control, think quickly, and act resolutely. These are indeed often life and death situations. This is a matter of taking deliberate action to deal with the emergency in the best way possible. The following seven points are the essential steps of the *fourth way*:

Fourth Way Perspective and Skills

1. You have a clear higher cause, a sense of a mission above yourself.
2. You have very specific priorities for which you are prepared.
3. You assert a leadership role and command with authority.
4. You accept necessary risks to accomplish your goals.
5. You remain focused and in complete, deliberate control of your actions.
6. You are able to ignore or tolerate all pain or suffering until you complete your mission.
7. You recognize that everything happens for a reason and a purpose so you prepare yourself to learn the lessons with dignity and respect.

The *fourth way* refers to using this set of superior skills including the nine Master Keys. Together these tools allow you to deal as constructively as possible with any catastrophe that requires a response. This does not mean that you avoid stress or resolve the problems completely. In reality, chaos can leave a wake of destruction in its path; there may be loss and misery. Still you don't want to lie down and get run over, especially if you can get up and fight for something meaningful.

How to cope with tragedy after chaos strikes?

Tragedy is an inevitable part of life. Bad things happen. Fortunately, the worst forms of chaos do not strike often, but when they do, it can really be horrible. For example, the physical loss of property that may have more sentimental than monetary value (your grandparents' home burns down). The emotional pain, like betrayal by a spouse who abandons you to run off with a mutual friend. Or the mental shock of some crisis, like becoming a paraplegic after a bad car accident. The common factor is that crisis is over; now it is only a matter of dealing with the consequences.

No matter how strong an individual is, these are the most difficult circumstances to find oneself in. Consider all the unspeakable tragedies that we hear about and honestly hope they never happen to us. The most painful experiences are the death of a child or a loved one; a serious and permanent medical problem (paralysis, a stroke, brain injury, loss of a limb, blindness, etc.), or a natural disaster that destroys some irreplaceable property. Now what can you do about it? Unfortunately, such tragedies cannot be reversed; however, you can learn to adapt and deal with the difficult consequences successfully.

Tragedy and what is the Fifth Way?

The *fifth way* refers to graceful adaptation to the most difficult situations life presents. This means that there is a constructive and positive way to deal with these tragedies. This requires a very unique perspective and a highly evolved self-awareness. The *fifth way* includes the capacity for transcendence; not only letting go of something important, but even embracing its absence. This is a step above and beyond acceptance because to transcend means to seek how a tragedy can be enlightening, liberating, a lesson in life, a special opportunity to experience the depth of our own soul and suffering. This is not meant to belittle or diminish the actual tragedy or loss. To the contrary, it is meant to help us find meaning, understanding, and then the strength to carry on.

The most common response is despair and anger at the loss incurred. This negativity truly cannot help. The *fifth way* is a manifestation of the most superior human spirit, that expresses the highest degree of endurance, dignity, compassion, respect, and grace. This enables us to accept the consequences of some chaos in a constructive way and not to give up, rather to harness strength and push forward with positive and adaptive actions. This obviously includes all the previous skills and keys reviewed.

Fifth Way Perspectives and Skills:

1. Superior clarity of awareness that acknowledges every aspect of the situation.

2. The courage to experience the full loss without denial, dissociating, or escaping.

3. The ability to truthfully empathize with the victim or family without inhibitions.

4. Embracing the higher self to merge objective and subjective perspectives to find the most optimistic perspectives.

5. Reaching a state of higher consciousness that enables you to transcend the tragedy and seek meaning, understanding, and enlightenment (a mystical or spiritual message).

6. Experiencing transcendence, releasing or letting go of the tragic aspect and finding ways to embrace the loss meaningfully. This includes discovering the spiritual or psychological lessons that can have positive consequences in the future.

7. To achieve a state of peace, compassion, and acceptance after shifting polarities away from any of the negative emotions up to the higher nature. This includes behaving with grace and dignity, not seeking sympathy, rather asserting a leadership role that expresses courage and strength. Building your personal sense of faith, believing in yourself, a spiritual reality, and/or God.

These are the special keys that we must be able to use when dealing with the aftermath of a catastrophe. These events are indeed the hardest experiences in life, those that can easily ruin a person's life afterwards; or if we find ways to adapt constructively, we can build upon these challenges. The most simple and frequent comment during such events is "Why me!?" This is our ego trying to defend our need for stability, protecting ourselves and our territory. The ego is not the higher self; the ego cannot make sense of tragedy. Only our higher consciousness is able to analyze such a painful situation and find meaningful answers.

The *fifth way* is the most adaptive, healthy, and constructive approach in dealing with tragedy. The reason for this is because you are prepared to acknowledge that the cause of this misfortune is attributable to the forces of chaos. Chaos – the forces of disorder – causes destruction continuously somewhere, mostly on a random basis, but sometimes it can even be intentional. Rarely is anyone actually singled out to be a victim of chaos; this is just the nature of reality. Even when chaos is caused by human intervention, as in terrorist attacks, it is not directed at an individual; yet that is how we feel when we are involved. The main point is that if you are to escape stress and adapt to some tragic event, you must rise above it, see it in the context of a universe of events, and not get caught in the normal negative emotional reactions.

The *fifth way* is above and beyond the other keys. It represents a deep human capacity for adapting and getting past the most difficult problems in life. Since it is possible to follow a superior path, then why not? It may not be easy. It does require extraordinary strength; it does work.

Conclusion:

This chapter reviewed the steps to escape stress under normal circumstances and what to do under the most extreme situations. The media is full of heroic stories about human endurance. These stories are examples of individuals following the *fourth or fifth ways*. Like the brave souls who were hijacked on Flight 93 and forced to crash on nine-eleven. These were not specially trained military forces; they were regular people who rose to the occasion. That is the incredible human spirit.

Since the total amount of energy we start with every day is limited, the less we use dealing with stress, the more we will have to apply towards reaching goals. The tools presented here are very efficient techniques to deal with stress, giving you more time and energy to achieve greater happiness. The last chapter describes more details about achievement.

Imagine all the people living life in peace. You may say I'm a dreamer, but I'm not the only one. I hope someday you'll join us, and the world will be as one.

John Lennon

Chapter 24

Spirituality and Your Higher Nature

Our life is what our thoughts make it.   Marcus Aurelius

Spirituality has been a controversial topic since the beginning of civilization. Some people are absolutely certain that it exists; others are equally convinced that it does not. Although a large majority believe in a spiritual dimension, there exist vastly different interpretations of what that spirituality is. The diversity of our beliefs is another product of the easily persuaded mind that creates problems.

It is the uncertainty in the universe that forces us to debate all the big "Why" questions. Either the incredible mysteries of the universe were created by God or they evolved by accident from nature. Secondly, either the amazing "spiritual" experiences we have are because we can become aware of that "invisible" dimension, or they are just biological "illusions" of the brain. Personally, based on decades of scientific research and many extraordinary experiences I have had, I am absolutely convinced of a spiritual dimension. However, let me explain both sides of the story.

This is a matter of the *Diamond Key*, your consciousness. Regardless of what you believe, it is your conscious awareness that reveals both possibilities! Your mind, not your body, is what perceives the universe as well as experiences the mystical or spiritual dimension. I find this fact paradoxical and amazing, that it is consciousness that enables us to believe in God or argue against the idea. It is every person's freedom to explore these ideas and experiences to eventually decide what he or she chooses to believe.

What is Spiritual?

The real problem is defining what we truly consider "spiritual" as opposed to the "material" world. There have been many explanations of what spiritual is or is not. Here I intend to offer you a very clear and simple description of what is spiritual. On the following page you will find Table 17 The Higher - Spiritual Nature vs the Lower - Biological Nature. The boundary between your lower nature and the higher spiritual nature is straightforward. Lower emotions are apparently in-born for our protection or survival. Higher emotions must be learned and developed over time to enable us to experience the benefits of surviving and feeling safe. That means that once you escape all the threats, you are supposed to enjoy the good, happy, fulfilling aspects of life. This is the origin of spirituality in my philosophical understanding.

The material world is based on your biological survival. The spiritual world is based on growing past mere survival by learning to express all the higher emotions and experiencing all the positive feelings. Being spiritual is not a matter of following a religion or having faith in God. Spiritual means learning to act from the higher mind, the higher nature, and not letting your lower nature dominate your life. We are all vulnerable to be controlled by the negative aspect of our minds; when you become aware of this and transform the negative urge or wish into a positive action, you are acting spiritually. The upper half of Table 17 represents a sample of the positive, spiritual emotions or attitudes that make us spiritual.

How to be more spiritual?

The entire universe continues to evolve on a cosmic, earthly, and personal level. This evolution represents a decrease in the forces of chaos and an increase of the forces of consciousness and order. This is a cosmic polarity shift in *Positive Directions*. On the individual level, we are growing more aware of the universe, our planet, and our humanity. More individuals are realizing that we do not need to worry about survival personally. Rather, it is a matter of cooperation among all people, taking care of our environment, and growing from within. We are on the brink of a major transformation of awareness. I refer to this as the *Third Renaissance,* a rebirth of the human spirit. The first renaissance was about an intellectual awakening, the second about architecture and technology; the third is about consciousness.

There are many more people today interested in developing their personal strengths rather than just their physical strengths, enriching their lives in more ways than just by becoming rich. This is a worldwide trend of a spiritual reawakening. People want to experience more of their own higher natures than their lower emotions. Shifting polarities is exactly the process by which this is accomplished, enabling you to transform the negative into the positive, higher spiritual energy.

It is easy to be more spiritual. Escape the mind's natural weaknesses by reversing directions and going up to the emotions of your higher nature (See Table 17). The key to transforming lower into higher emotions is to first identify the negative emotion, then find the most opposite feeling among the list of positive emotions (in the same upper column). Follow the steps outlined in Master Key 8 (page 178) to complete the process. The more time and energy you spend embracing spiritual emotions and attitudes – including the Master Keys, the *fourth* and *fifth ways* – the more you evolve the balance of consciousness around you.

Another aspect of this internal enrichment is that people are becoming less subjectively driven and more flexible about what will make them happy. That means the ***Third Renaissance*** also liberates people to find more ways to be happy, not just the ways they wish for, but any way that will work. This, in general, makes people less selfish and more interested in whatever serves the greater good.

What is the ultimate lesson in compassion?

The mind has its positive and negative aspects. The reason for most of our hardships is because the mind has an inborn slant towards the negative side, causing unimaginable grief. The moment you understand this problem, then you can easily transform frustration into compassion and tolerance. All the pain, anger, evil, stupidity, crime, and even war is the result of this imbalance in the mind. The more people recognize it and pass this little wisdom around, the more quickly we can decrease the negative aspects from destroying our world and lives. The world is changing and more people are striving to be more spiritual; being more compassionate is one major step forward.

What are the three principles of the Third Renaissance?

There are three principles that will push the ***Third Renaissance*** to evolve, the vast majority of people would like to embrace, if they knew how. The simple concept of sharing and cooperating among diverse peoples is exemplified by the principle of ***Unity***. The idea that we can transform any negativity into a positive energy results in greater tolerance, promoting the principle of ***Peace***. And the result of these two forces creates the third rewarding principle of ***Prosperity***. We live in an abundant world.

Recognizing our interdependence and need to work together will allow us to share the wealth the world offers. The reward is that each person grows his or her own prosperity, building greater wealth throughout the world.

Table 17 Higher - Spiritual Nature vs Lower - Biological Nature

Relaxed	Kindness	Free	Fun
Pleased	Embrace	Compliment	Rapture
Content	Approving	Cool	Ecstasy
Stamina	Open	Sweet	Humor
Youthful	Forgiving	Innocent	Beautiful
Heroic	Positive	Soothing	Loyal
Motivated	Powerful	Serene	Optimistic
Daring	Generous	Faithful	Bonded
Strong	Assertive	Blissful	Humor
Brave	Flexible	Celebrating	Attracting
Bold	Patience	Healthy	Admiration
Excited	Gentle	Relief	Stimulating
Secure	Peaceful	Hopeful	Interesting
Ambitious	Compassion	Balanced	Respect
Confident	Tolerance	Harmony	Pride
Courage	**Accepting**	**Happiness**	**Love**
⇅ ⇅ ⇅ ⇅	⇅ ⇅ ⇅ ⇅	⇅ ⇅ ⇅ ⇅	⇅ ⇅ ⇅ ⇅
Fear	**Anger**	**Pain**	**Disgust**
Anxiety	Frustrated	Sad	Boredom
Tension	Demanding	Dismay	Apathy
Nervous	Territorial	Agony	Ashamed
Scared	Bitter	Depressed	Inhibited
Panic	Mad	Grief	Hatred
Terror	Screaming	Hopeless	Repulsive
Dread	Rage	Desperation	Contempt
Trapped	Hostile	Suicidal	Pessimism
Worried	Aggressive	Guilty	Sickening
Hesitant	Vengeful	Sting	Vile
Shy	Irritated	Burn	Ugly
Doubts	Jealous	Throb	Nauseating
Distrust	Greed	Torture	Gruesome
etc.	etc.	etc.	etc.

The world is an infinitely diverse habitat. The greater the number of people who aspire to promote unity, peace, and prosperity, the more our diversity will develop our humanity. The ***Third Renaissance*** is building bridges through the internal spiritual awakening of compassion, tolerance, forgiveness, appreciation, admiration, optimism, and all the other positive emotions. With six billion people on the planet, we need perhaps only one out of ten to embrace these concepts in order to actually initiate a global change of consciousness for all. Many authors and luminaries believe, with me, that we are fast approaching the tipping point. When enough people become more spiritually oriented – what is a personal shift, will become a planetary enlightenment. I have such a vision that this is truly within our grasp at this time. I also realize that there are very dark and powerful forces that could stop our progress. I would urge you to do your part to promote positive concepts, and perhaps in our lifetime, the world will enjoy greater unity, peace, and prosperity.

Are you ready for the ultimate crusade?

If you are interested, on my website, **www.UltimateGoals.com**, you can see how you can participate in the Unity Crusade. This is a place for people who share a similar vision of the future to come together and find ways to promote a "spiritual" agenda. Part of this includes raising awareness of people around the world about how to act more spiritually. This has nothing to do with religion; rather, it is a matter of raising the level of consciousness in our civilization.

This crusade has a growing number of established goals for this century. The Unity Logo is a symbolic image of these ideas. It was registered as the logo for the twenty-first century in 1996. The axiom we advocate is: ***"Create what you can do best that the world needs most."*** This is the general concept designed to encourage people to contribute to the future of this world in a creative and positive way. (See a picture of this logo on the next page.)

Conclusion:

The notion of spirituality here is proposed to be a combination of the higher emotions (love, happiness, courage, and acceptance) along with the Master Keys, Gold Keys, and the *fourth* and *fifth ways*. Those who can exercise their freedom to express these positive feelings and attitudes will bring more spirituality into this world. Ultimately, spirituality is intimately tied to the concept and workings of consciousness. Those who are truly interested have the opportunity to explore the unlimited depths of conscious awareness or spiritual contact. I have seen and experienced incredible visions, feelings, and alternate realities. Allow your curiosity to bloom and take the courageous steps to learn more about your very own portal into the infinite universe – your consciousness! See the Appendix for ideas, workshops, and websites under "consciousness."

Chapter   25

Mastering the Art and Science of Life: Conclusions

Dream, love, love your dreams and love your life!

John Ryder

So what is the secret to life? Is there a secret formula to success? Perhaps there is. Have you been thinking that a part of the secret is found in the duality of opposite polarities? The East - West differences represent two very opposite styles of thinking and living. The East is more concerned with internal personal growth, while the West is more focused on external worldly achievements. Eastern philosophy believes that intuition, or introspective knowledge, is superior, while on the other hand, Western tradition relies on the rational, logic, facts, and details to find reality. One side is more flexible, holistic, idealistic, and timeless, while the other side is more rigid, structured, organized, compartmentalized, and ruled by time. Have you come to the same conclusion I have, that both systems are smart and powerful? Is it possible that either system is valuable without the other?

What to do about the duality of life?

Do you recognize the importance of the obvious polarities or duality of life? Should we ignore one part of life if we become immersed in a different part? Doesn't mastering life simply mean being open and flexible to changing perspectives? How could anyone know which side is better or stronger without considering both at least for a moment? There are definitely situations in which the Eastern approach is superior, and there are others in which the Western, more scientific system has a significant advantage. Consequently, isn't being able to shift between opposites quickly and easily a major advantage in life? This is the ultimate purpose of polarity shifting– to effectively deal with the duality of life by moving in *positive directions*.

When to be single minded?

Achievement, on the other hand, requires a single mindedness and focus on just one direction. Once you have a future vision, pushing in that one direction with every possible resource is the best guarantee that you will reach your goals. The complexity of life also guarantees that you will experience a great deal of stress because of the challenges, obstacles, or actual failures that occur on the road to success. Escaping stress requires you to embrace the duality of life to deal with your situation. The art of life explains ways that you could accept the "failure" as a new challenge, even appreciate the learning experience, and actually feel good once you are able to adapt to it. Doesn't that attitude make it easier to enjoy life and have greater fulfillment? It is just being positive and adaptive. The power of shifting polarities enables you to escape stress and adapt more effectively. Once you reestablish some balance, you can return to single mindedness to work on your goals.

What is Cosmic Consciousness?

The ultimate tool that will help you achieve greater mastery is your consciousness. The concept of your CQ represents what and how much you are aware of at any moment. Consciousness is the Diamond Key of life. That refers to consciousness being the only portal you have to learn the truth about reality. Curiously, we do not learn about reality directly with our senses, but rather through the intuitive and analytical mind working together to understand what we perceive. Hence, back to the duality of life. Being able to move back and forth between these two systems (analytical and intuitive) provides you with incomparable power to have the most fulfilling life.

The ultimate power of the conscious mind is that it can even transcend itself, escape the limits of the personal self, and embrace a bigger perspective. The key to our success has always been our consciousness, that superior awareness of more than just our bodies and personal needs. As we become more aware of life and the world, we open more pathways in our minds to have better ideas, which help us grasp more meaning. At the highest levels, our consciousness actually discovers our connection to God, the universe, as well as the planet, the environment, your country, your city or village, your colleagues, friends, family, and everything on the inside. Yes, it is possible for anybody to expand his or her awareness to gain a larger perspective, and no, it is not necessary to transcend all these levels to have a great idea. The moment we connect with the supreme inner awareness of our deliberate minds we enter what often is referred to as cosmic consciousness, a portal into very idea of infinity!

What do good vibrations create?

The interaction of the brain and mind combine to give us consciousness; every person has the same system. What is unique is how we direct it and what we pay attention to. That is how all the differences between people appear. In my opinion, the most valuable resource of the system is creativity. On the simplest level, this is just coming up with good ideas. If you find yourself in uncomfortable surroundings, you feel awkward; something unpleasant is disturbing your space. Try to move to a better place. Make your environment more comfortable and pleasant by either transforming it, transcending it, or finding a way to integrate into it. When you are in a pleasant space, it becomes easier to heighten your sensitivity to generate more new ideas. This starts with your conscious intent to search for new ideas. This can literally be anything; it can be simple, like going to a movie, or profound, like deciding that you want to become a parent. It is just an idea. My suggestion is that you produce many of them; this way, there will a mixture of simple, better, and a few great ideas. This almost seems silly, advising people to have more ideas, but the fact is we all could generate many more ideas than we normally do. This activity should be exercised by everyone constantly. Go have a great idea!

What is the last secret?

There are many secrets about life and success that are not hidden very well. I have shared with you many of the important secrets I have discovered. It has been my most sincere wish to empower as many people as possible to conquer stress and actualize their potential. This has been the intention of this book. These are the keys I believe will help you gain greater freedom from stress and achieve more of your dreams. Now it is up to you to take the next step, believe in yourself, and believe in your dreams.

One last secret key I wish to leave you with is a very simple idea that keeps getting verified over and over for me. An excellent example of this secret is Margaret. She is a very interesting woman who is on her fourth career; she is filled with enthusiasm, vitality, curiosity, passion, and many other virtues. She won a beauty pageant in Europe almost five decades ago, and she is still very attractive, looks almost half her age, with beaming eyes, glowing skin, and true happiness in her smile. I asked Margaret what her secret was. She replied with great exuberance, that '***she loves life***!' What a simple and wonderful secret. If you ***love*** life, your own best energy will keep you young and going in positive directions!

Appendix

Positive Directions

www. ShiftingPolarities .com

www.JohnRyderPhD.com

Mission Statement:

My ultimate goals are to enlighten and empower as many people as possible through the books, programs, and workshops that I have developed. Shifting polarities in *Positive Directions* is a universal technique to reverse any negative direction into the opposite positive one. This system creates a new spiritual path for any person to easily follow to escape the stress of life and achieve more of his or her goals. It is my intention to promote the tools to make life easier so that we can all enjoy greater unity, peace and prosperity around the world.

This book is enough to catapult some people to a whole new level of life. Those of you who have a superior skill of transferring written intellectual knowledge into action will witness your life transform. Most of us require additional experience in order to learn to use the information here to promote progress in life. For most people a multimedia presentation can accelerate learning and make it much more memorable. For this reason I have established several additional levels to this material than just the written book. Besides the audio versions (available as CDs, iPods, or MP3 players) I have several websites with more multimedia information and I intend to bring this work in the form of lectures and workshops to a city near you. This gives you the possibility of mastering the skills being described here in many more ways.

The Internet:

The main website (ShiftingPolarities.com) is this book's mission virtual address. You will find there many resources that will make your journey through life easier and more fulfilling. Go to this website and click on "**Resources**." There you will be able to access information or download materials you desire.

At any of Dr. Ryder's websites you can also learn about **Live Events** that may be scheduled in your area. There is a variety of workshops offered based on this book. Groups or individuals can sponsor a lecture or a workshop by Dr. Ryder that give participants the opportunity to experience various exercises that will help them develop and master these skills. To request or propose an event in your area go to JohnRyderPhD.com and click on Media & Speaking Engagements – there you will find the information you need.

The *Live Events* rely on a multimedia presentation that is specifically organized to stimulate all of your senses. Magic and illusions are used to dramatize major concepts during these presentations. They make your experience very memorable enabling you to maximize learning. The workshops deliver advanced content, along with a variety of experiential exercises that help you learn and develop these powerful tools.

Lectures:

Dr. Ryder has given numerous lectures and keynote addresses to audiences throughout the United States and internationally. He can accommodate your group with a presentation that is entertaining and educational that will fit your format. The lectures can elaborate the basic concepts from the book, illustrate the key points, and go through exercises to demonstrate the system, with time for questions from the audience.

Positive Directions Workshops:

Get Leverage - Develop Your Strengths

The first event is a short (2-4 hour) intensive about how to shift polarities. This workshop takes participants through the maze of illusions to the magic of insight. It leads people through three exercises, teaching you how to escape stress more easily and develop the power of intention. This process is called *Mastering the Art and Science of Life*; it contains the essence of the book's powerful secrets to live in the optimal way.

Get Leverage - The Master Keys Workshop

This is a full day event. It goes into greater depth, covering all of the nine Master Keys, along with twenty exercises designed to increase your awareness and will power to deal with life. This workshop develops your skills to more effectively manage the JEEP factors or any adversity and always feel like you are floating rather than sinking. I call this process **Walking on Water.** This experience gives you incredible confidence and determination to go forward and upward in life. Transforming anything negative into something positive. Learning how to leverage all of your strengths to live a more fulfilling life. A special workbook is included that guides you through the work to make life easier and more successful.

Express to Success

The two-day workshop goes through the same material the first day and then on the <u>second day</u> you are taken on a **Super Express to Success.** Everybody wants to succeed, to achieve peak performance and reach all of their dreams. This day is dedicated to take each individual on an experiential journey to be a winner, to speed up your progress to achieve the highest goals you have. This is a very pragmatic process that takes you through clearly defined steps. First, you identify the superior talents, skills, and abilities you have. Next, you are instructed on how to gain greater leverage with the resources you have. Then you work on developing a vivid vision of your goals and overall potential. This leads to establishing a detailed strategic plan that includes your vision, the resources required, the network of people to rely on, role models to emulate, and the motivation to accomplish these goals. This part of the workshop equips you with a very realistic, pragmatic, detailed plan that includes a time line of events to follow. You will go home charged with energy to realize your dreams. A special workbook is included to guide you through this process and continue to use as a reference.

Visit **www.ShiftingPolarities.com** click on live events.

The mission statement explains my desire to help you make life easier. Liberate yourself from the obstacles and small thinking. Think BIG! Let your imagination run free! Find more opportunities. Believe that you can change your life and even the world around you for the better. These are the skills of mastering the science of success and the art of life described here and in the other programs I offer. If you wonder whether you have made enough progress, do not lose hope, recognize that you must continue to apply these tools in more practical ways. The websites offer something different and the live events are stimulating and empowering. Embrace your life, think about what you really want and let me help you make it happen.

The Master Tool Kit:

The first step towards mastering your life is to gain better control of your intentions. Be clear that intentions are not urges, temptations, impulses, or desires from the lower nature. Intentions arise from the higher mind and are directed by the higher self, that inner core of your being that experiences consciousness and feels connected to life. There are many exercises that build your awareness and increase your control of these skills.

Anchoring a Power Move:

The process of "anchoring" is to condition your mind and body to react in a special way to a specific trigger. Just like most of us react to the sound of a siren behind us, you can train your body to respond to a special signal (Power Move) in a positive way. For example, slapping your thigh and exclaiming "yes!" when you achieved your goal. What if you practiced slapping your thigh and repeating "yes!" dozens of times while imagining that you have reached some fantastic goal. Your body would feel the excitement, your mind would practice experiencing the passion and success of achievement. So that whenever you would repeat this "power move" you anchor the positive energy and expectations to your body and mind. This is how every single high performing individual reaches outstanding levels of achievement.

The key to the power move is to find a distinct physical signal, a slap, snapping your fingers, punching the air or your hand, stamping your foot, or something similar, that you associate with a desired outcome. Once you decide what kind of power move you feel comfortable with, you must practice repeating it until it becomes a conditioned or automatic response. Then when you use it, this power move starts a cascade of effects in your mind and body that greatly facilitate achievement. You are creating positive expectations and programming yourself to utilize this energy more effectively. This increases your determination, motivation, and your ability to actualize your potential.

Will power is applying your intentions deliberately with no reservations. When you have complete faith and confidence in what you are suppose to do, then it is easy to have the will power and determination to see it through.

Relaxing and Letting Go:

This is a two step process that counterbalances our tendency to become tense and obsessively hold on to certain negative ideas or events. Relaxation is the process of releasing all tension – muscular, mental, and emotional. When you really are relaxed, you stop all the feedback from your body to your mind. The deeper you relax the less information from your body reaches the mind. This creates a state change in which your mind is liberated from the constant clutter of tension and activity of the body. Once you are completely relaxed, the mind begins to revitalize and energize. Watching television, or even reading a book is not being completely relaxed because you are still active. You do not need to meditate or sit in any special position for hours. A few minutes of deep relaxation is equivalent to hours of sleep.

The ability to let go depends more on your mind's skill of shifting attention away from what you would focus on otherwise. Letting go is the process of recognizing that the focus is unnecessary, unrewarding, and unproductive. Consequently, you make it your intention to shift your attention away from the unwanted focus. Shifting attention takes practice. As you improve this skill, it becomes easier for you to release ideas or events that are bothering you and let go of them. Then you can focus on something that will return much more to you.

Relaxing Exercise:

Step one. Set your environment. Find a comfortable place to lean back and relax. Turn down the lights and turn off the phones. Perhaps you need to ask others to leave you alone for a few minutes.

Step two. Make it your intention to relax. Get comfortable, let your body settle into a very comfortable position and continue relaxing your body. The paradox of this exercise is that you do not need to make an effort to relax, just let it happen.

Step three. Change your breathing. Normally, you breathe 22 times a minute, slow it down to about 10 times a minute, that is about 3 seconds in and 3 seconds out. Start by taking two or three deeper breaths about 5 to 10 seconds in and the same time out, very slowly, smoothly, easily, remember no strain.

Step four. Change your focus. Think about, or recall, or imagine a beautiful, peaceful place that you would feel very safe and comfortable in. This can be your special sanctuary where you go to in your mind to shift your focus away from everything else and relax. Visualize this place, imagine yourself there and what it would feel like to be resting in this wonderful place.

Step five. Embrace and enjoy this new state. Allow yourself to rest, relaxing completely and not having anything to bother you physically or mentally. Be here now. Enjoy this state of peaceful being for a timeless moment.

Step six. As you rest, increase your awareness. Notice the changes in your body and mind. Learn to recognize the progressive stages of relaxing and sensations of your body as it becomes totally relaxed. Releasing all the unwanted burdens, stress, and worries of everyday life you can now experience the inner peace. Even if it is only for a few minutes (ideally five to fifteen minutes) you are recharging your mind and body with renewed energy.

Step seven. Time to refocus and return refreshed. Once you have relaxed your body and rested enough prepare yourself to return completely revitalized and ready for the next activity. Your mind should be clear, your body energized. Take a few more deeper breaths that are faster (3 seconds) and more powerful. Refocus on your body, begin moving your fingers and toes a bit. Feel your body awakening and as you open your eyes be aware of the alert refreshed state of mind you are now in. Enjoy the rest of your day.

This is part of the exercises performed during a live event. You can also obtain one of several recorded CDs or download these exercises from the internet. I created a number of different programs for you to select one that suits you best. The more you practice these exercises, the faster and easier you learn to master this skill. (See details about *Relaxation Programs* on the ShiftingPolarities.com website.)

Letting Go:

This exercise can be combined with relaxing above or done on its own.

Step one. Increasing awareness of your focus. First, you must be clear about what is drawing your attention, how important is it, what can you really do about it, and does it deserve any more attention.

Step two. Make it your intention to shift your focus. Decide now to shift your attention to other matters. Let go of the unwanted ideas or events and allow them to fade away. Refocus on a new subject and continue to shift to new matters without returning to the old focus.

Step three. Gain control of your new directions. Shifting your attention should be directed by your higher mind and specific intentions with a purpose. By learning to let go of unimportant matters you can focus on more important ones. This is the process by which we make progress.

If you are being bothered by something that you should let go of, relaxing first may be helpful. Relaxation changes the state of your body and allows you to direct your attention more effectively. Using this exercise while relaxing is simple, just begin this process after step four of the relaxation exercise. This promotes a more complete shift of attention. The ultimate purpose of letting go is to escape matters that are stressful or unwanted. This is a skill that evolves over a lifetime of practice.

The *Letting Go Program,* is part of a series of exercises at the live events is also recorded on CD and is available on the Internet for those interested in experiencing these tools.

Open Visualization:

The key to shifting attention is to be aware of what else you can focus on that may be more important or useful. This exercise develops the skills of noticing and shifting attention. Remember that letting go is dependent on your ability to shift your focus. Practicing this skill is essential for a successful life. Most people are better at concentrating than at shifting. There are others who are much better at shifting attention than concentrating; they are often seen as very easily distracted (attention deficit disorder) which may not be a real impairment at all. That is the purpose of shifting polarities, developing both skills is important to a successful life.

The open visualization takes you on a journey to explore the inner world and the external universe in progressively deeper, faster, and larger shifts of focus.

The Open Visualization is another exercise performed during live events which is also available on CD and on the internet.

Cosmic Consciousness:

Those who are interested in exploring the farthest reaches of our consciousness are invited to visit my other website www.UltimateGoals.com where you will find many more resources about this topic. As I have described earlier, consciousness is the diamond key of life. This is the ultimate doorway to perceive and understand the world you live in. Most importantly, it is the only system by which you can learn more about yourself.

'Know thyself' has been a major axiom since the beginning of civilization. This does not refer to knowing your name or social identity. This is a matter of getting to know who you are at the core level, becoming more conscious of your higher self. Consciousness holds many secrets about our existence and reveals it to those who are curious and willing to make an effort to expand their mind. The road to inner awareness is open to all, however, it is a difficult path to travel. Cosmic consciousness refers to an experience of awareness that transcends the normal sensory information we process every second.

The opportunity to explore your consciousness and its infinite dimensions is always available to you even while you sleep with dreams. During the awake portion of your day, direct your awareness inwardly, first to your higher self and then make it your intention to expand your consciousness. This is a spontaneous process by which your awareness grows, but at the same time it may take a lifetime of effort to reach the highest levels of consciousness. There have been many prophets, seekers, and just regular people who have reported the extraordinary experiences of cosmic consciousness. It is by all accounts I have read, and by my own experiences, an extremely unique and powerful state of awareness. It does not compare to normal consciousness. The term "cosmic" is suppose to convey the meaning of universal awareness, which is accessible by transcending the mind itself. There are many unusual benefits to reaching this special state of consciousness. Those of you who are truly interested, I would like to encourage you to pursue this on your own and through the help of others as well. If you are interested in the Unity Crusade visit www.UltimateGoals.com. Check out the World Leadership Blog.

What do you really want?

Table 11 from page 121 gave you a number of choices about how you see yourself and how others perceive you. The true purpose of this exercise was to make you consider the differences between your subjective viewpoint and how others see you. The scores reflect how positive or negative your self image is. The scores range from 8 to 24. The higher your score the better.

The Artists:

Janusz Kapusta
philosopher, artist, inventor
www.K-dron.com
pages 142, 163,181

Yanusz Gliewicz
renaissance painter, designer, artist
www.FinishingDaVinci.com
page 45, 80, and logo design

Rob Corrao
Designer, Artist
www.SC-artdesign.com
page 299

Lilian Citron
Cover Design
New York City

References and Suggested Reading

1. Consciousness

Wilber, Ken. (2000) *Integral Psychology Consciousness, Spirit, Psychology, Therapy.* Shambhala, Boston.

Ornstein, Robert E. (1972) *The Psychology of Consciousness.* Harcourt Brace Jovanovich, Inc. NY

Swami Rama, Ballentine, Rudolph, and Weinstock, Allan. (1976) *Yoga and Psychotherapy: the Evolution of Consciousness.* Himalayan Inst., Il.

Bucke, Richard, M.D. (1961) *Cosmic Consciousness.* Univ. Books, Inc.

Tart, Charles T., ed. (1969) *Altered States of Consciousness.* John Wiley & Sons, Inc. NY.

2. IQ and EQ

Gardner, Howard. (1999) *Intelligence Reframed: Multiple Intelligences for the 21st Century.* Basic Books, NY.

Goleman, Daniel. (1995) *Emotional Intelligence Why it can Matter More than IQ.* Bantam Books, NY.

Sternberg, Robert. J., Forsythe, G. B., Hedlund, J., Horvath, J. A., Wagner, R. K., Williams, W. M., et al. (2000). *Practical intelligence in everyday life.* Cambridge: Cambridge University Press.

3. Nature - Nurture Debate

Herrnstein, R.J. and C. Murray (1994) "*The Bell Curve*" (Free Press)

Jensen, A.R. (1985) "The nature of Black – White differences on various psychometric tests; Spearman's hypothesis." Behavioral and Brain Sciences, 8, 193-263.

Bouchard, T.J., Jr. (1996) "Behavior genetic studies of intelligence, yesterday and today." Journal of Biosocial Science. Vol. 28 p.527-555.

Harris, Julie A., Vernon, Philip, Jang, Kerry, L. (1998) "A multivariate genetic analysis of correlations between intelligence and personality." Developmental Neuropsychology. Vol. 14, p.127 - 142.

4. Success in Life

Segal, Jeanne, Ph.D. (1997) *Raising Your Emotional Intelligence A Practical Guide.* Henry Holt, NY.

5. Rational Approach

Crick, Francis. (1994) *The Astonishing Hypothesis*. Macmillan Pub. NY.

Delacour, Jean. (1997) "Neurobiology of consciousness: an overview." Behavioral Brain Research. Vol. 85, p. 127 - 141.

Stout, Chris and Hayes, Randy, eds. (2004) "The Evidence-Based Practice: Methods, Models, and Tools for Mental Health Professionals." Wiley. NY.

6. Intuitive Approach

Gladwell, Malcolm. (2005) *Blink: The Power of Thinking Without Thinking*. Little, Brown and Conscious. NY.

Day, Laura. (1998) *Practical Intuition*. Random House, NY.

Sternberg, Robert, Wagner, Richard, Williams, Wendy, Horvath, Joseph. (1995) "Testing Common Sense." Am. Psychologist. Vol 50, p. 912- 927.

Metzner, Ralph. (1996) "The Buddhist six worlds model of consciousness and reality." Journal of Transpersonal Psychology. Vol. 28, p. 155- 166.

7. Self Improvement

Seligman, Martin, E. (1991) *Learned Optimism*. Knopf, NY. & (2002) Authentic Happiness. Free Press, NY.

Dalai Lama, H.H. the 14th and Howard C. Cutler, M.D., (1998) *The Art of Happiness: A Handbook for Living*. Riverhead Hardcover

Swami Rama. (1992) *Meditation and its Practice*. & (1977) *Freedom from the Bondage of Karma*. Himalayan International Institute. Pa.

Tracy, Brian. (1995) *Maximum Achievement: Strategies and Skills that Will Unlock Your Hidden Powers to Succeed*. Simon Schuster, NY.

8. Knowledge of Reality

Pelikan, Jaroslav, ed. (1992). *Sacred Writings: Confucianism*. Harper Collins, NY.

Zukav, Gary. (1979) *The Dancing Wu Li Masters*. Morrow& Co. NY.

Hawkings, Stephen. (1988) *A Brief History of Time*. Bantam Books, NY.

Jaynes, Julian. (1976) *The Origin of Consciousness in the Breakdown of the Bicameral Mind*. Houghton Mifflin Conscious. Boston, MA.

Wilbur, Ken. (2007) *A Brief History of Everything*. Shambhala, Boston.

9. Human Nature

Kabat-Zinn, Jon. (1995) *Full Catastrophe Living: Using the Wisdom of Your Body to Face Stress, Pain, and Illness.* Delacourte Press.

Chopra, Deepak, M.D. (1990) *Quantum Healing Exploring the Frontiers of Mind-Body Medicine.* Bantam, NY.

Penfield, Wilder M.D. (1975) *The Mystery of the Mind. A critical study of consciousness and the human brain.* Princeton University Press, NJ.

Goldstein, Kurt (1963) *The Organism. A Holistic Approach to Biology Derived from Pathological Data in Man.* Beacon Press, Boston MA.

10. Nature vs Nurture

Canfield, Jack and Switzer, Janet. (2005) *The Success Principles: How to Get from Where You are to Where You Want to Be.* Harper Collins, NY.

Sternberg, Robert (2004) "Culture and Intelligence." American Psychologist. Vol. 59. p. 325- 338.

Neisser, Ulric; et al. (1996) "Intelligence: Knowns and Unknowns." American Psychologist. Vol.51, p. 77 - 101.

11. Maslow Hierarchy of Needs

Maslow, Abraham (1968) *Toward a Psychology of Being.* D. Van Nostrand Conscious. NY.

12. Anthony Robbins' Six Human Needs

Robbins, Anthony. (1997) *Unlimited Power: The New Science of Personal Achievement.* Free Press. NY.

13. How we get conditioned

Andreas, Steve and Faulkner, Charles, eds. (1994) *NLP: The New Technology of Achievement.* Morrow and Conscious. NY.

Araoz, Daniel, Ed.D. and Carrese, Marie, Ph.D. (1996) *Solution-Oriented Brief Therapy for Adjustment Disorders, A guide for Providers Under Managed Care.* Brunner Mazel, Inc. NY.

14. Autonomic Nervous System

Everly, George, Jr. And Rosenfeld, Robert. (1981) *The Nature and Treatment of the Stress Response: A Practical Guide for Clinicians.* Plenum Press. NY.

Netter, Frank, M.D. (1983) *Nervous System: Anatomy and Physiology.* Ciba-Geigy Corp. NJ.

15. Body response to stress

Roizen, Michael, M.D. and Oz, Mehmet, M.D. (2005) *You: The Owners Manual.* Harper Resource, NY.

Chopra, Deepak, M.D. (1993) *Ageless Body, Timeless Mind: The Quantum Alternative to Growing Old.* Harmony Books, NY.

Baumeister, Roy, et al. (2001) "Bad is stronger than good." Review of General Psychology. Vol. 5, p. 323-370.

16. Automatic Mind

Pribram, K.H. (1991) *Brain and Perception: Holonomy and Structure in Figural Processing.* Lawrence Erlbaum Associates, NY.

Bargh, John, and Ferguson, Melissa. (2000) "Beyond Behaviorism: On the automaticity of higher mental processes." Psychological Bulletin. Vol. 126, p. 925- 945.

Bennett-Levy, James. (2003) "Mechanisms of change in cognitive therapy: The case of automatic thought records and behavior experiments." Behavioral & Cognitive Psychotherapy. Vol. 31, p. 261-277.

Langer, Ellen, Ph.D. (1998) *The Power of Mindful Learning.* Perseus Books, NY.

17. Brain Power

Landry, Susan H. (2000) *Turning Knowledge into Action.* Texas Univ. Press.

18. NLP – Modalities

Dilts, Robert, Grinder, John, Bandler, Richard, & Delozier, Judith. (1980) *Neuro-Linguistic Programming: The Study of Subjective Experience.* Meta Pub. CA.

19. Judgment and Decision

Plous, Scott. (1993) *The Psychology of Judgment and Decision Making.* McGraw Hill, NY.

___ see also Canfield, Jack

___ see also Robbins, Anthony

20. Your Potentials

Hillman, James. (1996) *The Soul's Code: In Search of Character and Calling*. Warner Books, Inc. NY.

Buckingham, Marcus and Clifton, Donald, Ph.D. (2001) *Now, Discover Your Strengths*. The Free Press, NY.

Moore, Thomas. (1992) *Care Of The Soul, A Guide for Cultivating Depth and Sacredness in Everyday Life*. Harper Collins Publishers, NY.

21. What is stress

Benson, Herbert, M.D. and Klipper, Miriam (1975) *The Relaxation Response*. Avon Books, NY.

22. Psychological defenses

Cummings, Nick, Ph.D. and Sayama, Mike, Ph.D. (1995) *Focused Psychotherapy*. Brunner Mazel, Inc. NY.

Freud, Anna. (1966) *The Ego and the Mechanisms of Defense*. International Universities Press, Inc. NY.

23. Coping Skills

Seligman, Martin, Ph.D. (2002) Authentic Happiness. Free Press. NY.

Lazarus, Arnold, Ph.D. and Lazarus, Clifford, Ph.D. (1997) *The Sixty Second Shrink: 101 Strategies for Staying Sane in a Crazy World*. Impact Pub. CA.

Beck, Aaron, M.D. (1976) *Cognitive Therapy and the Emotional Disorders*. International Universities Press, Inc. NY.

Bandler, Richard and Grinder, John. (1982) *Reframing: Neuro-Linguistic Programming and the Transformation of Meaning*. Real People Press, UT.

24. Theories of psychology

Millon, Theodore. (1973) *Theories of Psycholopathology and Personality*. Saunders Conscious. PA.

Nicholi, Armand, Jr. M.D., ed. (1978) *The Harvard Guide to Modern Psychiatry*. Belknap, Boston.

25. Intelligence

Savant, Marilyn vos and Fleischer, Leonore. (1990) *Brain Building in Just Twelve Weeks*. Bantam Books, NY.

Gardner, H. (1983). *Frames of mind: The theory of Multiple Intelligences.* New York: Basic Books.

McClelland, David.   (1976) "Testing for Competence rather than Intelligence", appearing in: *The IQ Controversy*, Block and Dworken, eds. Pantheon Books.

26. Achievement: talents and potential

Eker, Harv, T. (2005) *Secrets of the Millionaire Mind: Mastering the Inner Game of Wealth.* Harper Business, NY.

Carnegie, Dale. (1936)   *How to Win Friends and Influence People.* Simon and Schuster, NY.

Hutchison, Michael. (1994) *Mega Brain Power.* Hyperion Books, NY.

Csikszentmihalyi, Mihaly.   (1991) *Flow: The Psychology of Optimal Experience.* Harper Perennial, NY

27. Other Suggested Reading

Madanes, Cloe (1991) Strategic Family Therapy. Jossey-Bass

Sinetar, Marsha. (1987) Do What You Love, the Money Will Follow. Dell, NY.

Stoltz, Paul G.   (1997) Adversity Quotient.   Turning Obstacles into Opportunities. Wiley, NY.

Redfield, James. (1993) *The Celestine Prophecy; An Adventure.* Warner Books, NY.

Williamson, Marianne. (1992) *A Return to Love.* Harper Collins, NY.

Weiss, Brian, M.D.   (2000) *Messages from the Masters: Tapping into the Power of Love.* Warner Books, NY.

Lipton, Bruce, Ph.D. (2005) *The Biology of Belief: Unleashing the Power of Consciousness, Matter, and Miracles.* Elite Books, CA.

Demartini, John. (2006) *Count Your Blessings: The Healing Power of Gratitude and Love.* Hay House, Inc. CA.

Riklan, David, ed. (2007) *101 Great Ways to Improve Your Life. Vol. 3.* Self Improvement Online, Inc. NJ.

Index

The Author

John Ryder, Ph.D. is a psychologist with a private practice in the heart of New York City. He was educated in both the Western science of the brain, and the Eastern philosophy of the mind. He was trained at Mt. Sinai School of Medicine, where he served as an Assistant Professor specializing in how the brain functions. He has published more than a dozen articles of his scientific research. His work and quest for knowledge have taken him on extensive travels around the world. As an achievement coach, he consults ambitious individuals, corporations, schools, and various organizations to leverage all potential. Dr. Ryder conducts workshops and lectures nationally, and internationally. He also has recorded a variety of programs based on his work to deal with stress more effectively and to enhance performance to promote greater achievement.

For more information refer to the Preface or the websites.

Visit these websites:

www.PositiveDirectionsBook.com   To purchase the book

www.ShiftingPolarities.com   Resources about the book

www.JohnRyderPhD.com   Resources about Dr. Ryder

www.UltimateGoals.com   Resources for better balance
    and harmony in the world – the 21st century crusade
    to promote unity, peace, and prosperity to all.

Buried Treasure!

No digging, just click your way to this
website and claim hundreds of dollars of rewards
www.ShiftingPolarities.com/Treasure

F R E E

- ♦ Audio recording – Relax and Recharge
- ♦ Strategic Planner for Your Achievement
- ♦ List of Super Positive Affirmations
- ♦ Links to other great offers
- ♦ Video Vision Manifesto Positive Directions
- ♦ Positive Directions Ezine
- ♦ Plus prizes, poems, music & pictures

Visit the website to download your treasures
and accelerate your journey in the most
Positive Directions!

Thank You
for your interest in my work.